THICKER THAN WATER

THICKER
THAN
WATER

History, Secrets and Guilt:
A Memoir

CAL FLYN

WILLIAM
COLLINS

William Collins
An imprint of HarperCollins*Publishers*
1 London Bridge Street
London SE1 9GF
WilliamCollinsBooks.com

First published in Great Britain by William Collins in 2016

1

This book has been written with the assistance of
Creative Scotland and Arts Trust Scotland

A catalogue record for this book is
available from the British Library

ISBN 978-0-00-812660-5

Page ii: unknown Aboriginal man, Gippsland, c. 1858–9
Page iii: Angus McMillan, c. 1860

Map by John Gilkes

Printed and bound in Great Britain by
Clays Ltd, St Ives plc

MIX
Paper from
responsible sources
FSC
www.fsc.org **FSC˘ C007454**

FSC is a non-profit international organisation established to promote
the responsible management of the world's forests. Products carrying the
FSC label are independently certified to assure consumers that they come
from forests that are managed to meet the social, economic and
ecological needs of present and future generations,
and other controlled sources.

Find out more about HarperCollins and the environment at
www.harpercollins.co.uk/green

To my parents,
who make everything possible

Contents

AUSTRALIA

40 miles to Melbourne

Dargo

Mitchell River

Wood's Point

Macalister River

Iguana Creek

Perry River

Avon River

Bushy Park

Stratford

Thomson River

Ramahyuck mission station

Lake Wellington

Drouin

Latrobe River

Sale

Yallourn

Warrigal Creek

Port Albert

Corner Inlet

B A S S

Wilsons Promontory

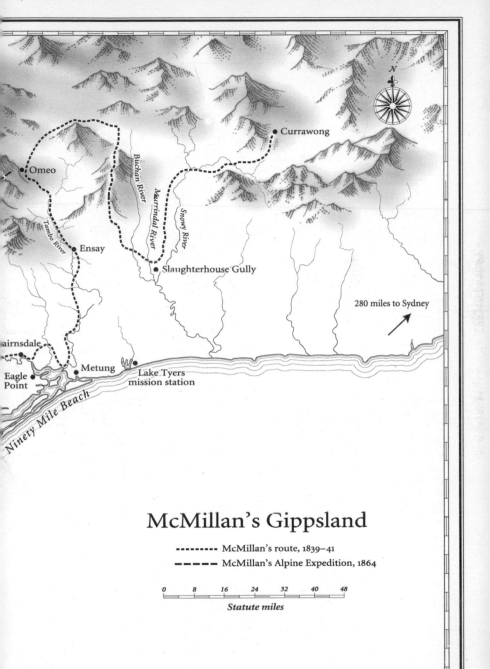

N

Currawong

Omeo

Buchan River

Marrindal River

Snowy River

Tambo River

Ensay

Slaughterhouse Gully

280 miles to Sydney

airnsdale

Eagle
Point

Metung

Lake Tyers
mission station

Ninety Mile Beach

McMillan's Gippsland

- - - - - - - McMillan's route, 1839–41
- - - - - McMillan's Alpine Expedition, 1864

0   8   16   24   32   40   48
Statute miles

S T R A I T

Prologue

Gippsland, Victoria. July 1843

Ronald Macalister was dead. The blacks had killed him.

Angus McMillan's stablehand found the body at the side of the track a half-mile from Alberton, a mess of blood and gore. They had dragged the lad from his horse. Dragged him flailing and yowling to the dust, dispatched him with their wooden clubs, and later, once he was dead, they had cut him.

Though Angus knew Ronald well – had known him for years, in fact, since he'd worked for the dead man's uncle – he had barely recognised him. The corpse had been stripped naked, the face disfigured, the insides left spewing out upon the ground. There were slashes in the gut where the Gunai attackers had cut the fat from around his kidneys.

All the settlers were in uproar; this time the blacks had gone too far. Not a sheep, nor a bullock, not even a shepherd or a stockman; this time they had killed the nephew of the big man Lachlan Macalister himself, and a crime of this magnitude could not go unpunished. There must be reprisals. Angus felt the heavy weight of responsibility settling down upon his shoulders.

For who else could lead the men of Gippsland? He was the founding father, the man who had led the way from the withered plains of the colony over the Great Dividing Range. He was the one who had hacked through the snarls of stringybark and tea tree and finally guided them down into these green and fertile pastures. He had gathered his countrymen around him in the new land and shown them the way they must now live. There was no one else.

In the end, retribution was not so difficult to organise. The men were fired up, just waiting for the touchpaper to be lit. It didn't take much persuasion to amass a hunting party; by the next morning every Scotsman in the district with a gun and a sound horse was assembled, ready for the off, baying like the hounds. Baying for blood. They called themselves the Highland Brigade.

A cry went up and the mob were off. The horses skittered under them, sensing but not understanding the tension in their riders, whose reins were short and faces set as they cursed in their native Gaelic, guttural and emphatic, and struggled for control. And all the time their eyes flitted along the skyline, searching for sign of the Gunai.

Overnight every one of the Aboriginal workers had melted away into the bush, abandoning their posts on the homesteads and the cattle stations. They were as spooked as the horses by the strange charge in the air, the rumbling among their workmates and masters. The murder of Ronald Macalister had set something in motion that they couldn't yet predict, but they didn't want to be around to find out what it was.

Word spread amongst the Highlanders that the blacks had been gathering down by the coast, where the sea pummelled its soft fists into the silver sweep of Ninety Mile Beach. Someone had heard that natives had been seen wearing the clothes of poor dead Ronald, clothes they must have stripped from the lifeless body before the blades were drawn. Clothes that would be spattered with the dead man's blood.

Another said that when the attackers were disturbed they were squatting down beside the body, with the clear intention of eating the man's flesh. They were inhuman, said someone, and they all agreed. They were dangerous, murderous vermin that needed exterminating.

Later it would never be clear who had said exactly what to whom; at that moment they were of one body and one mind. They looked around and saw only brothers and equals united in pursuit of a common enemy. This was more than revenge: it was about securing the safety of their homes, the virtue of their women and a future for their children. It was white against black, good versus evil, the triumph of civilisation over barbarism.

It would be impossible to identify the culprits of the Macalister killing, for what separated one black from another? Each was as murderous as the next. And was not the life of a Macalister worth ten, or twenty, of the natives? The loss of a Macalister must be answered with whatever punishment was necessary to ensure that no white man would ever find harm at the hands of the blacks again.

The Highlanders were armed, organised and angry. When suddenly they came upon the Aboriginal encampment, on a flat by a waterhole nestled in a wide bend of the creek, no one needed to tell them what to do. They advanced stealthily towards the camp, fanning out in a line until they stretched between the banks of the creek on either side, like the string of a bow. It was a fine trap: when the first shots were fired there was nowhere for the Gunai tribesmen to run to.

Crack. Crack. Rifles fired into the centre of the camp, scattering men, women, children. Some of them clutched infants to their chests, as if their frail bodies could protect them from firepower.

Crack. Crack. Bullets began to rain down upon the Gunai. The screams of shock and fright would soon intermingle with the wails of the wounded.

Crack. Crack. The Scots advanced, bloodlust in their eyes. Those still able to run, ran. They ran blindly from the muzzles of the guns, tumbling down the steep banks and into the waterhole. Others made a desperate break through the line of horsemen, eyes fixed on the cover offered by the scrub beyond.

Crack. Crack. The deep water offered solace, but only temporarily. The terror and chaos were contained in another room. Underwater even the gunfire sounded different: a distant drumroll, more felt than heard, and the strange suction sounds of bullets through water.

Lungs burning, the fleeing Gunai were forced to raise their heads to breathe. As they surfaced, the Highlanders fired again. Again and again, until there was no one left to fire at.

The water was red with blood. Fresh blood, vivid and unreal. Thick and opaque, like the paint in a pot. It swirled and eddied, leaching from the corpses, flecked with a white frothy scum where the water had churned up.

When all was quiet, Angus stepped forward to inspect his men's work. There were too many dead blacks to count: dozens of them. Warriors, shamans, hunters, gatherers, fathers, mothers, sons, daughters, infants, elders, all dead. One of the Scotsmen pulled a young Aboriginal boy from the water. He was around twelve or thirteen, and still living, although he had been hit in one eye with a shotgun slug. Later they would christen him 'Bung Eye'.

On, ordered Angus. Let's move on.

They marched Bung Eye ahead, made him lead the way. There must be other camps, they said. Take us to the other camps. They waved their guns in his face. He didn't have much choice.

They walked on across endless flat land under an endless flat sky, pushing through the starburst heads of kangaroo grass that grew up as high as their stirrup irons. Three miles to the south they found another camp, on another flat by another waterhole. The midden nearby attested to a long residency: layers upon layers of discarded shells. A handful each from every meal, built up over hundreds of years.

Again the Gunai were surrounded. Again the shotguns fired. Crack. Crack. Crack. And on again, Bung Eye! Lead on! Once more they advanced across the plain, to another creek, another waterhole.

Crack. Crack. Crack.

The massacre at Warrigal Creek was one of the bloodiest episodes on the very bloody Australian frontier. In all, somewhere between eighty and two hundred Gunai people were slaughtered that day, wiping out in a single assault a substantial portion of the southern Bratowooloong clan.

The leader of the Highland Brigade, Angus McMillan, was a Scot who had fled the horror of the Highland

Clearances, during which thousands of his countrymen were forced from their land to make way for sheep, only to re-enact brutal clearances of his own upon this new land: Gippsland, the south-eastern corner of Australia.

He was a tough man, a pious man, a lonely man. A man who had struggled through miles of unknown territory, built new homes with bare hands, met tribes who had never seen or even known of white skin. He was a man who cut tracks, fought bushfires, felled trees, shot strangers dead.

He was 'the Butcher of Gippsland'.

He was my great-great-great uncle.

1

Blood Relatives

I've spent the last decade of my life scrambling for foot-
holds and handholds, pulling myself ever onward, ever
upwards. Shift – move – adjust – and shift again. It was
only when my bough began to bend, and creak under my
own weight, that it occurred to me to think: How did I
get here? Where did I come from? Who is behind me?

The summer I turned twenty-five was the first time I felt
the wobble. On paper everything seemed ideal. I had landed
my dream job as a reporter on a national newspaper, and
since then I spent my days high on adrenaline, making bad-
tempered phone calls, arguing with lawyers and scanning
the news wires for excitement. My nights were spent blowing off steam in East End bars, nights fuelled by alcohol and
enthusiasm that could fire off in any direction at any time,
end up anywhere. It was exciting. *I* felt exciting.

But more and more I was feeling something else as
well. Everything seemed very precarious somehow, as if,
when I next turned to take hold of all the strands of my
life, my hands might slip through space, finding nothing
solid to grip onto. I had a mounting sense of dread.

For despite the business cards and the security passes
and the smart-casual work wardrobes, it wasn't working

out quite the way I'd planned. Over the past three years I'd seen too many of my contemporaries slipping suddenly from their rungs and sliding down the snakes back to the start. Pumped up by the big talk of the graduate recruiters, we had graduated right into the worst of the financial crisis, and all the overconfidence – ours, theirs, everyone's – was coming crashing down around us.

The easy, breezy lives we'd been promised at those Magic Circle, Big Four, get-rich-quick corporate-sponsored drinks parties had vanished in a puff of smoke; after all the champagne hysteria the next few years had come on in a flood of disappointment and stifled ambition. One of my university peers spent weeks in the papers as a photo of her, looking dishevelled but fragilely beautiful as she carried a cardboard box of belongings from the Lehman Brothers office, was wheeled out by the picture editors again and again. The face of the recession, of hubris, of financial calamity; we recognised her.

London had seemed a shining city of hopes and dreams, but now it had transformed into a dark and terrifying place, where jobs stuttered and vanished but the rents were still rising up in front of us like a drawbridge. I had no security. None of us had any security. And for the first time in my life I was scared. Low-level and not such low-level anxiety buzzed in the background of all my thoughts.

On the one hand, I was lucky. I had a job, and I held it tight. But everyone knew that newspapers were a doomed industry. The internet was rendering us obsolete. It was all we talked about, in hushed voices in the office. 'Get out now while you can,' senior reporters told me in harsh whispers. 'It's too late for me. I'm too old to retrain. Save yourself.'

After work I wandered through the docks, looking at all the yachts and skyscrapers and cocktail bars, and I couldn't remember what I was doing there. I picked up my phone. Dialled.

'Can I come home for a while?'

'Of course,' said my mother. 'Whenever you want.'

Home for me is the Highlands. This is a detail about myself that has always been a disproportionately large source of pride and the basis for a bizarre game of one-upmanship I play secretly, constantly, with everyone else, smiling quietly to myself as others recount with self deprecating humour the banality of their suburban roots in Luton or Wolverhampton or Wigan.

Never mind that I fled at eighteen, as soon and as fast as education allowed – first to India and later to university in England, both in their own way the most antithetical environments to the Highlands that I could imagine – or that by now I'd lived for so long away from 'home' that my accent had slipped so low as to be imperceptible. They say that ex-pats make the best patriots, and I believe them. I can't help it. I love the place.

My childhood summers were spent paddling with Highland ponies in the biting cold waters of Loch Ness, then charging – kicking their barrel sides and flapping my reins – together up the muddy tracks in the hills above. In the autumn I walked home across the field, gorging on brambles, stumbling through nettles. We swam in the loch behind my house, climbing into a rowing boat at its centre and jumping off again until our fingers turned blue. When we were older my friends and I threw parties in fields, drinking cheap cider amid clouds of midges, lying back on our jackets to watch shooting stars. And in the winter, if we were lucky, the northern lights.

The Highlands are a place where it's easy to escape and walk out all alone, except for the sheep and the honey-sweet aroma of the gorse. It's a place where you can go entire days, even in the middle of summer, without seeing another soul. To me it seems the only place to be from.

Now it was to the Highlands that I had the urge to return. I was suddenly grateful for the grandeur of the landscape and the reassurance of family, newly apprecia-tive of the importance of knowing and understanding my place in the world. Fed up with being a lone wolf, I was turning tail back to the den.

With two weeks' leave to play with, I set off with my mother on a jaunt around the island haunts of her youth. From our home on the Black Isle we headed west, through the green pastures of the east coast and up into the bleak stretches of heather moor that characterise the north and west, skirting the lochs that split the country along its weakest fault. Mum's a nervous passenger, and she clutched the door handle and held her breath on the corners, but between the bends we talked about family, her family – all these vivid characters to whom I am bound inextricably but have never met, the people who define so much of my identity.

When my grandmother was still alive we would make this journey often, rushing to catch the ferry from Kyle and rumbling the car down the concrete slip and onto the diamond plate of the metal ramp. I would peer out at the other cars, crammed together like a herd of cows, and the big metal rivets that held the walls together. Everything

that went on and off the island came via that ferry –
horses kicking the backs of their boxes, sheep packed
two-storey into trailers with their ears poking through the
air vents, lorries bearing food and supplies that shifted the
balance of the ferry perceptibly as they came on board.

Once aboard we had to leave the car and clamber up
the metal ladder to the wet-sprayed deck or the striplit
waiting room in case the vehicles started moving around
during the voyage. It was just a short jump by Hebridean
standards. You could see our destination, Kyleakin, across
the water, and the hills of Skye, whose southerly arm,
Sleat, loomed up in front of us as the little ferry set off
gamely across the waves. After twenty minutes we all
trooped back down the ladder and into the cars to drive
off up the ramp. It was my favourite part of the trip.

Now the ferry is gone, replaced by a road bridge that
skims across the water like a stone, shooting straight out
from the mainland and skipping off Eilean Bàn – 'the
White Island' – barely missing the lighthouse and its keep-
er's cottage, the impact sending it arching in a high para-
bolic path above the sea before alighting on the Skye coast.

Skye is central to my family's history. It's where my
mother grew up, and where her father's family was from,
and it's also where my parents met, when my father came
to work with my maternal grandfather in the Portree
court. We drove north along the edge of the island, stopping at sites of family significance. 'That was my granny's
house,' said my mother as we reached Breakish, a scattering of crofthouses set back from the road. She pointed to
a whitewashed cottage with a neatly hatched slate roof.
Triangular dormer windows poked through the tiles at the
front like eyes, in the local vernacular.

Across the road sat the family croft — a narrow strip of land stretching away towards the sea, a traditional island smallholding held under an unusual form of Scots law, whereby tenants rent the land from the local estate, build their own houses on it, and pass on the tenancy when they die. Mum's brother Myles was still the official tenant, although the grass was quietly being grazed by a neighbour's bedraggled sheep in his absence. We stopped to look, but I felt odd and underwhelmed. The croft is a ghostly, wordless presence in many of our family's discussions of Skye, a reference point around which stories and lives rotate. But in reality, there was nothing marking it out as ours.

I had heard that it didn't have any buildings on it any more, that the house had been sold off separately decades ago, but I hadn't really processed that. Seeing it in person for the first time in years, this soggy paddock didn't feel much different from any of the others around it, or the thousands we'd passed on the drive. Still, I felt that it meant something to have gone there, that it existed. There was a link between our family and this rocky patch of earth, something more material than memory alone.

A track led down from the road across a flat expanse of reeds and heather to the Breakish graveyard, where my forebears lay quietly on a rise overlooking the beach, dark kelp drawn up tight over the sand like a blanket.

I remembered this place from my childhood: windswept, the black sea bottomless under a sombre sky. Cattle standing on the track. The large cartoony petals of carnations in their metal colanders and the fabric flowers stabbed into oasis foam, cloth leaves fluttering in the cold wind.

We laid flowers at the graves of my grandparents and of my uncle Niall, who died when I was young. Afterwards we drifted through the kissing gate into the oldest section of the graveyard, behind a low dry-stone wall. Here the gravestones were larger, monumental, almost Gothic. Marble angels crouched with heads bent, in mourning for entire families. Celtic crosses stood proudly; a row of neat matching stones remembered unnamed sailors.

There were family stones here for us too. We browsed, looking for the name.

'Wait – here.'

It was a neat grey stone, almost as tall as me, the stone left rough along its edges. Engraved ivy climbed up the left side. 'In loving memory of Myles McMillan, died 14th December 1899 ...' began a roll-call of the deceased. There, at the foot of the list, came '... and Angus, Christina, who died in Australia'.

I had a camera in my hand. I lifted it, focused on the stone. Snap.

Portree was a thirty-mile drive north from Breakish along the coast, through the seaside village of Broadford and darting between the feet of the red Cuillins – Beinn na Caillich, 'the hill of the old woman', with her grizzled and scree-strewn face, then Marsco and finally the perfect, conical Glamaig. The black Cuillin ridgeline loomed up in the west beyond, jagged and forbidding.

To our right we looked out across the water to the tiny isle of Pabay and her big sister Scalpay, then the south end of Raasay rose out of the water, with the familiar shorn crown of Dun Caan, flat like a tabletop.

Portree is a small town – a big village, really – clasped between the three steep sides of a fishing harbour. We wandered along the water's edge between stacks of green-stringed lobster creels and the neat cottages that line the quayside; painted baby-blue and rose, sage-green and amber. The evening sun caught the sides of the fishing boats and buoys that speckled the sea loch further out, and burnished the rocky slopes of the isles beyond.

On the way back through the village we passed the butcher's ('New recipe!!! Irn Bru sausages: £6.98/kg', a handwritten sign promised) and then the courthouse where my grandfather – my mother's father – was the procurator fiscal for many years. Her family lived just outside Portree in a big, chaotic house of brothers and sisters and animals.

Heading north out of town towards the house, we rounded a bend and the Old Man of Storr swung suddenly into view – a startling pinnacle of rock jutting from the hillside so abruptly it seemed almost to stand up.

'There –' said Mum, knocking me out of my reverie. She slowed the car and craned her head to look past me out of the passenger window. 'Our house was just behind those trees.' But it wasn't there any more: the line of trees turned out to screen a cul-de-sac of modern bungalows. We stopped the car.

'Creag an Iolaire,' I read aloud from the street sign. Craig an yo-lara. Eagle Rock.

'That was the name of my house,' she said, and stopped as if to catch her breath. 'I remember when they planted those trees.'

At the top of the little street, her former driveway, on the site of the family home, was a stubby, white-harled block of flats. A sign outside declared it 'Macmillan House', after my mother's maiden name.

You often hear about people who return after long absences to their childhood homes and knock on the door to ask if they can have a look around. They try to remember what it looked like under the coats of paint, the new wallpaper, before the extension was built. The house is the same, but not the same, as if one day you had miscounted the steps and walked into a neighbour's home: in the image of your own, but the colours all wrong, and everything in the wrong place. What a curious sense of loss this is, when we know that things cannot stay the same.

We drove on glumly, past the Storr and along the coast road, echoing the curve of the ridge, until Portree and the cul-de-sac were long behind us. The land there is stark and bleak, grass holding to the slopes where it can, wrinkles in the hillside where the earth has slipped and settled again, peaty water settled in the clefts levelling the uneven pitch of the ground. Further out on the headland, white cottages cling on to the rocks like limpets.

We spent the night in a B&B that sat out alone on the heather near Staffin. The scale of the place unsettled me – the great malevolent forces that shaped the earth writ large across the land. And the colours too: the vegetation was not green, but crimson and orange and gold. 'Like the surface of Mars,' said Mum.

It was late by the time we arrived, the sky the strange dusky twilight it will stay all night this far north in the summer, and we realised we hadn't brought anything for dinner. There was not a shop or pub for miles around. Too embarrassed to beg for food from the landlady, we pooled our resources and split a pack of breath mints and a cellophane gift bag of tablet between us in a bedspread picnic. All that was missing were the plastic cups and the cuddly toys.

I noticed with relief that I had no signal on my phone. For the first time in months I felt safe.

Back in Portree, we found ourselves drawn in by an A4 poster promising an exhibition on the Skye diaspora in the new archive centre, in the old boys' boarding house at the high school.

The exhibition was small – photocopied documents pinned up on blue felt display boards, black-and-white photos of kilted Highlanders in their brave new worlds: America, Canada, Africa, India – and the archive smelt of carpet tiles and the chlorine from the school swimming pool across the carpark, but we dallied, reading each label slowly, waiting for the rain to die down outside.

There were aged, curling registers in glass cases that recalled in long lists the names of those who sailed from the west coast of Scotland in the eighteenth and early nineteenth centuries in search of a new life. They were the refugees from the Highland Clearances, an agricultural revolution that saw the removal of thousands upon thousands of Highlanders from their traditional land by their clan chiefs. In Gaelic they call this time *Fuadaich nan Gàidheal*: the expulsion of the Gael.

From Skye, most left for Nova Scotia, Canada, where even now one can still hear the lilt of Gaelic song and the beat of the bodhran – almost a third of its population still self-identify as ethnically 'Scottish', as opposed to Canadian. But not all. The emigrants fired off in every direction, and the displays in front of me charted how the thin tendrils of kinship stretched out from this island across the world.

I was enchanted by a copy of an old, hand-drawn map, a segment of coastline blown up on the photocopier to cover an A3 sheet. Seas and rivers had been delicately shaded blue by some devoted archivist with a pencil. A mountain range stretched across the top of the page, coloured purple, and a set of unknown straight-edged boundaries upon the land had been rendered in green.

The 1845 map of Gippsland on display at the Portree exhibition.

There was something fantastical about it, like a real-life treasure map, with names straight out of J.M. Barrie's imagination: 'Snake Island', 'Shoal Lagoon', 'Mount

Useful', 'Sealer's Cove'. But there were names I recognised too: one peak was labelled 'Ben Cruachan', like a mountain in Argyllshire; a settlement called 'Glengarry', like the Lochaber village; another called 'Tarradale' – wasn't that in Ross-shire? The green squares too bore names I knew: Campbell, Macalister, Cunningham.

I couldn't identify the country by its coastline. In thick copperplate, carefully traced and filled in with a pink coloured pencil, the words SOUTH PACIFIC OCEAN rose out of the empty space of the sea.

I gave up, let myself check the information tag: 'Robert Dixon's map of Gippsland, Australia, showing the stations occupied by the squatters, 1845 ... The detailed insert shows the Macalister River, named by explorer Angus McMillan after Captain Lachlan Macalister (1797–1858), a grandson of Alexander of Strathaird. Angus McMillan was born in Glenbrittle, Skye in 1810.' There was a monochrome portrait of the explorer stapled to the board alongside: a sober, severe-looking man with strong features and a white chinstrap beard. He wore a tweed three-piece and cravat, and looked off into the middle distance from under heavy brows.

I smiled, watching the rain lash against the windowpane. I tried to imagine sailing all the way from Skye to the South Pacific. Landing on Snake Island.

'Angus McMillan,' came Mum's voice from behind me. 'He's a relative of ours.'

I wasn't listening. The thought was still turning itself over in my head. 'Get on a boat here, and don't get off until you get to Australia,' it went. 'Sealer's Cove,' it said. 'Mount Useful.'

'What?' I asked, belatedly.

'He's a relative of ours,' she said again. 'I remember my father telling us about him when we were children. He was very proud of it. Angus was an explorer in Australia when it was first being settled. There are whole areas named after him. You'll have to ask your uncle Myles, he'll know more about it.'

'Huh.' I looked at the map again, impressed. There was a mountain in the north-west corner of the map that had been labelled 'Mount Angus'. I drew this small source of fuzzy pride close to my chest, like an otter with a clam shell.

Until this moment I had never understood the appeal of family history, the draw for all those anoraks poring over their bloodlines in the back rooms of libraries. I knew it would be hard to explain the significance of my discovery, in the same way that the relating of last night's dream is never as interesting for the audience as it is for the teller. Sheer self-indulgence. Yet it was strange how much this revelation had cheered me. How this whole trip had cheered me.

I couldn't be sure why it had affected me so much to learn of this swashbuckling relative. His story, after all, did not appear to have had much bearing on my life thus far. But, I told myself, wasn't it this sense of context that I was seeking when I returned to Skye? Of course our lives should stand alone, to be considered on their own merits, but didn't it add something to step back and see myself as the latest episode in a longer series? As part of a family epic, whose themes reverberate down the generations?

There is a certain comfort, I realised, in accepting the existence of some kind of folk destiny, wherein the prede- cessors' achievements confer some inherent advantage, some easing of paths on the present generation; the very simplest form of predestination. One can almost imagine the nods of approval from the family portraits in the great hall ...

For this reason I was glad that McMillan was an explorer. I could use this familial detail as a hook to hang my wanderlust from – the yearning for escape that rears up in me even in the most pleasant of circumstances, the restlessness that has driven me from gainful employment and fulfilling relationships and onto aeroplanes instead, time and again, to hike along the Yangtze, or cruise the backwaters of Kerala, or snowshoe in the Arctic. With this new information, I could reimagine myself as the latest in a line of notable wanderers, rather than a deadbeat who simply found it hard to settle down to work.

I have often daydreamed of how I too would have been an explorer, had I been born into another century. It grieves me that there is now so little on earth to explore, truly explore – only the final dark crevices of deep-water trench and polar crevasse. Meanwhile the breaching of the new frontiers, beyond our own planet (stars spinning past the portholes, one-way trips to Mars), remains decades away.

What I'd give to touch down on a strange beach and walk out into unknown land. To draw the first map and write on it my own names for what I saw.

I was in the habit of following leads, so I called my uncle Myles, as my mother had suggested. He lives in London now, in a terraced house with a Greek wife and two young sons who speak with English accents, but the white walls bear his oil paintings of the Skye landscape in red-browns and mustard yellow and the deep blue slate of the Atlantic.

Myles's reluctance to give up the tenancy of the croft at Breakish reflected a wider reluctance in both him and his wife Eleny to accept that they would stay in London, despite having lived there for nearly thirty years. Every time I visit, one or the other of them is apt to mention some new scheme they've been discussing recently – a house swap with a Highland family, perhaps, or a new start somewhere on the English coast. Something, anyway, that would pitch them directly from inner city to remote location. The boys do not want to go.

For my uncle, that croft kept up a tie between him – and, by association, the whole family – and Skye like an umbilical cord, a legal paper trail of personal heritage that signified so much, but in actuality boiled down to only a strip of scrappy pasture that we don't even own. I was a Skye man, it said. And, although I've changed, at any point I could return to this place and be a Skye man again.

Myles did know more about the family explorer. Angus was his great-grandfather Martin's uncle, he said. 'He discovered a region in Australia and opened it up for the British. The area he discovered was called Gippsland, after Sir George Gipps, the governor then. You might have to go and find out all about it.'

I made a non-specific sound. 'Maybe I should.'

'The McMillans were a big family, and most of them went abroad. Dad was always telling us stories about their adventures. Martin was a captain on the clippers sailing round the Horn and back with wool. One brother took ill with measles on board ship and died. He was put ashore and buried on Tierra del Fuego.'

I smiled wistfully to myself, visualising and then weighing the phrase 'latest in a long line of adventurers' in my mind.

Myles also seemed wistful. He was a wanderer too, in his youth, a traveller who carried his home on his back. 'Personally I've always yearned to see Australia. To see the coral, swim around the Great Barrier Reef. Those red deserts ... Angus has a statue somewhere over there, apparently. I'd like to see that too.'

'Where?'

'In Gippsland, which I'm told is in Victoria ... More research needed, I think, before you go booking any tickets.'

More research needed. I took it as an order, and started to read.

It started promisingly, with the entry in *The Australian Dictionary of Biography*:

Angus McMillan (1810–1865), explorer and pioneer pastoralist, was born on 14 August 1810 at Glenbrittle, Isle of Skye, Scotland, the fourth son of Ewan McMillan ... He arrived in January 1838 with letters of introduction to Captain Lachlan Macalister, who made him ... manager at Currawang in the Maneroo (Monaro) country and he began there in February 1839. In this year he learned much bushcraft, befriended Aboriginal tribes and after an eventful journey in May climbed Mount McLeod and glimpsed the plain and lakes country of Gippsland.

McMillan pioneered Gippsland and spent the rest of his life contributing to its welfare ... He died

while extending the boundaries of the province he
had discovered. Although he received little wealth
from Gippsland, his journals and letters and those
of his contemporaries reveal him as courageous,
strong and generous, with a great love for his
adopted country.

I read the entry with a thrill of pride, printed it out and
basked in the reflected glory. Soon after, I stumbled upon
a second-hand copy of Ken Cox's florid hagiography, *Angus
McMillan: Pathfinder*, online ('the story of one man's battle
against natural obstacles'), and when it arrived I pored over
it like a gospel, underlining the most flattering passages.

On the inside cover I found a ballpoint inscription
declaring the book the property of 'Cllr Robinson, Port
Albert', and a map of the first European explorers' routes
through and around the state of Victoria and its surrounds,
showing McMillan's explorations in their proper context.

Each was given a different mark to denote their routes.
The first forays into the region were confined to the coast.
The earliest, marked COOK 1770 and characterised by a
trail of dots and crosses, was shown to swoop in from
New Zealand to the south-east, hit the Gippsland coast at
Point Hicks, turn and follow the coast round Cape Howe
and north towards Botany Bay, in the southern suburbs of
modern-day Sydney.

Cook was not the first European to encounter this
mysterious continent – a series of seamen working for the
Dutch East India Company had sailed along the northern
coast and skiffed the underside of Tasmania over the previous century – but his expedition would prove crucial to
the future of the new land. Evidence submitted to

Parliament by members of his party (notably the onboard botanist Joseph Banks) would lead to the founding of the first convict colony in 1788.

Short choppy dashes showed BASS 1797 sailing south from Sydney in a whaleboat as he sought to prove the existence of a strait separating Van Diemen's Land (now Tasmania) from the mainland. He skimmed Wilsons Promontory, where the tiny Little Penguins come ashore, briefly touched land at Western Port Bay, before shooting back the way he came.

Then came GRANT 1800 (long, confident dashes), the first to sail Bass Strait from west to east, and MURRAY 1801 (the dot-dash, dot-dash of Morse code), discoverer of Port Phillip Bay, a shallow inlet leaping with dolphins and whales, on the shores of which Melbourne would later be founded.

Inland, it was another twenty-three years before HUME AND HOVELL 1824–25 (Xs and dashes) made the first inroads into Victoria, hiking south with a party of convicts from the former's home at Lake Hume, trying and failing to cross the Great Dividing Range at what they christened Mount Disappointment, before finally forcing their way over and down to the coast at Port Phillip.

From the Monaro plains of New South Wales, McKILLOP 1835 shortly came tripping down in a line of tiny cross-stitches, coming to a halt at Lake Omeo. Then HUTTON 1838, represented as the noughts to McKillop's crosses, edged in along the coast from the east, reaching the golden shore of Lake King before turning back. Despite these incursions, an enormous stretch of land between these lakes and Port Phillip Bay remained – to the Western colonists – entirely unknown and unexplored.

At last, the name I was looking for: McMILLAN 1839–41. In dense black dashes he was shown tumbling down the Snowy River gorge to Mount Macleod, where he was pulled up short by the hard going and the threat of hostile tribes, turning north to McKillop's outpost at Omeo, then immediately south again along the banks of the Tambo River. Finally successful, he headed west, fording rivers as he went, then south across flat plains to hit the coast at Port Albert. He did not know it then, but this fertile country would become his adopted home, where he would shoot from obscurity to high society.

A final set of marks – circles separated by lines – shows STRZELECKI 1840 piggybacking along McMillan's tracks to the Macalister River, before striking off towards Western Port Bay. The so-called Polish 'Count' Paweł Strzelecki's overlapping journey and rival claim to the title of 'discoverer of Gippsland' would come to trouble my relation greatly in his latter years.

I devoured the book in a couple of days, a fanciful portrait of a daring hero that even I found overblown, and turned back to the internet for more. My appetite for information was limitless. But there was plenty to find: photos of cairns built in his memory, a panoramic painting of the view from his homestead (lush grassland, blue-tinged mountains far behind, Aboriginal children playing on a fallen tree) by the Austrian-born artist Eugene von Guérard, and facts, facts, facts, each sending me spinning off on another internet spiral.

But one too many searches brought me finally to an uncomfortable discovery. It started with a single, sobering sentence in a news report dated 2005.

A Scottish pioneer revered as one of Australia's
foremost explorers faces being erased from maps
amid accusations that he was responsible for the
cold-blooded murder of hundreds of aborigines.

I skimmed it quickly, expecting more praise, more admiration, and didn't digest the words completely until an odd
dropping sensation alerted me to the new discovery. I
recognised the feeling at once, an uncomfortable, visceral
reaction I've had sometimes while working on investigations – a new scrap of incriminating evidence, perhaps a
footnote in a company's accounts or an unexpected name
on a title deed, will set my nervous system clanging like
the sounding of a gong before I've even realised what I've
found.

'Wait, what?' I thought, sending my eyes spinning back
up the way they came.

I read the sentence again, and felt a gradual unspooling
inside me. The next paragraph hammered the point home:

The aborigines are calling for the electoral district
of McMillan in the southern state of Victoria to be
renamed out of respect for the men, women and
children they say were slaughtered by Angus
McMillan and his 'Highland Brigade' in the
massacre of Warrigal Creek. The 1843 massacre
was one of several attributed to McMillan,
originally from Glenbrittle, Skye, and his band of
Scottish settlers, who ... are accused of carrying
out a genocidal campaign against the aborigines for
a decade.

'Oh,' I thought. Just: 'Oh'. Not sadness or disappoint-
ment or the trundling, wondering, what-does-this-mean?
All of that came later. I was simply stopped short. I
opened up the search bar again and began to type. 'Angus
McMillan', I started, then paused to assemble my thoughts.
As I hesitated, a list of suggestions popped up unbidden:

Angus McMillan Gippsland
Angus McMillan explorer
Angus McMillan massacres

I clicked the third option, with a thrill of anxiety. Soon I
had drawn up a list of dates and places and sketchy details
of what, I learned, have become known as 'the Gippsland
Massacres'. The placenames alone invoked a chill.

1840–41, Nuntin: Angus McMillan and his men kill
  unknown numbers of Gunai people in skirmishes
  during 'the defence of Bushy Park'
1840, Boney Point: During one such skirmish, 'a
  large number' of blacks pursued and shot down
  at confluence of Perry and Avon rivers by
  McMillan's men
1841, Butchers Creek: McMillan's stockmen chase
  and shoot down 'a party of blacks' at a headland
  to the north of Bancroft Bay
1842, Skull Creek: Unknown number shot down
  west of Lindenow in reprisal for death of two
  white shepherds
1843, Warrigal Creek: More than 80 (as many as
  200) shot down by Angus McMillan and his men
  following the death of Ronald Macalister

1844, Maffra: Unknown number killed in rumoured
  skirmish
1846–47, central Gippsland: 'At least 50' shot
  during the search for a white woman supposedly
  held captive by Gunai people
1850, Slaughterhouse Gully: 16 thought to have
  been shot down near the 'Pyramids' rock
  formation by the McLeod family and their men
1850, Brodribb River: Unknown number shot
  down during 'hunt' along riverside

I realised that I had stumbled upon a dark secret. Far from
the romance of our family folklore, Angus McMillan
appeared to be a dark character responsible for some truly
terrible deeds. And more than that: over recent years, his
name has come to symbolise some of the very worst
excesses of Australia's violent colonial past.

It is easy, as a Scot, to assume a certain martyr complex.
Historically speaking, we have been cast as the plucky
victims who struggled bravely on in a fight that was
weighted against us from the start. And without thinking,
I had absorbed the national story as my own.

Every past injustice is hammered home in history lessons
at school: wars upon wars in which our plaid-wrapped
men ran fearlessly to their deaths, armed only with clay-
mores and shields, their throaty war cries harmonising
with the skirl of the bagpipes and the shrieks of the bloody
and bruised in the great symphony of battle.

We remember the sacrifices of our people *en masse* at
every football match, every rugby match, at the end of

concerts and parties, with voices raised and quavering with emotion:

> O Flower of Scotland
> when will we see
> your likc again,
> That fought and died for
> that wee bit Hill and Glen
> and stood against him.

We remember our scorn for the colonising English, who took our land, stole our freedom and stamped on our culture as well, suppressing traditional music, our national dress, the Gaelic language. But, we tell ourselves, we have not been cowed. Our national pride, our *hunger* for freedom, for self-determination, remains:

> But we can still rise now,
> and be the nation again
> that stood against him.

The belief in our nationhood is as strong as ever, our indignation still bubbling. We are proud still, and angry, and self-righteous. And quite right too.

But, as in everything, the full story of the Scots is complex. It is full of threads that will not tie neatly together, and details that do not always flatter that sense of self-righteousness. Even the Battle of Culloden – the great slaughter that finally crushed the Jacobite rising in 1746, so often invoked as a symbol of the triumph of the ammunition of the English over the courage of the Scots – was the culmination of what was as much a civil war as a war between nations, as clan turned against clan, seduced by the sophisticated south or the desire to settle old scores.

Many of the most enthusiastic proponents of the British Empire would emerge from among the Scots. Only a year after the bloodbath of Culloden, Prime Minister Henry Pelham declared that 'every Scotch man who has zeal and abilities to serve the King should have the same admission with the administration as the subject of England had'. It was a shrewd move on the part of the British government, and one that would see the colonial administration becoming increasingly Scotch in character over the following decades.

Britain sent at least forty governors of Scottish descent to America before it declared independence in 1776, including General John Campbell, governor general of Virginia and commander-in-chief of British forces in North America during the Seven Years' War (he was later replaced by James Abercrombie, another Scot).

As the American colony grew restless, it was Pitt the Younger's Edinburghian right-hand man Henry Dundas — bitterly nicknamed 'the uncrowned king of Scotland' — who called most vocally for the harsh punishment of the rebels. He also devoted much time and energy to blocking attempts to outlaw the slave trade — according to one estimate, he single-handedly delayed its abolition in the British Empire by ten or fifteen years through his 'skilful obstructions'.

As Home Secretary, Dundas acted to open India to his fellow Scots, and they soon came to dominate the administration of the colony and the East India Company. The first three governors general of India were Scots, and later, seven of the twelve viceroys. Others, like Sir Arthur

Hamilton-Gordon, son of the Fourth Earl of Aberdeen, skipped from colony to colony, serving as governor of Trinidad, Mauritius, Fiji, New Zealand, and finally Ceylon (modern-day Sri Lanka).

Thus in America, India, the Caribbean and the Pacific, the hand of empire stretched out in the form of opportunistic Scots, as the colonised became the colonisers. In Gippsland, Australia, Angus McMillan wreaked destruction upon the indigenous people in the name of British expansion.

I had known – however vaguely – that men like him had existed. Men who had fled a homeland made miserable by colonisation, then made it their lives' work to extend the empire, some of them, like McMillan, killing wholesale in its name. But whereas previously they had been aberrations, incongruous footnotes to a rousing narrative, now here he was, right there in the family tree. Part of my story, part of my heritage, part of *me*.

I returned to London determined to put the whole sorry business out of my mind. I took another job, at another paper, and tried to concentrate on fitting in and getting on. But I couldn't forget what had been, for me, a momentous discovery. It rolled around in the back of my head, unsettling me. All my easy assumptions about my heritage had proved to be flimsy.

What I was feeling reminded me of a concept I'd once stumbled across in a book: 'intergenerational guilt'. It described a generation of Germans who felt a profound sense of guilt and remorse for their nation's role in the Holocaust, although they had not been born at the time it took place. At the time I had flicked through the pages with indifferent curiosity, but now I rolled back through their reasoning. I couldn't help but wonder: what responsibility for our ancestors' actions do we all unwittingly take on?

It seemed to me that McMillan's story sat at the very crossroads of what makes a person victim or aggressor, good or evil. From my reading I had been presented with two characters: McMillan the hero – the hard-working, generous Scot honoured with plaques, portraits and cairns – and McMillan the villain – a bloodthirsty tyrant who rampaged through the bush, cutting down unarmed women and children. But what was the truth? I was left with the task of fitting both together to construct the image of one man, seen from two different directions.

Was it the views of his contemporaries or the harsh realities of life in the outback that had prompted such an apparent transformation – from virtuous Presbyterian lad to cold-blooded killer – or even the ravages of the landscape itself? I struck upon the idea of travelling to Australia to retrace his journey, as closely as I could, in search of the answer. Perhaps I might find it wandering still the rough tracks through the bush in the Snowy River gorge and the foothills of the Australian Alps. Perhaps it was grazing with the cattle in the Gippsland pastures.

There too I could confront the true legacy of McMillan's actions by seeking out the present-day representatives of the Aboriginal group he had terrorised. What state were they in? What could I do to help them? Would they want my pity? I had no way of knowing; I would have to go there to find out.

2

But for the Sea

It started with a departure, as so many stories do.

Friday, 8 September 1837. Angus McMillan stood on the dockside in Greenock, looking for the ship that would carry him across the ocean. All his goodbyes had been said, all his belongings stowed in sturdy wooden trunks. He was an emigrant – or rather, a would-be emigrant. All he needed was to secure his passage to the other end of the earth.

McMillan had a vessel in mind: the *Minerva*. His friend Allan MacCaskill was already booked to travel on it to the colony of New South Wales. Or 'New Holland', as McMillan still called it, an old name that conjured up some of the old mystery: unknown coastlines, islands of knowledge swimming in great seas of empty mapspace. He had seen her too, her great bulk at the quay, the bright flags flying, readying herself for flight. But there was no room, said MacCaskill. All her berths had been filled.

Half of Scotland seemed to have got there ahead of him, and they all seemed to have planned in advance. Men in plaid, cheekbones protruding like broken glass; hollow-eyed women with children hiding in amongst their skirts; families with everything they owned slung onto their backs. All desperate for passage on board, an escape, pouncing upon what tickets there were. They were rats from a sinking ship, and McMillan was one of them; paws scrabbling for purchase on polished decks as an entire country upended beneath them. Those who had lost their grip were flooding out through the ports across the ocean, looking for a new life in the New World: New Zealand, New South Wales, New York, Newfoundland. They'd go anywhere there was room to sit down.

He, like many of his compatriots, had mixed feelings. Sailing out from Barra, only three days previously, he had pressed himself against the rail to watch the retreating shores of the beloved island slipping away from him, *not for their sake*, as he told his journal, *but for the love of some of its ever to be remembered inhabitants*.* Clear light danced on a rippling sea, flecked far off with the fins of basking sharks soaking up the late-summer sun. But none of this could cheer him, nor his friend Finlayson Kilbride. *Alas he had no cure for the deep wounds of my tortured heart.*

Still, it had been set in motion. The future beckoned, and however reluctantly, he had heeded its call. *O'er the blue waves I go.*

After a long day trudging the docks, from agent to ship and back again, McMillan retired to his inn and MacCaskill with no news to speak of. The ship's crew had only confirmed MacCaskill's warning: there were no second-class berths, and all the first-class cabins were already filled. *As for going in the hold*, he wrote, *I could never dream of it.* The *Minerva* had not long retired from her career as

---

* Italicised text is directly quoted from McMillan's own journals.

a transport for convicts, and conditions on board were little better now than they had been then. He could not face all those weeks below deck: the double layer of bunks down either side, no ventilation, no natural light. Two to a bed. For four months! God only knew the horrors of the hold, the filth and the lice and the disease that would whip through the steerage passengers as they lay packed together at night, waves slamming the hull by their feet. For all this they would pay £21 a head. No. He did not have much, but it had not come to that, not yet.

But what were the alternatives? A whole day's enquiry had turned up little else. There was space in the cabins on the *Bullant*, but that would cost £74 – his entire savings. Or he could try Liverpool, and spend yet more of his dwindling funds getting there, with no promise of a better offer. All around him, others were making the same calculation: what worth pride, when with every day their financial position was weakening? But then, to arrive ragged in the port at the other side, one of those pale, faceless hundreds – poor wretches – *that* could cost a man more than could be bought back at the other end.

McMillan at least was saved the trade-off. A breakthrough came that evening just as he undressed for bed, still wrangling with his own pride and preparing for another day of ships' agents and haggling. A gentleman arrived at the inn seeking him by name: the captain of the *Minerva*, he said, had sent him with a message. There was a berth in Captain Furlong's own cabin, which McMillan could have for £55.

The deal was done. Now there was little to do but write his last letters home, and wait with nervous anticipation as the *Minerva* finished her toilette. He bought copies of the New Testament in town, and sent them on a boat bound for the Western Isles to the young women of Barra: his sisters, Miss Finlayson Kilbride, and his *dear Miss Margaret* — his first love, who he was leaving behind. Oh, the agony of waiting! With every passing day he was forced to renew his resolve.

God's will be done. And God's will, he reminded himself, was that he must go. On Monday, seeking solace in prayer, he went to the kirk twice, both in the morning and in the afternoon. But it left him cold. *The clergymen I heard were strangers.*

Hold steady. Tuesday dawned and they filed aboard, heavy trunks stowed neatly under narrow bunks. Anchor up, sails unfurled. Course set for the south. After all the anticipation, all the hanging around, there was a carnival atmosphere. At night the steerage passengers ventured up onto the decks and danced under the stars in delight. But McMillan was in no mood for celebrations. *They should employ their time to better advantage*, he thought darkly, and retreated to his cabin to scribble in his journal and dwell on the dark coast that drifted ceaselessly by, inch by inch, behind him into the night.

He would never go home again.

At twenty-seven, he was already a man with some experience of the sea. An islander by birth, he had grown up in and around boats; he knew well the whip of the wind and salt spray on the face, the constant shifting of the deck beneath him.

He and his family had spent their lives skipping between the Hebridean islands, as his father Ewen sought out suitable positions to support his growing brood. Angus was the fourth of at least fourteen children, a large family even in those times; and though the McMillans were not poor, relatively speaking – Ewen was a tacksman, a sort of intermediary between clan chief and the peasantry, the closest equivalent to a middle class in traditional Highland society – their position was unstable.

The agricultural revolution sweeping Scotland was rendering the role of the tacksman obsolete as more and more English managers and 'land economists' were brought in to commercialise the vast Highland estates. Change was afoot; the McMillans kept on the move. They had started in Glen Brittle on the Isle of Skye, at the foot of the forbidding Cuillin ridge. It was the domain of Macleod of Macleod, the clan chief who – when not in London – lived at Dunvegan Castle, twenty miles to the north-west.

As tacksman Ewen had made a name for himself as a grafter and an innovator, importing new, improved breeds of sheep from the mainland, before he met and married Marion, a well-connected local girl both well educated and deeply devout. Their growing brood had been instilled with the importance of religion and education, of leading a moral life, and the skills for self-sufficiency necessary in a remote community.

But across the Macleod estate, rents were rising like the tide, and there was no extra money coming in to pay them with. When their nineteen-year lease came to an end, the family packed up and sailed west, first to South Uist, and then to Barra, a jewel of an island just to the south, where Angus spent his formative years. The then laird, General Roderick MacNeil, had converted from Catholicism, and brought numbers of Protestant outsiders onto the island after inheriting the estate in 1822; the industrious – and numerous – McMillans took to their subsidiary role as lay missionaries as energetically as MacNeil could have hoped.

It had been an outdoor, practical, windswept childhood; one spent trudging through rain and snow and hail, mending fences and lambing sheep, navigating small boats through the wild gales that howled their way down the Minch. So, on board the *Minerva*, he stared up at the sails and out to the horizon with a critical eye, and noted the ship's pace and progress in his journal each day. Within a few hours, his spirits began to sink: *our craft does not appear to be a good sailor.* But conditions were good, at least. The coast of Ireland appeared within the day, and then Wales. *Fine leading under single reef top sails.* The wind was behind them, blowing them straight down the Irish Sea, and out into the Atlantic Ocean.

I too was now twenty-seven. It had taken eighteen months to get things in order – or, more accurately, sufficiently disordered – so that I might head off in pursuit of Angus McMillan. I'd left my job, left London, amassed some (already dwindling) funds, and booked my own passage to Australia.

Before I left, I returned to Skye for a last look. I need to get closer to him; to nestle in close to the heart of this strange man and listen for his pulse. I was thinking of the tombstone with his name *in absentia*, of the black gabbro cliffs of the ragged-edged range that loomed over McMillan in his infancy. I wanted to see it all afresh, start at his beginning and work from there.

I had dragged my boyfriend with me. Well, 'dragged' is unfair. Alex loved the Highlands as much as I did – more, even. He was a Londoner who dreamed of moors and mountains, who saw the whole of Scotland as a sort of adventure playground of snow and rock, of peaks to be scaled and troughs to be traversed. He'd been dragging me to remote parts, to the tops of mountains and to icy trig points – fingers of cement rising out of the rock, shrouded in mist, encrusted in windsculpted ice – for months.

It was winter now; we'd been living together since the spring. Our reckless love, a whirlwind of promises and declarations, had culminated in a hasty move to the countryside. Each of us had seen in the other an easy solution to problems we had not yet been ready to voice. But now, in our house in a village in the north of England, each of us had been sitting in separate rooms, making separate plans for the coming months. We had made a deal: meet you back here in spring. 'We'll be fine,' we each said to each other. 'It's not so long.' And we smiled with our mouths but not with our eyes. This trip would be our swansong, but we were not yet ready to voice that thought either.

Since my visit with my mother, my brother Rory had moved to Skye with his wife to start a family. Mum and her siblings had been almost euphoric at the announcement; the family claim to the island had been shored up, brought from the academic into the actual and made solid again. Myles was in the process of handing over the family croft so my brother might build a house on it.

Alex and I drove north, the car packed with everything we owned, love blooming in my heart as the neat dry-stone-wall stitching of Cumbria gave way first to the long slow slopes of the Southern Uplands, and then to the bleaknesses and steepnesses of the Highlands. Winter was closing in, and with it came the all-encompassing dark. At Cluanie we slowed to a crawl, wary of the red deer that had come down off the hills to amass along the roadside, lantern eyes glinting in the darkness like some terrible premonition. I nosed the car into their midst, taking care not to touch one with the bumper and jolt this dream sequence into the real, and slid to a halt as the largest stag stood his ground in the centre of the road. He raised his head, many-pointed antlers silhouetted against the gloom like a great pair of wings opening. Then slowly, insolently, he turned and bounded down the bank, white rabbit-tail flashing in the shaft of headlight.

Poring over the map that night, my eyes alighted on a small grey square near a bay pockmarked with the stippled texture signifying pebble beach. 'Glenbrittle House', said the label. McMillan's childhood home. I waved Alex over, but his eyes snagged instead on the mass of contours to the near east: the Cuillin ridge, all tumbling crags and chutes of scree. He cared little for my murdering relative; he ached instead for the feel of cold rock under his hands. We made another deal.

In the morning we set off again for the hills, heating on full blast and rain blattering at the windscreen. Talking in undertones, still half asleep, we nearly didn't see the bird hunched in the middle of the road, watching our approach with wide yellow eyes as he guarded some small prey in his talons. Alex slammed on the brakes as the bird took off, but too late and in the wrong direction. He launched and flew directly into our path, glaring in at us through the windscreen. At the last moment he lifted, but not enough – he clipped the roof of the car with one wing. I shrieked and craned around to see him whirl and right himself in the air, wings outstretched and as unsteady as a drunk.

A golden eagle. I'd never seen one before, not in the wild. Only those depressed, scrawny specimens on their Astroturfed perches at game fairs, shackled at the ankle. 'Is that a good omen or a bad one?'

'Good,' said Alex definitively. 'He survived.'

'Yes,' I said. 'I hope so.'

The road wound a slalom path down into Glen Brittle, through a neat-penned conifer plantation. Stray larches pressed against the wire, stretching their feathery arms out between the strands. Dead pines swayed, monuments to themselves, bare of needles but shrouded entirely in thick white lichen like cobwebs, or lace – bridal somehow, so many Miss Havishams in their veils.

Snow had gathered in this sheltered nook, where ploughs rarely ventured. A single car had preceded us that morning, and its tracks wriggled down over the narrow strip of tarmac, bunny-hopping at places where the driver had nearly lost control. Neat heaps of grit had been left at five-yard intervals along the worst stretches by the council, so the locals could help themselves.

The Cuillin rose up on our left as we descended, recent snowfall exaggerating the terribleness of its crags, each crack picked out in the sharp black and white of a Victorian engraving; the jagged line of the ridge stretching above dark and forbidding, sharp enough to skewer a cloud to its highest peak. At its foot, the hillside was a magnificent technicolour of the clashing orange vegetation, darker bracken and flashes of bright, almost neon green where burns had overflowed and spilled out across the face of the slope.

We abandoned the car and hiked in to where the water rushing down off the mountains rumbled through a series of perfect turquoise ponds: the Fairie Pools. The noise was tremendous as the water crashed between levels, then slowed and stilled in the deep, dark channels between the rocks. I clambered down to a pool partway up the chain that had been split in two by an elegant underwater arch, and dipped an arm in up to the elbow. The water was gloriously, bitingly cold, numbing my fingers almost instantaneously.

Alex was impatient to be on his way, and set off alone towards the start of the ridge. I watched him go, then turned back towards the road, with the roar of the falls in my ears. Water was everywhere, slipping between the rocks, dripping on my forehead, resting in still pools and puddled on the ground, which was sodden as a dropped cloth. Where tributaries had cut down into the hillside, stripped birches huddled for warmth out of the wind, naked branches crimson. Erratic rocks dotted the burned-red hillside, teetering where they had sat so unsteadily for hundreds of years.

I waited at the car until I caught a glimpse of him silhouetted against the sky on the crest of the ridge, then drove down into the township along a single-track road, scattered with sheep-droppings. Here and there amongst the heather and peat bog that lined the foot of the glen clumps of hut circles nudged mushroom-like from the earth.

There wasn't much to Glenbrittle: a youth hostel, closed for winter; a mountain rescue base; a clutch of cottages, barely enough to call it a hamlet, where the glen opened up by the water's edge. Three lush fields, spotted with heavy-set sheep, led down to a dark pebble beach. The landscape was stark and unforgiving, the colours rich: the burgundy of the heather, the rusting bracken, the bare purple birch, the hawthorn's scarlet berries, the gleaming white snow of the peaks.

Glenbrittle House was easy to identify; a somewhat tumbledown, but nicely proportioned stone building, its grey-harl façade patched up in places with concrete. I was hovering outside, considering my options, when a young man stamped across the puddled road, enveloped in thick, kelpy green oilskins.

'Excuse me,' I blurted out, stupidly. 'Do you know which one is Glenbrittle House?'

He paused. 'The big grey one.'

I nodded and made to leave, but he spoke again. 'Do you mind me asking why you want to know? Only, it's my granny's house.' He was friendly enough, and about my age, with dark hair crammed under a beanie hat. He led me up the garden path and peeled off his waterproofs at the door as if shedding his skin, leaving his trousers cinched into his rubber boots. 'I'll fetch her for you. She often doesn't hear the bell.'

I stood politely on the doorstep in the rain, craning my neck to get a look inside. The interior was big and roomy, but dated – the hallway papered with photo-detail brickwork. Finally the owner came out, and blinked at me, cautious. She clutched a copy of the *West Highland Free Press* in one hand, holding it to her breast like a shield.

'Angus McMillan?' she said. 'Oh, no. I don't know. When was this?' She was a tiny, white-haired woman.

'1810?' I hazarded. She batted the air, letting out a puff of air – ho! – as if to say, 'Well, I'm not that old!' and her grandson and I laughed.

'It's been in our family, the MacRaes, for seventy years now,' she told me. 'Though it's not ours, you realise. We're tenant farmers. The whole lot belongs to Macleod of Macleod at Dunvegan.'

I nodded. Some things never change. 'Who else lives round here?'

She considered. 'There's just us, really. Our family.' She looked fondly at her grandson. 'There's a few moved in from elsewhere, but' – a bit disapprovingly – 'all just holiday homes.'

Down on the beach, I picked my way across the coloured pebbles and the seaweed lying thick and variegated as autumn leaves. Hailstones drew a white-rim tideline along the shore, like foam swept in off the sea. A band of rain drew across the bay like a curtain.

It was such an isolated spot. A man with thirteen siblings – perhaps more: records from that period are very partial – would never be lonely. But his parents would have been instrumental in the formation of his character. They were his only role models.

Out across the water I could make out the faint outline of the island of Canna. Directly behind it, unseen in this weather, was South Uist, the family's next stop, and to its south, McMillan's beloved Barra. Each of these islands has its own personality. South Uist, the flat sandy isle, tucks its head down out of the wind, its back grown thick with a fur of wildflowers upon the machair in summer: eyebright and lady's bedstraw, harebells and butterfly orchids, corn marigolds and sea bindweed, field gentian and red clover. Barra is a rougher, readier sort of place, its one green peak looming from the sea, slipping the earth from its shoulders like a shawl, smooth rocks poking through the slopes like clavicles, smoothed by the wind.

I visited Barra too, alone this time, and camped on a silver cockle beach unseen by any other; then, tramp-like, on a grass verge on the outskirts of Castlebay, the only village. I cycled the circumference of the island on a borrowed bike, otter-spotting, calling out in greeting to the curious seals that followed me along the water's edge, singing them nonsense songs and the scraps of pop music that popped into my head.

The McMillans' solid Georgian farmhouse at Eoligarry, on the north end of the island, has long been demolished, but I cycled up anyway, finding the tide out and the enormous expanse of white sand now employed as a runway for the tiny airport. Wind battering my face, I watched a twelve-seater propeller plane land, wheels bouncing on the sand, sending salt water up behind it in a sheet, carrying the post and groceries. Five figures ventured down the steps and out into the rain, bent double against the wind. Even today, I thought, this is a remote outpost of humanity.

Angus McMillan never explicitly explained in his journals why he left the Hebrides, but it is not hard to paint a picture of the prevailing tides that swept him from their shores. Scotland at that time was in crisis, both financial and existential. In the century since the union with England the ancient clan system had been dissolving, and dissatisfaction among the poor was growing.

Historically, the clan chiefs had held a position of paternalist responsibility over their subjects in a subsistence economy. However, since the advent of the United Kingdom, the lairds were becoming increasingly embedded in the moneyed society south of the border, frequenting the gentlemen's clubs of Mayfair and dabbling in Westminster politics. Keenly aware of their aristocratic status in Highland society, but without the vast incomes of the English landed gentry, they began to turn their attentions to generating new profits from their estates.

There has been much discussion of the motivations that underlay the turmoil of the subsequent decades, but whether the chiefs' decisions were driven by personal greed or simply market forces, the transition to capitalism would be a painful one. The great Highland estates underwent a seismic shift which saw unprofitable tenants, who had depended on the lairds for their livelihoods, displaced – initially to provide a workforce for the burgeoning kelp industry, and later to make way for sheep. To the peasantry, these upheavals were a profound betrayal of the trust they had placed in their traditional patriarchs.

Between 1780 and 1880, an estimated half a million people left the Highlands – some under their own steam, many under duress – permanently skewing the country's demographics towards the newly urban south and sending tens of thousands across the oceans to the New World.

It was not only the destitute who left, although many were destitute. For many young men like Angus McMillan, this was a chance to better themselves in new, more egalitarian countries, where land was cheap, or even free.

Coming from a culture where land equated to power more than money ever had, this was a startling opportunity.

Australia in particular was becoming a hub of migration from the Hebrides. Visiting Skye in 1840, the novelist Catherine Sinclair commented that every family she met seemed to have a member settled in or en route there. In Angus McMillan's immediate family, for example, it is known that four of the brothers lived at some stage in Australia: Angus himself, and his brothers John, William and Donald – who had also lived in Jamaica for some years before he joined Angus in Gippsland. A fifth brother, Norman, travelled to South America, only to drown in the Amazon.

The newspapers of the day were full of advertisements for cheap passages to the US, Canada and the new colonies of the far-off Southern Ocean, Australia and New Zealand. Some offered government assistance towards the cost. One such advert from 1835, placed by the Colonization Committee of South Australia, noted, 'Commissioners are also prepared to receive applications from such intending Settlers as may wish to have their Servants or Labourers conveyed to the Colony FREE OF CHARGE by means of the Emigration Fund.'

As the rural population dwindled, entire villages fell empty and were abandoned to the elements and to the blackfaced sheep that now grow fat on the grass that grows high amid the ruins. Huge round stones slip one by one from their places in crumbling walls to the ground; roof-less buildings shrink and sink as they are reclaimed by the land.

*

Balnabodach is one such village. It lies on the north-west edge of Barra, four miles from the pier at Castlebay, overlooking a tiny pebbled cove. I spotted it from the road as I cycled back from the airport, left my bike unlocked on the verge, shimmied under the fence where the sheep had got through, and headed down to inspect. A fat-rumped roan pony watched me uninterestedly as I waded through drifts of sphagnum moss, thigh-deep in places, as wet and as soft as a cloud. Within seconds my feet were squelching in their boots, peaty water oozing between my toes, my jeans soaked to the crotch.

The remains of the old village were rendered in texture and colour, most house sites made visible only by the changes in vegetation – rectangles of sheep-cropped grass gleaming amidst crowds of dark, rubbery reeds and the burned-out orange of the bracken. A single cottage was roofless but otherwise almost perfectly preserved, with a doorway and shoulder-height walls, the rocks dry-stacked, slotted together perfectly, its good condition a testament to the skill of its builder. Its windows had been sealed with rocks sometime in the distant past – the mark of the plague.

Across a stream and up a bank huddled four or five more ruins, in poorer condition. The walls had tumbled many years before; now grown over, but sitting proud to the ground, the same rounded humps of old graves.

It is a lonely prospect. In Angus McMillan's time – the 1820s and '30s – this would have been a busy, bustling township: a tight huddle of one-roomed blackhouses thatched with reeds, cattle penned at their backs as dogs and chickens roamed loose between the walls. But now there was nothing. Less than nothing; a palpable absence. A negative.

In the course of those two decades, a financial drama unfolded that would see the island's ownership fall from the hands of the MacNeils of Barra, who had held the title since the eleventh century. General MacNeil, who had brought the McMillans to the island, found he had inherited an estate shackled by legalities and weighted with liabilities. Although he had served with distinction at the Battle of Waterloo, this had apparently not been enough to impress his father, Colonel Roderick, whose lack of faith in his son's financial acumen had manifested itself in the imposition of a deed of entail upon the estate before his death to prevent its being sold off piecemeal; it had then been further bound with a large number of settlements to the colonel's other children. At the time of his death it was already foundering.

That same year, 1822, the bottom fell out of the Scottish kelp industry when the lifting of import restrictions after the defeat of Napoleon saw the market flooded with cheaper European alternatives. Until then, lairds had been able to produce a ton of kelp for around £3 – gathering seaweed from the beaches and burning it down to create soda ash – and sell it on as fertiliser for £20. By these vertiginous profits the MacNeil accounts had been buoyed. Without them, it sank without trace.

MacNeil the younger turned to ever more desperate means of staying afloat. He established an alkali works, so the kelp could be processed on the island and thus sold at a higher price, at which the islanders were forced to work. It failed miserably. He threatened local fishermen with eviction if they sold their catch in Glasgow or to passing boats rather than at Castlebay, where he could take his cut. He seized his tenants' cattle, and later their sheep.

There was not much else to take: 'The poverty of the people is beyond description,' their parish priest wrote in 1831.

For all of the islanders it was a time of enormous stress and uncertainty. Even the tacksmen, like Angus's father, were not safe: his counterpart in the south was evicted from his farm at Vatersay, which had been passed down in his family for generations.

The estate reached crisis point in 1837, when the general finally admitted defeat. As MacNeil was facing bankruptcy and preparing to sell up, Angus McMillan packed his bags and sailed for the mainland with the intention of joining his friend Allan MacCaskill on the boat to New South Wales. He was not alone. That same year, 1,253 other emigrants left Scottish ports for Australia, 2,391 for the American colonies (including Nova Scotia), and 1,130 for the United States.

This sorry tale forms the backdrop to McMillan's departure. He was, however, fortunate to have left in time to miss the very worst the Clearances had to throw at the island.

The Barra estate was sold to an outsider, Colonel John Gordon of Cluny. Gordon was a notoriously ruthless man of vast means – 'the richest commoner in the kingdom' – who on his death would leave £2 million and numerous estates scattered across Scotland as well as lucrative plantations on Tobago. Over the following decade the destitute tenants would be pushed from the estate, initially in a trickle and finally in a great torrent now regarded as one of the most brutal clearances of the period.

During the 1840s, a series of crop failures left the island in a constant state of near-famine. In one particularly bleak period, the minister reported 'a scene of horror' as starving families scratched in the sand for cockles, without which 'there would have been hundreds dead this day'. Gordon found that, far from the estate being an investment, he was now responsible for supporting the majority of its two-thousand-strong population. And so he began to evict them.

By the winter of 1850, the piteous state of Gordon's expelled tenants had attracted the concerned attention of the Lord Provost of Edinburgh, who heard reports that a number of families from Barra had arrived in the city 'in a state of absolute starvation'. A few months earlier, 132 families had been removed from their crofts, a feat accomplished by 'demolishing their cottages, and then, after they were cast out desolate on the fields, getting them shipped off the island'. None 'could speak a word of English' – only the heavily accented Gaelic of the island.

These wretched families had been dumped on the island of Mull, and from there some had struggled to Edinburgh in the hope of appealing to the colonel himself, who kept his headquarters there. But Gordon was not to be found.

Even if he had been present to meet his former tenants, it is unlikely that compassion would have been forthcoming. The next year he would call his poorest tenants to a public meeting to 'discuss rents and arrears', with a threatened £2 fine for non-attendance. The meeting was a ruse: 1,700 people from Barra and nearby South Uist were forced – begging, pleading and struggling – onto an emigrant ship bound for Quebec. Those resisting were dragged from the caves and mountains and handcuffed together on a boat that carried them from the tiny, wind-swept island to a vast, unknown wilderness of dense, dark forest and frozen wastes. When, finally, they were let loose on dry land there was an ocean between them and everything they had ever known.

In Balnabodach, all eight families still resident were forced on board ship, with only the clothes they had on. Not one of those recorded as living there in 1841 was to be found in the census of 1851. Today the name Balna-bodach can still be found on maps – a label for the smat-tering of modern white-harled cottages set high and apart along the road, far back from the ruins at the water's edge, to house people who have come here for the peace, the quiet, the tranquillity.

Standing there in the dell, out of sight, I realised that I had not spoken to another person all day. For the first time I appreciated the bittersweet nature of that Highland solitude I had thought so quintessential, so central to its character. Many of the most silent spots in the Highlands and Islands today were once the most densely populated – indeed, the devastating impact of the crop failures and the kelp-industry collapse had been attributed by some commentators to overcrowding. The emptiness of the glens is as artificial as once was its congestion.

I was alone that trip, but I had not felt lonely until now.

These lost generations maintain a presence in Scottish culture more than 150 years later. Songs and poetry writ-ten in the times of the Clearances circulate and recirculate, the hot breath of each singer taken in by the next, a constant oral reliving of that turbulent age.

The most famous, perhaps, is Sorley MacLean's 1954 Gaelic poem 'Hallaig', an elegy for an abandoned village on the author's native island of Raasay (*'Mura tig 's ann theàrnas mi a Hallaig/a dh'ionnsaigh Sàbaid nam marbh,/far a bheil an sluagh a' tathaich,/gach aon ghinealach a dh'fhalbh'*; 'I will go down to Hallaig,/to the Sabbath of the dead,/where the people are gathered,/every single generation gone'). Or perhaps it is The Proclaimers' hit 1987 song 'Letter from America', which addresses the emigrants directly ('I've looked at the ocean/tried hard to imagine/the way you felt the day you sailed/from Wester Ross to Nova Scotia').

They are songs of loss, of heartbreak, of the pain of being left behind. The departed wrote songs too, songs filled with the crash of the sea and the tug of the heart. Thoughts of home pull from deep inside, behind the navel, somewhere delicate and bruised and inarticulate. The emigrants are rootless, anchorless, their homesickness trailing like a long lead behind them, with no one holding on to it. Oh! for our dispossessed brothers. Oh! for the land of bleak beauty. Oh! for the touch of soft rain on the skin, for the peat smoke from the hearth, for the mud of the well-trodden path.

They have a saying in Nova Scotia, an expression of longing: *Ach an cuan* – But for the sea. But for the sea we'd be together again.

At Sabhal Mòr Ostaig, the Gaelic college in Skye, I watched a group of singers who stood stiff-armed at the centre of the dance floor; their leader alone at first, tapping her foot, eyes to the ceiling, harsh Gaelic consonants chopping through the low, rich tones of her voice.

Thicker Than Water

Thoir mo shoraidh dhan taobh tuath
Eilean Sgithanach nam buadh
'N t-eilean sin dan tug mi luaidh
Àit' is bòidhche fo na neòil
Thoir mo shoraidh dhan taobh tuath.

Bear my greetings to the north
To the Isle of Skye and all its graces
That island to whom I gave my love
The most beautiful place under the clouds
Bear my greetings to the north.

From those exiled abroad, this song had crossed the miles
and the years to pop up among us like a message in a
bottle. Heard now afresh, it was a mournful keening to a
long-lost homeland which sat only a few miles to my
north, behind the Cuillin ridge, the Macleod estate:
Dunvegan, Duirinish, Glenbrittle. The land of Angus
McMillan's childhood.

A sharp intake of breath, and then the others were singing too, the warbling, flat-noted melody calling to mind
the nasal tone of the chanter. And then, all around me,
one by one, the voices of the audience were coming
together too, soaring loud and clear and high up into the
rafters above:

B'fheàrr leam fhìn na mìle crùn
Mi bhith nochd air tìr san Dùn
Mi gun coisicheadh le sùnnd
Rathad ùr aig clann MhicLeòid
Thoir mo shoraidh dhan taobh tuath.

But for the Sea

I'd pay a thousand crowns
To be tonight ashore in Dunvegan
I would happily walk
Clan MacLeod's new road
Bear my greetings to the north.

Many of the singers that night had themselves travelled from what was once the New World back to the Old World, to rediscover their lost links to the Highlands. So many studying at the college were Canadians, Australians, New Zealanders, with names like MacDonald, Fraser and Munro.

They felt a tie, they confided by the bar late at night, a complex bond that is difficult to explain or understand. They felt compelled to return to a homeland they had never seen. Thousands of the diaspora return to Scotland every year; I watched them in my childhood, trooping through the village in their tour groups, keeping the tweed shop in business, cheering for the pipe band. Many are better-informed on the ins and outs of Scottish history than Scots themselves. Clan membership, particularly, is now dominated by overseas members who trade notes on the minutiae of family trees that have spread their branches across continents. Perhaps the locals feel they have nothing to prove; the visitors, with their foreign accents and long-lensed cameras, much.

But it was hard too for those left behind – those left standing in empty glens, watching first as the thatch of the empty homes collapsed, and then the walls. Imagine the desolation of the empty township, the abandoned schools, the silent churches. In Croik church in Sutherland, the dispossessed scratched messages in the glass of the windows as they sought shelter from the driving rain: 'Glencalvie people, the wicked generation'. They thought they were being punished for their sins.

The old ways were dissolving under their feet. The warriors who had once commanded fear amongst even the most stout-hearted Englishmen now found their skills and courage in battle repurposed for the furthering of the British Empire. What else could they do to earn money, in a world that now seemed to revolve around it? They knew of no other way to live.

The old tongue too was in the process of being phased out. Since the seventeenth century, the Highland nobility had been obliged by law to send their children to English-speaking schools in the south; more recent attempts to Anglicise the wild and rebellious population of the Highlands and Islands had resulted in the prohibition of the Gaelic language in schools, even in solely Gaelic-speaking areas — a ludicrous policy resulting only in classrooms filled with uncomprehending faces and dire literacy rates.

By Angus McMillan's time, Lowland policy had been relaxed somewhat, in that it allowed the teaching of the scriptures in Highlanders' mother tongue, so as not to inhibit their religious education at least. As a result Gaelic had begun to take on the quality of a spiritual mode of communication, a speaking in tongues. It was the vernacular of the church and the home, an unwritten language of confession, of conviction, of off-the-record conversation, while English became established as the language of the learned, the landed, the future.

But only the old language has the vocabulary to describe that particular flavour of Highland melancholy. Edward Dwelly's great dictionary, *Faclair Gàidhlìg* (1911), records forty-nine different words for sadness, each with its own special quality. *Snigheadh* sadness: also the act of falling in drops, the shedding of tears. *Mùig* sadness: darkness of mood, gloom, also snot, snivelling nose. *Mì-fhuran*: a churlish sadness, joylessness, a disinclination to welcome or congratulate. *Aithridh*: the sadness of repentance.

Longing finds twenty-four ways of expressing itself. In *fonn*, a carnal longing, also land, earth, plain, the drone of a bagpipe. *Leid*: uncomfortable longing, also a shake-down or bed made on the floor, a temporary fireplace. *Deòthas*: the longing for a loved one, as of a calf for its mother.

There are other words too, more subtle descriptions of a land that finds itself emptied of life.

> *Aibheis* (noun): An expanse of sea or air, an abyss; a place full of fairies, or in ruins or unkempt.
> *Tannasgach* (adjective): Abounding in spectres or ghosts.
> *Sporthail* (noun): A subdued rattling noise, such as is made by a stone wall about to fall.

3

The Fever Ship

A month passed. Time moved slowly.

The *Minerva* was making heavy work of the voyage, and McMillan grew bored with watching sails appear on the horizon behind them only to speed by with demoralising ease, leaving the *Minerva* in their wake. He wished he had gone in another ship.

Daily he stared out at the sea, calculating their progress, growing impatient in his impotence: *Wind is fair this day, also E by S, steering SW, going about 5½ miles an hour. Lat 20 59 Long 22½°. Very warm.* They were surrounded by ocean on all sides, with nothing but their own company as they chased the horizon across its infinite expanse. McMillan's eyes raked the skyline as a man walking out at night casts around the circle of light given out by his lantern; he was watching for the coasts of new lands, the masts of strange ships that dipped in and out of sight on their unknown courses.

Four days before, they'd seen the Canary Islands, specks of rock in the far distance, but they hadn't sighted land since. Shoals of flying fish skimmed the surface of the waves, driving themselves into the air with slashing tails, then smoothly soaring on stained-glass wings. The heavily laden *Minerva* sat low in the water, and as the fish glided unseeingly forward they grazed the tops of the rails and came in to land, gasping, on the deck. They tasted like mullet, fat and sweet.

The shores of Cape Verde lay still a few days to the south, somewhere over the horizon, unseen. The passengers were listless, settling heavy as sand into the rhythm of life on board: biscuit and salt pork, lime juice, the strictly rationed water grown stale in its barrels, inertia. The stutter and sigh of conversation drying up. A Sunday service in the German missionary's stilted English marked off the weeks like the tally on a prison wall. But although his body was confined, McMillan's mind roamed free across the ocean, coasting on the thermals like a seabird; forward into the unknown, then inevitably backwards, to the comforts and the consolations of home.

He retreated to his cabin, braced himself against the rolling of the ocean, dipped a pen, and opened his journal. *Bright fancy brings me to the distant shores of green Barra, for my heart will throb with warm affection at the mention of thy ever remembered name. Often do I think of thee amid this wilderness of water, when nothing is heard but the roar of the tempest and nothing visible beyond our back but the lowering heaven and the rolling sea.* He knew that the lives of those he had left behind would still be rolling on without him as he trod water and stewed on his present condition: his past choices, his future chances, his lost love.

For McMillan the journey was uneventful. But below him, in the hold, the mass of his fellow passengers ran the full gamut of human experience. A young man, *in a poor state of health*, disappeared from his bed one day and was never seen again; over the side, presumably, but who could say for sure? His poor wife, who had left his side only to prepare him a drink, would pass the rest of the journey scouring the ship in desperation. The German missionary held a funeral, in case. Afterwards, McMillan turned back to the ocean to regard the *merciless wave* afresh. He did not want to die, he thought, not without ever seeing his home again.

The German held another ceremony, a wedding for a young couple from Kintyre. Afterwards, McMillan eyed the lovers fondly as they danced on deck long into the night. He envied them. They would arrive in the New World together, secured to each other, and linked too by the other to their former existence. As for him, he would have to face the future alone: *I must own my weakness on thinking of dear — that loved me while I lived near her, and I hope will preserve my memory while in a foreign clime and under the heat of a tropical sun.*

He mourned the loss of his old life, with no aspect of the new one yet in view. He wrote to his brothers, his sisters, his mother, his father, his *Miss Margaret*, but the *Minerva* made no stop at any port, and the letters sat, unsent and unread, in his cabin. By the time they were sent, by the time he heard back, the news would be long out of date: they had been split apart like firewood, and there would be no putting them back together.

Time passed in an interminable haze of sorrow and introspection. He resolved that on arrival at his destination he would be a better man, *hereafter to do whatever I think to do my duty and work for the good and advantage of mankind. To be sweet and benevolent, quiet, peaceably contented, generous, easy company, humble, meek, diligent and industrious, charitable even of aliens.* He cleaned and waxed his boots. He set himself arithmetic problems. He wished for a faster ship. He prayed.

Though progress was slow, it was constant. Celestial signposts marked their advance: every day the sun rose higher in the sky; by now it was nearly directly overhead at midday. Constellations whirled in nightly dance, slipping down and down, taking their leave as they reached the edge of the dance floor, allowing new sets to take their places from the opposite horizon.

He grieved for things it had not occurred to him that he would miss. *Last night there was an eclipse of the moon. Totally eclipsed about 10 for it was quite dark then and the stars appeared beautifully, but I've almost lost sight of my friend the Great Bear.* He took the time to examine every facet of the life he had left behind and store it carefully in a file marked *home.*

It is not only distance that creates lags in communication. A gulf between my boyfriend and me had begun to grow even in the moments when we lay next to each other in bed. In the rush to clear our house and catch my plane, we had left important conversations unspoken and said a goodbye more ambiguous than I'd expected.

It had been a sorry parting, and one that I felt guilty to be causing. Before we left the house I had pressed my forehead to his chest and promised everything I had, and made him promise too, again and again. But this much I knew: all our belongings were either in our backpacks or in the boxes stowed away in my childhood bedroom awaiting a plan of action, of which we had none.

Still, I was on my way. And when I found myself safe in my seat on the first of several flights, uncontactable, in transit, my initial reaction was one of relief. Out of touch, out of office, out of sync with the world, I have always found the still point at my centre. My mind is always steadiest when my body is in motion.

It was late morning when I took off from London, but there was barely time for lunch before the dark came upon us and we flew on into the night. Lights were dimmed and blinds pulled low. The frequent fliers put their eyemasks on and tried to catch up with the world we were heading towards. Twelve hours later I was reluctantly awake in the gilded purgatory of Dubai International Airport, swilling the milky dregs of a double-strength coffee and watching the flights on the departures board tick up and up and up.

Unlike in McMillan's time, when it was a tangible and gruelling process, travel today is experienced in the abstract. On board a plane, the passenger moves extraordinary distances with relative immediacy, while signing over all autonomy to the cabin staff. One has no need to worry about food, or water, or even amusing oneself, while in the hands of these unreliable timekeepers who slow or speed the passage of the day depending on the direction in which you are flying: skipping from breakfast to dinner, or working their way down the aisles shutting out the light, heralding in the artificial night even as the sun burns fiercely upon the fuselage outside

I ate what food I was offered, drank what wine was given to me, slept whenever my eyes fluttered closed. I got drunk and confused, got off one plane and onto another, drank more wine. I passed out across a bank of empty seats, then snapped at the hostess when she woke me for my meal. Breakfast again. How long had I been travelling? It was an unedifying state of affairs. At least on a ship, as the mercury of the thermometer inches up degree by degree, and the stars slip from view to the underside of the earth, there is time for adjustment. Time to come to terms with the distance, both mentally and physically.

They understood time differences in McMillan's day — the disparity between the 'noon' of a clock set to Greenwich Mean Time and the actual noon observed from on board the ship had been used as a navigational tool since the seventeenth century — but in the nineteenth century it was not so pressing a reality as it is today, given the lack of immediate communication and the slow speed of travel. To those on board, it would not have been apparent that day by day their body clocks were adjusting themselves, that day was becoming night and night becoming day — that they were not, in fact, staring together with their loved ones up at the same moon every evening.

Jet lag began with the advent of high-speed travel, and it is hard, or at least it is hard while suffering from its effects, not to interpret it as nature's payback for tampering with the natural way of things: that long-distance travel should be appropriately protracted. It put me in mind of an aside in Douglas Adams's *The Hitchhiker's Guide to the Galaxy*, which quotes 'an ancient Arcturan proverb': 'However fast the body travels, the soul travels at the speed of an Arcturan Mega-Camel.' This would mean, it adds, 'in these days of hyperspace and Improbability Drive, that most people's souls are wandering unprotected in deep space in a state of some confusion; and this would account for a lot of things'.

Certainly, I arrived in Australia in a state of physiological and emotional confusion, my sense of purpose and understanding of my mission trailing some way behind, perhaps over Eurasia, certainly a considerable distance from civilisation.

I tottered through the streets of Melbourne, made top-heavy by rucksacks strapped to both my back and my front, navigating the gridiron central business district where tall glass skyscrapers jostled for space in their neat plantations. I was used to tangled, sprawling old cities, had always thought of the 'central business district' as a construct of urban development rather than as an actual physical location. But here it was, in poker-straight rows and columns like a computer simulation, every corner tipped with pedestrian signals at each axis, emitting a low, rhythmic chirrup in stereo from all around. In turn, they rose from their drumbeat in a crescendo of solid noise, cicadas taking the air on a remote hillside. In the still night streets it was disconcerting. At least navigation was easy: walk four blocks, turn, walk four blocks. Addresses here were like a game of battleships.

The hostel was an enormous, elderly institution close to the Queen Victoria Market. Downstairs was very jolly, all neon colours and glossy posters, but the bedrooms on the fourth floor had the atmosphere of a Victorian boarding house. At home, I calculated, it would nearly be time to get up. I lay sleepless on a metal cot in a cell-like room, and waited for the clock to tick round and the sun to right itself.

Angus McMillan, I thought. I need to find Angus McMillan, and then tie our lives together again.

*

McMillan and his fellow voyagers came in the second wave of immigrants to New South Wales: free men, who had decided to make the journey to the convict colony of their own accord.

Those aboard the *Minerva* were for the most part law-abiding, conscientious men and women, many of whom had been inspired to travel to the far side of the world by the writing of John Dunmore Lang, the first Presbyterian minister in Sydney, who was presently in Glasgow seeking recruits with whom to improve the colony. Lang deplored the wickedness and sexual licentiousness he saw in Sydney; an inevitable result, he wrote, of its beginnings as a repository for the criminal outcasts of British society. In a series of convincing polemics he called for willing members of his flock to populate a country that was, to his eyes, rich in opportunity yet poor in virtue.

These 'very superior' immigrants were promised land, an improved standard of living, higher wages, and an escape from the destitution of their homeland. Lang secured sponsorship for 140 Scottish tradesmen, much in demand among the largely unskilled population of New South Wales, and persuaded around four thousand more to emigrate under their own steam over the course of a decade.

McMillan himself carried a copy of Lang's *An Historical and Statistical Account of New South Wales* when he boarded the *Minerva*, which he read from cover to cover over the course of the voyage. It was a *very flattering account* of the country, he thought, and he was taken with one of Lang's poems, which he copied out in full during a bout of homesickness.

No parent, sister, brother
Can greet me now – nor other
Earthly friend.
The deep sea lies before thee
But Jehovah's shield is o'er me
To defend …

McMillan's own writing reveals him to be as devout a recruit as Lang could have hoped for. At his weakest moments he turns his gaze to the heavens, prostrating himself before the Almighty, he *who has the boundless ocean in the palm of his hand*. He repeats his motto again, and again, until his mind is still: *God's will be done. God's will be done. God's will be done.*

When the sailors slaughtered a sheep on the Sabbath, the young Highlander was outraged. The German missionary too attracted his wrath when McMillan spotted him whistling on the poop deck after a sermon. It was not the Gaelic way, McMillan said. (It's true – it is not. Even today the Sabbath is widely observed throughout the Highlands and Islands, particularly in Eilean Siar, the Outer Hebrides, where on Sundays many still refuse to work, watch television, exercise or drive a car except to travel to church. On Lewis there were protests when ferries introduced Sunday sailings in 2009.)

He tried to arouse the indignation of the other passengers, but there were few takers. His neighbour Taylor quoted the apostle Paul: 'Whatsoever is set before you, eat, asking no question for conscience' sake.' The German himself only *took a slow look of me and left me to discuss my argument alone.*

McMillan felt angry and isolated aboard this ship of heathens. Were they not on a mission to improve an ungodly land? He shut himself in his cabin and refused the meat, turned his face from the world. The captain, *a moderate man*, tried to talk him down. He was older, made wise by experience. McMillan was quite right, of course, he assured him. *He'd defy any one on board to say otherwise as I have the word of God on my side.*

But the realities of life in a primitive colony might loosen McMillan's chokehold upon right and wrong, the captain warned. *He said if he met me 40 years hence I would be of a different opinion.*

I knew where to find him. His words, at least. His journals – kept during three crucial phases of his life – are held in the State Library of Victoria, a neoclassical pile on the corner of Swanston and La Trobe.

I was there as soon as the doors opened, filed my complicated request forms and waited in the drab manuscript room in the bowels of the building. They arrived quickly, in cream accordion envelopes tied with string, and I unpacked them, fingers quivering over creased, delicate documents in their protective plastic sleeves. At last, the insight I was looking for, file 268/1: 'Journal of a cruise from Greenock to New Holland, 5 September 1837–22 December 1837'. In flowing hand, on the tall, thin pages of a handbound notebook, the thoughts of the young McMillan. I had found him.

It was strange to think that his inner thoughts, scrawled down in a cabin on the raging sea, were present in the here and now, in this buzzing bright-lit room more than a century later. Did he ever consider that they would be read by anyone other than himself, never mind pored over and parsed phrase by phrase by generations of researchers? By me? I suppose we all must, we diarists. Otherwise, what would be the point of recording our thoughts at all? If it were merely the act of writing we seek, we could write upon a slate and then wipe it clean.

I read as fast as I could, my eyes straining to find words in the looping, old-fashioned cursive. When the library prepared to close I stood on a chair and photographed each page, of this and the two later documents, and retreated to my hostel to continue detangling his words from the screen of my laptop. It was my first insight into the character of this man I had hitched myself to.

Much had been made of the negative aspects of his character – his superiority, his outspoken piety ('sanctimonious, intolerant and churlish', as one historian has described him) – but I was unconvinced. They should read *my* diaries, I thought, if they're looking for a case study in intolerance and churlishness. There was something sturdy about him, his optimism and his faith; his resolve to devote himself to work and to the furthering of mankind.

And there was a romance to him that I had not anticipated. During a storm far out in the ocean he listened as the wind *moaned in most melancholy tone through the rigging*. Outside, *a dark haze extended itself over the whole southern sky*. As sail upon sail was taken in and hatches secured, McMillan headed out onto the deck to stand in the lashing rain. *I stood silent and alone, thinking of Him who overrules the deep as well as dry land and gladdens our weak hearts when infused with fear.*

He had a comic turn of phrase, too. In another such storm, as the ship rocked *most fearfully*, he noted how *some of the passengers were thrown on their beam ends and rolled from side to side, like so many seals.* His sketches of his dinner-table companions were lacerating: the captain was a *gentle-manly fellow*, but a skipper from Greenock travelling as a passenger was of *a very cannibal appearance*. The German missionary was a *fat greasy man*, whose wife was *so extensive in raising the little finger for I have seen her gulp five glasses of wine and a tumbler of beer before 3 o'clock*. (*Oh, for a Highland lady,* he mourned. *She would hardly put her rosy lips to the glass.*) An Englishman called Simpson came in for special criticism: *a down right ass and a fool of all the company*. A Mr Mitchell, on the other hand, was *no better than a guttural mumbler*.

Ha. Perhaps it was my tiredness, my sense of being out of sync with my surroundings, but his particular brand of misanthropy appealed to me. As I sat alone in the hostel's bar, adrift in a sea of backpacker hedonism, I found myself strangely drawn to him, so tightly bound by his standards and his islander integrity.

Endless streams of European youths filed out of the main doors into the Melbourne streets, only to be replaced by yet more backpackers coming in, weighed down like packhorses with their rucksacks and carrier bags looped through and over every arm. Girls slept sprawled on the bar sofas, their backpacks like totem poles in every corner. The PA stuttered into life from the speaker above my head every few minutes with the Australian call to prayer. 'Come on down to the bar,' a disembodied voice whee-dled. 'Half-price vodka, free beer pong until 10 p.m.'

'I can't wait for tomorrow night,' a Brummie lad told a pretty Czech girl beside me. She smiled blandly back at him, inviting explanation. 'I'm going to get muntered.'

In my tired, cantankerous frame of mind, I was enjoying McMillan's catty remarks and his Eeyore-like air. *This life*, he reminded me, in schoolmasterly reprimand, *is only a scene of variety which soon passeth away and affords no solid satisfaction, but in the consciousness of doing well, and in the hope of another life.* He was a strange, earnest young man. If he were to exist in the here and now, I reflected, he might have been sitting with me, nursing a glass of wine, glowering at all the fun-havers with as much venom as I was. The thought gave me heart.

Across the room, a rowdy drinking game came to some orgiastic conclusion as a stocky young man reared up and half-ran, half-fell out of his seat while his companions roared and heckled. He barged sideways, unseeing, into the nearest sofa, lost his balance and tipped bodily over the back and onto one of the sprawling sleeping girls. Pandemonium. The girl, thrust suddenly from dream into alarming reality, screamed in shock and fear. Strangers clapped and catcalled. The PA coughed again, theme and variation: 'Come to the bar before 10 p.m. tonight for free beer pong and half-price jugs!'

'McMillan,' I couldn't help thinking, 'if only you were here to see this.'

I turned back to my screen, read again McMillan's response to the captain's warning that in forty years he would have reconsidered the rigidity of his beliefs. McMillan would have none of it: *I answered, if I was spared to see another forty years that I hoped to be guided by the same guide.*

His comment came down upon me like a weight. Forty years later, I knew, McMillan would be dead. Within five, he would already have the blood of innumerable innocents on his hands.

I felt myself pulled by a complex tug of emotions. I'd come looking for a killer, and had instead found an earnest, headstrong man of my own age, full of ideals and expectations. What happened to him?

They had crossed the equator and found the earth upside down. Each change rang through him with a piercing tone: the new moon, when it appeared, had inverted. It looked strange, but also just the same. The southern sky at least was beautiful. At night he lay on his back on the boards and traced his finger down the sweep of the Milky Way, joined the dots of the Southern Cross, smoothed the smudges that marked the Magellanic Clouds.

And across that glorious sky in the daytime came *great flocks of birds*. Birds of all stripes: sea swallows and storm petrels; fowl of a sort the sailors called the stormy pheasant – *they put me in mind of the common plover, but much brighter in colour* – and another they called the castle pigeon, its back spotted with black and white. Albatrosses too, in their dozens, their six-foot wingspans *in beautiful dun colours*, dark eyes rimmed with white.

But while McMillan's eyes turned upwards, death stalked the deck, and down below, in the hold, all hell was breaking loose. Fever was taking root among the steerage passengers, spreading from bunk to bunk. McMillan was right not to have travelled there: they were dropping like flies. Almost every other day seemed to herald a new death.

The first victim, a three-month-old child, had died a month into the voyage. All the passengers had attended the service as the tiny body was consigned to the deep. A few days later, more bad news – the young woman who had been married on board was sick: *our surgeon reports her to be in a dangerous way.*

By the end of November, McMillan reported that ten of the steerage passengers were ill. He fretted that they must be suffering from a contagious fever, though the ship's surgeon assured him it was 'only a cold'. *I am grieved to say that I cannot rely much on his judgement. Fearful consideration if it proves infectious – no one has a chance to escape its ravages.*

And so it proved. A young unmarried man from Greenock was the next to die, and within hours another, a shepherd, laid low *by the strong arm of the King of Terrors.* McMillan worried for their souls – *how poor a time to meet God, when the mind is infected with disease* – and prayed that there would be no more deaths. But to no avail. The surgeon soon grew to regret his earlier confidence, as first his own father and then his mother were taken. *His oldest sister, by every appearance, is on the brink of the grave.*

By late December, another sixteen or seventeen were confined to the hospital. Far from help, the *Minerva* sailed on. They were far out in the Indian Ocean, thousands of miles from dry land. McMillan was running out of paper. He used his last scraps to prepare himself for the worst, and to reassert his faith. *If it is thy holy will to call me Lord, grant that all who are dear to me may be forever united in thy kingdom. Thy will be done and may I be submissive to it.*

He was resigned to his fate, whatever it might be. He crammed his last entry into the bottom corner of the page on 22 December 1837, still a month's journey from Sydney: *It is a beautiful day.*

*

The *Minerva* finally staggered into port on 23 January 1838. 'THE FEVER SHIP', as Lang's newspaper the *Colonist* greeted it, had by then lost fourteen to typhus fever, while eighty-six of the 198 steerage passengers had contracted the disease, including the surgeon, who was in 'a dangerous state'.

At that time it was not known how typhus was spread (via lice), but an inspector saw enough to attribute the cause of the sickness to the 'overcrowded state of the 'tween decks', where the steerage passengers slept crammed together. 'I am informed,' he added, 'that when the vessel left Scotland, the space between decks was [also] crowded to excess with lumber, which was made a receptacle of refuse provision, and filth of every description.'

McMillan and all the others travelling in the cabins had escaped its grip, but were obliged to spend three weeks in quarantine on board the ship, under a yellow flag in Spring Cove, before they were finally allowed to disembark.

Arrival in Sydney would have been a shock to the system for a good Presbyterian boy from Skye. In 1838 the colony was celebrating its fiftieth anniversary, but while Sydney and Parramatta were now under stable government, the rougher edges maintained a lawless, frontierland air. Around a third of the population still were serving prisoners but, in terms of numbers, the dominant group was now the former convicts who had served out their sentences. Unable to afford the return fare, they were marooned indefinitely in a continent-sized prison. Many were now pursuing their own interests, searching for suitable land on the margins of the colony

There, conversation tended towards the coarse, and justice towards the brutal. Survival required cunning and self-interest, with little call for manners or sympathy for one's fellows. New arrivals often wrote home shocked by the discovery of how the realities of Antipodean life had robbed the colonists of human decency.

The very earliest arrivals had had the worst time of it. They had been dispatched from Britain in 1787 as a matter of urgency after the American Declaration of Independence in 1776 halted transportation of convicts there, generating enormous pressure on British jails. In Westminster, politicians watched with concern as elderly vessels were anchored in the Thames for use as prison ships, and convened an emergency parliamentary investigation: where could all these convicts go?

Evidence submitted by those aboard Captain Cook's expedition in 1770 – the first European encounter with Australia's eastern seaboard – was enough to convince the desperate policy-makers to send a fleet of boats carrying around 1,500 passengers, roughly half of whom were convicts, to establish what is now Sydney.

Incredibly, due to the time constraints, these reluctant colonists were sent out without any further reconnaissance. It took a gruelling eight months to reach Botany Bay, the proposed site of the new settlement, and perhaps another ten minutes after that to realise that this was not the green and pleasant land so stirringly evoked by Cook's botanist in the oak-panelled committee rooms of the Palace of Westminster, but instead a dry and alien habitat where the plants were unrecognisable, the soil arid, the climate treacherous and the animals unknown and often venomous.

They might have arrived on the surface of Mars for all they knew or understood about their new environment, and they were woefully ill-suited to master it. As the art critic and historian Robert Hughes has explained, 'The colony that would have to raise its own crops in unknown soil had only one professional gardener, and he was a raw youth of twenty. It would need tons of fish, but had only one fisherman. There were only two brickmakers, two bricklayers and a mason for all the houses that would need building [and] no sawyers.'

It was, to put things mildly, a very uncomfortable few years for those first arrivals, who struggled by on starvation rations as their crops failed year after year. Watkin Tench, an officer whose account of the colony's founding was published by Debrett's, wrote of those first, desperate months: 'Famine ... was approaching with giant strides, and gloom and dejection overspread every countenance. Men abandoned themselves to the most desponding reflections.'

The arrival of these incompetent pioneers had been met with surprising good humour by the local Aboriginal population. The Eora people, who populated the Sydney basin, had made some show of aggression on first contact, gathering in great numbers on the clifftops to brandish their spears and chant threateningly. ('*Warra warra*,' they shouted. '*Warra warra*.' Go away.) But they were intrigued by the new arrivals, and soon came down to investigate, leading to a scene of some geniality. 'They came round ye boats & many little things were given them,' the future governor Philip Gidley King recorded in his journal. 'Hatts was more particularised by them, their admiration of which they expressed by very loud shouts, whenever one of us pulled our hatts off.'

This initial bonhomie would soon give way to anger and resentment as boatload upon boatload of the British began to arrive: the Second Fleet in June 1790, the Third Fleet in July of the next year. Thus began the trickle, which became the flood. In all, 825 convict ships were sent to Australia, averaging around two hundred prisoners aboard each. These white interlopers spread inland from Port Jackson like a plague, occupying the most fertile land and encroaching upon a culture that had successfully existed in its present form for tens of thousands of years.

It is impossible to overstate the disruptive effects that these settlers would go on to have upon the lives of the Aboriginal people. Of these, disease would be the most devastating, jumping from tribe to tribe, racing across the continent far in advance of even the most adventurous Europeans. Of the Aboriginal nations of south-east Australia, only the Gunai people of what became Gippsland and their neighbours the Ngarico avoided the smallpox epidemics that cut down their countrymen like scythes, first in 1789 and again between 1829 and 1831. They were probably saved by their hostile outlook and lack of interaction with rival tribes. How sad, then, that they would be so devastated by the Gippsland pioneers led by Angus McMillan.

Today's Sydney, with its clean, breezy streets, gleaming skyscrapers and iconic harbour, is unrecognisable from the fleapit that McMillan encountered, but it is still a mecca for travellers and immigrants. Arrivals at Central Station are faced with a street of towering youth hostels and hotels, while nearby George Street, where dim sum and noodle restaurants vastly outnumber any other type of shop – apart from, perhaps, the backpackers' travel agents offering budget tours – has a distinctly international feel.

I stopped there overnight, still brooding on the future that beckoned to the serious young man I had encountered in the journals. But I felt calm. I had direction again – I was back on a path he had beaten before me. From his arrival at the quayside, he turned inland into the dry interior, and set about learning the skills for life in the fledgling colony.

I paused just long enough to take in the sights – but like Angus, I wasn't stopping long. I was off in search of cowboy country.

4

The Cattle Station

The train line from Sydney wended through mangrove swamps and bays toothed with sharp island outcrops before twisting in on itself and heading north-west into the dry interior.

I had booked onto the New South Wales railway as I would a plane: handed over ID, checked in my luggage, printed out a boarding ticket in advance. The whole aesthetic evoked 1960s air travel: wide, blocky reclining seats, cup holders, metal ashtrays carved into cubby holes in the walls. The buffet car served hot canteen lunches: roast chicken with vegetables or spaghetti bolognaise, $9 each and served in foil-covered TV-dinner trays, ordered from the conductor before 11 a.m. and picked up in person at noon.

My carriage was nearly empty, but an uppity lady steward paced the train, checking and rechecking that no one had moved from their assigned seat or carelessly allowed their belongings to spill into the empty place beside them, as if the headmaster had recently offered her the chance to prove herself as bus monitor. Her silver bob was scraped back under a black velvet Alice band, lending her a waspish look. Every ten minutes she spoke in chiding tones into the intercom. 'For anyone who was planning to hop out at the next stop for a cigarette – smoking in train stations is *prohibited.*'

North of Newcastle the lush, thickety vegetation petered out and the land opened out into a wide plain. Abandoned buildings scattered the landscape, collapsed in on their withered beams like elephant carcasses picked over by scavengers. Corrugated-iron roofs were striped with rust the deep red of clotted blood. In the middle of nowhere we came upon an enormous stopped freight train made up of dozens upon dozens of linked cars, an endless centipede of industry. A mining company was stripping the earth of her jewellery. The Australian heartland may be bleak on the surface, but underneath there is endless wealth. Each year mining companies unearth more than A$100 billion (£50 billion)-worth of iron ore, bauxite, uranium, natural gas and other resources.

Outside, the temperature was floating somewhere over 40°C, warping the tracks and limiting our progress to two-thirds of the normal speed. We trundled listlessly through a succession of towns whose names aroused confused pangs of recognition in me: Lochinvar, Aberdeen, Scone. A route map on the side of the carriage told me that the track would terminate at Armadale. The settlers' habit of naming their new homes after their old homes struck me as oddly poignant; the reassuring familiarity of the names immediately offset by the clanging disparity between the two places.

I looked out at wide, sun-bleached avenues and backyard swimming pools, but thought of the razor winds of the North Sea, and the rain that slices horizontally through the granite city. I thought of the Armadale ferrymen whiling away long workless days in hotel bars as a freezing gale outside whips the ocean into an impassable fury. What would prompt someone to link these places with those? What a strange and illogical way to help yourself feel at home.

Even weeks later I still felt that odd shock of recognition on spotting familiar names on road signs, the way you feel on meeting someone who shares a name with your brother, or the school bully, or a childhood pet. It doesn't dissipate; the associations are too deeply ingrained. Mark, an English friend of my brother's who I met for brunch in Melbourne, had laughed when I mentioned this. 'Yes, it's so strange. The names are all so incongruous. Chelsea here is down and out, it's Camberwell that's full of the ladies who lunch. Croydon is north of Bayswater. We're through the looking glass.'

'And there's St Kilda,' I added, referring to the beach-side suburb in south Melbourne, newly fashionable after decades of infamy as the city's red-light district.

He raised his eyebrows, inviting me to continue, so I told him about the tiny, wave-battered island that sits alone far off the west coast of Scotland, about the odd hobbit people who lived there for generations, scrambling barefoot over the rocks, stealing gannets' eggs and wrenching up limpets, until the British government finally evacuated the island in 1930. The stench of seafowl and rotting fish.

'Well,' he said, 'maybe that one's not so different.'

I disembarked at Tamworth, the self-appointed 'country music capital' of Australia, whose main attractions are an annual music festival and the oversized golden guitar on the outskirts of town. The festival was long gone; the streets were deserted. The few human figures I spotted outside were eerie metal statuettes of country musicians making themselves comfortable on benches or mooching on street corners.

I was to be picked up the next day by Tim Skerritt, the owner of a cattle station an hour's drive out of town. Tim's 1,280-acre property offered greenhorns and travellers an opportunity to learn the skills required for station work: aspiring station hands (or 'jackaroos' and 'jillaroos') might try their hands at mustering sheep and cattle, learn the basics of field and fence care, and take away the all-important letter of recommendation to show potential employers. These incomers would help to fill a growing shortfall of capable station hands in areas where many of the local youngsters have been lured away by the six-figure salaries available in the mines — not so much a brain drain as a brawn drain.

Stockwork is still vital for the Australian economy, which was founded on the proceeds of the wool trade, and it lies too at the heart of the self-image of a country that owes so much of its creation to the never-ending wanderlust of the cattlemen.

When Angus McMillan arrived in Australia he came armed with a letter of introduction of his own, which quickly secured him work as a station manager on the Clifton cattle run owned by a fellow Highlander, Captain Lachlan Macalister, near Camden, New South Wales.

McMillan's link to Macalister was fortunate: the captain was a prominent settler, local magistrate and former head of the mounted police who had been granted this extensive tract of land in what was then known as the valuable 'Cowpastures' district, around fifty miles south-west of Sydney, as a reward for his distinguished military service. He had also acquired a 16,300-acre estate further south, near Goulburn, which he named 'Strathaird' after the peninsula on Skye where both he and McMillan were born.

By this time, 1838, the colony of New South Wales had outgrown its original boundaries and spilled over the Blue Mountains to the west into the vast plains the settlers found beyond. The colony was still a wild place, but with increasing numbers of free settlers arriving in their boat-loads, drawn by promises of land and opportunity, a fledgling bourgeoisie was forming, and society was beginning to settle into its component layers. Three classes were emerging: the convicts at the bottom, still to be spotted in unhappy rows working the roads, shackled together under the baking sun; the 'Emancipists', former convicts who had worked out their sentences; and finally the 'Exclusives', free men who had been posted abroad, or had even *paid* for the privilege of moving to Australia, and who were now at pains to distinguish themselves from the other sorry lot.

Camden, the nearest outpost of civilisation to Macalister's property, was moulded by the pretensions of the Exclusives. Today it is a town of 50,000 people, and the sort of place Australians like to prefix with the word 'historic' on road signs: full of redbrick post offices, ornamental street lamps and two-storey, net-curtained, bay-windowed houses. Later, I stopped by for an afternoon out of curiosity, parking my hire car by the public pool, and a sports field and Victorian grandstand neatly enclosed by white post-and-rail fencing like a racecourse.

There was still a steamy, colonial feel to the place. In town, Whiteman's Arcade sat in unfortunate placement across the high street from White Lady Funerals. A backstreet lined with rows of old brick agricultural stores led to the equestrian park, Cobbitty Pony Club and Miss L. Davies' Town Farm Community Gardens, where oddly stylish scarecrows decked out in dresses, straw hats and necklaces were crowding between the lavender rows and tangled English roses.

The streets were lined with weeping willows, elms and apple trees, all reassuringly familiar to European eyes in a country where nothing looks or works quite the way you expect. As one early settler wrote, in Australia the 'swans are black, the eagles white, the cod fish is found in rivers and perch in the sea, the valleys are cold and the mountain tops warm, the trees shed their bark annually instead of their leaves'. Another wrote of 'birds without wings, as large as deer, their bodies covered with hair instead of feathers; [and] beasts with the beaks of birds'.

For Angus McMillan there was a lot to learn about this baffling country, which could not have been more different from his beloved green Hebrides. The industrious Scot set to work at Clifton with gusto, and soon marked himself out to his employer as a man of solid constitution, steadfastness and Presbyterian work ethic. In short, he showed great promise. Before long he found himself Macalister's right-hand man.

But McMillan also found himself on the precipice of the class divide. There was no true 'upper class' in New South Wales in the traditional sense, but men like Macalister and the pastoralist John Macarthur, owner of the adjoining Camden Park estate, sat on the very surface of society like gold leaf. They were becoming very, very rich men, and much of this success had been gifted to them. Not only had the land they called their own arrived in the form of a government grant, they had also been assigned a steady supply of unpaid labour in the form of the convicts.

By this time more than 75,000 offenders had been deposited in New South Wales, many of whom had since been funnelled out of the chain gangs and into private enterprise. Convicts assigned to work on cattle and sheep stations had often started their sentences in the gangs, before being 'promoted' to an assignment following good behaviour. But the experiences of assigned convicts were very mixed. Some unlucky souls found their new bosses at least as merciless as the officers supervising the chain gangs, and were rendered 'nearly stupid from hard toil and cruel treatment' at the hands of 'demon incarnate' masters.

An abolitionist described one superintendent as 'in the habit of putting handcuffs and leg irons on them, and throwing them into a dungeon on the estate, where they remained generally for three days without meat or drink ... [he had] drawn as much blood from the flogged backs of his assigned men, as would make him to swim in human gore'. And for some, the psychological challenges of remote work were at least as harmful as the lash. Shepherds were expected to wander for months in the bush, on foot and without even the company of a sheepdog, struggling back and forth under darkness each night to collect their meagre rations. Alone in the bush, guarding his flocks and listening to the howls of the dingoes, a man could quickly lose his mind.

It seems that the masters on Macalister's station at Clifton were of the less compassionate sort, for McMillan found the treatment of the convicts unsettling, once even testifying in court about their abuse. An entire work squad had been put on trial for refusing to work during a thunderstorm. McMillan relayed the outcome of the case to a newspaper: 'I was put in the witness box, and on giving my evidence that I would not ask anyone to work on such a day, the police magistrate at once announced that his men were at work, and there could not be such heavy rain as sworn to within five miles of his place, and sentenced the men to fifty lashes each. His children were dismissed from school to enable them to enjoy the torture of their fellow creatures, and I believe his wife also attended the flagellation.'

Sickened by this 'inhuman' conduct, McMillan requested a move further from the heart of this 'accursed colony', and towards the straggly edges of the map, where each day the frontier drifted further into unknown country.

Cattle drovers, pushed forward by a constant need for fresh grazing, were effectively the new explorers. Although legislation limited settlement to within a rough arc around Sydney of about two hundred miles – the so-called 'Nineteen Counties' – there was not much the government could do to prevent these itinerant men roving ever further inland; self-sufficient, bush-wise, always on the move, they slept under the stars in the swags they carried and laid claim to new pasture with makeshift huts constructed from slabs of bark. As Don Watson described in his book *Caledonia Australis* (1984), they were the 'factotums of white civilization in Australia, in a sense the flux in the transition from black to white occupation of the interior'.

These rough and ready pioneers retain a special place in Antipodean folklore. Much of Australian literature, well into the twentieth century, revolves around heroic accounts of their 'battling against' harsh landscapes, the movement of the cattle and lives lived around the billycan on the campfire. 'Pioneers' by Banjo Paterson, the best-known of the 'bush poets', is a good example of the genre:

They came of bold and roving stock that would not
fixed abide;
They were the sons of field and flock since e'er
they learnt to ride,
We may not hope to see such men in these
degenerate years
As those explorers of the bush – the brave old
pioneers.

'Twas they who rode the trackless bush in heat and
storm and drought;
'Twas they who heard the master-word that called
them farther out;
'Twas they who followed up the trail the mountain
cattle made,
And pressed across the mighty range where now
their bones are laid.

McMillan's year on Macalister's cattle station was an education that taught him the skills that would serve him well as an explorer and pioneer pastoralist: how to muster cattle on horseback; how to build a bark hut; which of these unknown plants were edible; which of these unknown animals were venomous; how to navigate steep, bush-tangled slopes that spread out into the distance, unmarked by track or trail.

Tim arrived in Tamworth in a spluttering, aged minibus to take me and his latest batch of trainees to the farm. I recognised him immediately: a strong, capable Crocodile Dundee lookalike in a wide-brimmed bush hat and torn jeans. His shirt was dirt-coloured and the top buttons long lost, revealing the skin below in a swatch of deep brick.

The homestead was half an hour by road out of town, followed by a long drive up an unfinished track through sharply rolling landscape. The orange-gold of scorched grass was interrupted only by the occasional irrigated garden, neat fenced-off patches made luminous with life. The earth of the steep banks and bare patches was red, but at the bottom of the empty, weed-strewn creekbeds the rocks were a dull steel-grey. The few animals around seemed oddly sleek and healthy for this desiccated environment: piebald magpies disregarding a scarecrow in jeans and an old bush hat, gleaming stockhorses flicking at the flies with their tails, and cattle ripping greedily at the last scraps of edible grass. A dead fox lay baking at the side of the road, red fur luxurious against the dust.

Within a couple of hours we were saddled up and riding onto the high ridgeline looking for Aberdeen Angus cattle. After a brief quizzing and a quick lookover Tim had teamed me with a pretty chestnut mare called She Oak. 'She's fast,' said George, one of the stockmen, when I asked about her. 'Just let her go if she wants to go, don't grab at her mouth. And watch her with the other horses. She's a bitch.'

I loved her on sight. She Oak had a silken, unpulled mane, a white snip set at an angle across her nose and three white ankle socks, like a naughty schoolgirl who'd let the other slip down. She wore a home-made rope bridle – a big knot at each cheek holding the bit in her mouth – and an Australian stock saddle equipped with solid knee blocks and a high cantle to keep the rider secure in rough terrain or on a difficult mount. A leather breastplate held the saddle in place as we shinned up terrifyingly steep gradients. She tackled hills with brio, breaking into a trot or a canter if I let her, her ears pricked forward as the sweat lathered where the reins touched against her neck. No matter how long we were out, she was always ready to pull ahead and run and run and run.

She Oak and her colleagues were Australian stock horses, a breed derived from horses imported by the British, starting with the nine carried over on the First Fleet in 1788. The stock-horse blood originated largely among English thoroughbreds, Welsh mountain ponies, Arabians and the sturdy little ponies from nearby Indonesian islands. They have the delicacy and dished faces of Arabs, the hardiness of polo ponies, the lucky-dip colouring – buckskin, roan, blanket-spotted, leopard-spotted, wall-eyed – of the American quarter horse.

The type is nicely characterised in another of Banjo Paterson's works, his classic 'The Man from Snowy River':

> He was something like a racehorse undersized,
>   With a touch of Timor pony – three parts
>   thoroughbred at least –
> And such as are by mountain horsemen prized.

He was hard and tough and wiry — just the sort
that won't say die —
There was courage in his quick impatient tread;
And he bore the badge of gameness in his bright
and fiery eye,
And the proud and lofty carriage of his head.

The skill of the riders forms a core to the pioneer mythology; the man from Snowy River races up and down the gullies until his horse's sides are heaving, and bloody 'from hip to shoulder from the spur'. In McMillan's time, the English settler John Pettit wrote of the stockmen of Gippsland: 'In riding in horses and cattle they go full gallop thro' the Bush no matter how thick the trees turning sharp around them almost touching, jumping over all fallen logs in the most astonishing manner going over such ground as would capsize any horse not up to it.'

At Tim's the riding conditions were no better, but I found myself desperate to prove myself to this terrifyingly capable man, particularly when I heard that the jobs generally available to female trainees in the outback were as nannies or cooks. Tim himself had three young men tasked with the livestock and landcare and riding, while the three girls' main jobs seemed to be cooking, cleaning and looking after the two children he'd fathered with a young woman more than twenty years his junior, originally hired to do his admin.

The macho outback culture owes much to the days of the pioneers, when men were *real men* and women were scarce (in 1838, the year of McMillan's arrival, white men outnumbered white women in rural New South Wales by seventeen to one). I was already becoming used to the slow, patronising blink of the Australian male as I grappled with uncooperative sheep and heaved my own bags into the back of the ute. But then, I've always liked a challenge.

I'm a strong rider, so I pushed myself forward in the mustering, looking for approval. Coming down the steep, stony hillsides I sat ramrod straight, reins held loosely in one hand, heels down, hips jerking side to side with She Oak's steps. Whenever a calf or cow made a break for it, I urged her into a canter, looping wide around the escapee, then walking calmly back towards it, hooting long low notes that curved up in glissando to a high whoop that I'd copied from the stockmen.

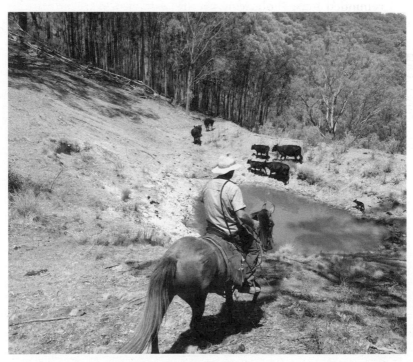

Tim Skerrit musters cattle on horseback at his station near Tamworth.

We gathered the cattle from every corner of the property and brought them down towards the yard, funnelling them into two small paddocks with a tall metal fence and a crush separating them. I jumped down to help split the calves from the heifers, whipping long sticks into the dirt to spook them and drive them apart, grabbing the small ones and pushing them bodily through the gate. Sweat soaked my shirt and beaded in unexpected places – my neck, my cheeks, the smooth skin on the inside of my forearms.

I was rewarded when, after a long day under a merciless sun, Tim eyed me approvingly and asked what I would be doing the next week. 'Heading to Gippsland,' I reminded him. 'Following the old exploratory paths.'

'Ah, yeah?' He'd clearly forgotten the entire reason I was there. I didn't really mind. Actually, I was hoping he was about to ask me to throw it all in and help them with the mustering all season, but instead he nodded once and turned back to the cattle. 'Get the branding iron,' he said to the boys.

On our return to the homestead each afternoon we shed our sweaty clothes onto the ground and jumped into the dam beyond the fence – a small artificial reservoir that collected rainwater. The water was mud-coloured and refreshing, warm on top but deadly cold in the deep. When we swam we set it swirling, cold fronts whipped up from below and sent spinning across the surface like a typhoon.

A wooden walkway jutted out into the empty air above our heads, a clear indication of how far the water level had fallen since winter. We took it in turns to jump off, legs wheeling in mid-air as we fell ten feet into the water. I felt my feet press into the spongey bottom and pushed off, surfacing with a gasp, lungs burning. 'Look out for yabbies,' said one of the boys. 'Got pincers like lobsters. Sometimes you feel them brushing against your legs.'

We staggered back to the yard in our bare feet, dodging dry cowpats and the thorniest of the weeds to drink bush tea by the fire from a billycan, brewed until it was bitter and chalky from the milk whitener. There were fat wedges of damper – a basic milk-bread stuffed with raisins and baked around a tin can so it came out shaped like a Bundt cake with a thick golden crust – made in the fire using a thick-lidded pot. One night we ate fried bullock testicles, fatty globs of gore we had cut off with a scalpel earlier that day and gathered in a hat for safekeeping.

To a sun-starved Scot it was glorious: clear skies, forty degrees, no phone reception and no internet. I was enjoying being carefree and cut off. The books I'd brought were sitting unread at the end of my bunk; I'd half-forgotten Angus McMillan and the rest of my quest. But to those living on the station, the heavenly weather was beginning to cause some concern. 'It's the driest summer since the sixties,' said Tim. 'At least. My da reckons it's the driest he's ever seen, and he's seen a few. He's ninety this year.'

By Wednesday evening the torridity was coming to a head. It had been muggy and hot all day, but clouds had crept in unnoticed with the dusk, quietly fading in as if they had been there all along. The thunder cleared its throat, then the flash of first lightning came from somewhere over the hill out of sight. A tiny spattering of rain. 'Not enough,' warned one of the Australians. 'The lightning could start a fire, and this rain wouldn't be heavy enough to put it out.'

The pasture where Tim's horses grazed was golden with close-cropped grasses that lent a velvety fuzz to the curve of the hill. It was so dry the blades would crunch and break under your soles as you walked. Further up, the bush grew in grey-green knots of spindle-armed trees and the creepers that choked them, the earth pale and sandy between their roots. Everywhere the ground was littered with the long, slender limbs of the gums that seemed simply to have let go; huge branches, half the tree sometimes, would have peeled themselves off and crashed to the ground. The long curved leaves of the eucalyptus, the size and shape of kukri knives, gold, tan and greenish brown, curled in the heat and piled up like tinder, ready to go up at any moment.

The Australian ecosystem has been sculpted by flame. Many plants thrive in or depend upon fire at key points of their life cycle; the release of the seeds of the saw banksia and the flowering of the grass tree are both triggered by bushfire. Others are simply highly flammable: the ubiquitous eucalypt, for example, whose resinous sap and paper-like bark are perfectly designed to catch and spread fire.

Bushfires have the effect of stripping out younger, less established plants and providing breathing room to the biggest trees. These brutes are then free to grow tall and strong and freestanding, lending the land the appearance of an English country estate, a feature made much of in the writing of the earliest arrivals. Sydney Parkinson, a draughtsman on Captain Cook's 1770 voyage along the eastern coast of Australia, wrote of his surprise at the pleasant, cared-for aspect of the newfound 'wilderness' of New South Wales: 'The country looked very pleasant and fertile; and the trees, quite free from under-wood, appeared like plantations in a gentleman's park.'

There is a false impression that Aboriginal people lived an idyllic lifestyle, 'in harmony' with the environment, hunting and gathering at such low intensity that they left no trace on the landscape. In fact, it was their continent-wide habit of 'firestick farming' – burning out the scrub, grasses and under-canopy of the forests in complex rotation to encourage new growth or lure larger fauna into better hunting ground – that resulted in this distinctive habitat. It killed off fire-sensitive plants and selected for the fire-friendly – in effect, it altered the entire ecosystem of the continent. As Edward Curr, one of the earliest settlers along the Murray, wrote: 'It may perhaps be doubted whether any section of the human race has exercised a greater influence on the physical condition of any large portion of the globe than the wandering savages of Australia.'

Man-made fire was still widespread at the end of the eighteenth century – making its first appearance in English literature in the verse of Thomas Muir, one of the 'Scottish martyrs' transported to New South Wales for their Jacobin sympathies in 1794:

> To clear the forest's dark impervious maze
> The half-starv'd Indian lights a hasty blaze
> Then lifts the Torch, and rushing o'er the Strand
> High o'er his head he waves the flaming Brand
> From Bush to Bush with rapid steps he flies
> Till the whole forest blazes to the skies.

The arrival of the European settlers was followed by a sudden fall in the bushfire. Those who build houses and farms rather than temporary shelters flinch from the destruction that such fires bring. As a result, the fire-friendly plants have been growing in their thickets ever since – fuel for the fires builds over years, just waiting for a spark. The result has been some of the most destructive fires in human history. In 1851, 'Black Thursday' raged through five million hectares of Victoria, killing twelve people and more than a million sheep; 'Ash Wednesday' in 1983 killed seventy-five and razed 2,500 buildings; most recently 'Black Saturday' of 2009 killed 173 and left an estimated seven thousand homeless.

Two years before my arrival, a bushfire swept through the hill behind Tim's homestead, barely missing the buildings. Tim packed his wife, children and female staff off to a neighbour's property, away from the flames, but stayed on with the other men to fight the fire with hoses, buckets and whatever water they could get their hands on.

They saved the house, but the burned-out trees still stood in swathes, poking limbless from the ground like fenceposts. Close up, I saw that their blackened trunks were wreathed in new sweet, green leaves, bursting through from the living tree underneath all the way up their lengths. And so the Australian flora regenerates.

On Thursday night the weather finally broke. I was swimming in the dam, racing the dogs to sticks that Mariánne, a Norwegian girl on the jillaroo course, was throwing in from the water's edge. Lightning was flickering again, somewhere in the corner of my vision, and the thunderclaps were growing louder and more frequent, until they came so close together they might have been simultaneous. Heavy drops began to hit the water around my head and shoulders, spot-spotting at first, before suddenly the sky unzipped and they came down on us in a torrent.

We whooped in delight, girlish squeals that sent the dogs skittering in the shallows, delighted by our excitement. A flash, the boom of the thunder again, directly above us now. I howled happily up into the sky like a wolf, rain splashing my face.

'You guys?' It was Tim's wife. 'You'd better get out of the water before you get fried.'

It was the droughts of New South Wales that finally sent the settlers south over the Australian Alps. By May 1839, less than a year and a half after McMillan's arrival at Clifton, conditions were growing desperate.

The *South Australian Gazette and Colonial Register* reported that 'the present year must be looked upon as the most calamitous the colony has ever experienced, occasioned by the long continued drought'. It carried extracts of reports from across New South Wales (a title which at that time referred to the entirety of the mainland colony, from present-day Brisbane in the north to Melbourne on the south coast, with a pocket of uncharted land – Gippsland – beyond the Australian Alps in the south-east), noting that 'the state of the interior is represented as deplorable in the extreme':

Bathurst – The drought continues, and no words
    can express the miserable appearance of the
    country; there is not supposed to be enough

wheat left for seed – no milk – no cheese, and no vegetables.

Patrick's Plains – There is neither food for man nor beast; the plains are as destitute of grass as a turnpike road.

Paterson, Hunter's River – The country is in a desponding state for want of rain; there will be no maize. God knows what will become of us all if some change does not take place very soon.

Port Phillip – The country is altered much for the worse; all the grass is burnt up, and the greatest difficulty is experienced in procuring food for the cattle. Several of the well-known fords of the rivers Hume and Ovens are quite dry, and the rivers have become a chain of ponds.

King – The drought continues with unabating severity, stock of every description are beginning to fall off for want of pasturage; things are in a dreadful state.

Murrumbidgee – The river has decreased so considerably as to become dry in many places, and fish may be seen lying in a putrid state on the bed of the river.

Wellington – The country is burnt up; sheep are dying by hundreds; the cattle have all long since been dead. For the last twelve months there has not been rain for two consecutive days.

This drought did not only affect the settlers, of course. The hard times were driving the British and Aboriginal populations into competition over the meagre supplies. One correspondent from Port Phillip, the large bay where

Melbourne had been founded four years previously, reported: 'The blacks have killed forty head of cattle belonging to Mr. Faithfull, and thirty six sheep of Colonel White's since you left. You may expect to hear shortly of some wild work taking place here, the blacks are so continually encamping near us.'

The dark allusion to 'wild work' was in fact a euphemism for what might, in modern terminology, be described as an ethnic cleansing. The previous year, 'great numbers' of the Kamilaroi people of New South Wales – the group indigenous to the Tamworth area – had been killed over the course of several months in what the local magistrate described as 'a war of extirpation' (*extirpation* – to pull up by the roots). The bloodiest episode, the Waterloo Creek massacre, took place in January 1838, when the officer in charge, Major James Nunn, claimed to have killed between two and three hundred Kamilaroi (although later estimates have placed the upper limit at around seventy).

The infamous Myall Creek massacre took place the same year, about a hundred miles north of Tim's homestead, when twenty-eight unarmed members of the Kamilaroi's Wirrayaraay tribe were tied to a rope, marched from their camp and slaughtered. Witnesses later described how the children had been beheaded, before the adults were forced to run as three stockmen brandishing swords slashed at their bodies.

The Wirrayaraay victims were well-known to their killers – many had been given English nicknames: Charlie, Davey, Martha, Old Joey, 'King' Sandy – but the extent of the betrayal and brutality is not what has singled out the Myall Creek incident; rather it is the only massacre in Australian history following which white Europeans were tried and executed for their role in frontier killings of Aboriginal people. In all, eleven settlers were tried for murder, of whom seven were found guilty and hanged: Charles Kilmeister, James Oates, Edward Foley, John Russell, John Johnstone, William Hawkins and James Parry. An eighth, John Blake, was cleared but later committed suicide.

The Myall Creek trials and hangings caused enormous controversy in their time. The defendants argued that they had not realised that killing an Aboriginal man was a crime, so common was the sport on the frontier. The newspapers took up the cause of the settlers: 'The whole gang of black animals,' argued the *Sydney Herald*, 'are not worth the money the colonists will have to pay for printing the silly court documents.'

But the judge reminded the court that the law made no distinction between the murder of an Aboriginal man and that of a white man. For the Kamilaroi this was a rare glimmer of justice. It must have seemed that finally the lives of the black population would be valued and protected. It must have seemed like a turning point. It wasn't. The effect of the prosecutions was to foster a culture of silence among the settlers. The killings did not stop, but instead became concealed in layers of secrecy and doublespeak. Settlers realised that talking openly about massacres and murders was no longer safe; that boasting of your kills could bring about your own execution.

Living in rural New South Wales through 1838 and into 1839, Angus McMillan could not have been unaware of the Myall Creek trial and its outcome. He would have discussed it among his fellow workers over a dram, even as the drought drew the settlers and the Aboriginal tribes into ever-closer conflict.

I was discussing the events of Myall Creek over a drink myself one evening when one of the girls on the course, a pretty, strong-looking teenager, overheard me and volunteered the fact that she had an Aboriginal father.

'Oh,' I said, surprised. 'I suppose you have the colouring for it.' She had a golden, sunkissed glow about her, a sweet snub nose, dark eyes under unexpectedly fair hair.

She nodded. 'I don't usually tell people. It's not something to be proud of.' I raised an eyebrow. 'They've got a pretty bad reputation. Drink. Drugs. Hitting their women. You know?'

I shook my head. 'Not really.'

'Have you not heard about Palm Island? It's off the coast of Queensland, where I'm from, an Aboriginal settlement. Pretty famous. Mad stuff goes on. Fighting, drugs, rioting, no control. Had to send commandos in one time after they set the police station on fire. It's one of the most dangerous places in the world.'

Her boyfriend was nodding at me, eyes wide, as she spoke. 'Yeah, man,' he chimed in. 'Shit gets pretty crazy in the settlements.'

'Anyway,' she added, 'I didn't know my dad ever anyway. Didn't stick around. They don't, usually.'

Tim was working nearby, checking some heavy tools. He inspected each one before piling them into the back of the ute.

I called over. 'Hey, Tim? Are there still Aboriginal people living in the Tamworth area?'

He half-turned as he considered his answer. 'Some,' he said, a noncommittal Australian tic which can mean anything from wild understatement to reluctant accedence. There was a pause while I waited for him to elaborate, but he didn't.

'Where might I find them?'

'The pub.' He waited until I feigned the required snort of amusement, before giving me a slow smile. 'Ah, there's a few. But I've probably got darker skin than the lot of them. They're all half-white, or most of them. I reckon I could claim welfare about as well as them. Go into the bars on Friday night and ask around and you'll find them.'

After a week on the cattle station, wearing the same filthy shirt and torn jeans every day, I quite fancied an evening out in any case. Mariánne the Norwegian was a willing accomplice. She'd just been offered a job at one of the neighbouring stations, and this would be her last chance to hit the town for months.

By 10 p.m. we were a bottle of wine down each, and feeling confident in our conversational skills. We stalked the main streets, trailing from empty bar to empty bar in search of new friends, finally alighting on the thump thump thump of dance music we could hear on the still night air as our final destination. The only club in Tamworth! We had to go there.

We weren't the only clubbers in Tamworth, but it was a close-run thing. A lone DJ stood on the stage, pluckily pumping up the volume as red and white spotlights strobed the empty dancefloor in the manner of school discos everywhere. Mariánne and I took to the floor without hesitation, on the basis that the lack of other dancers meant all the more space for us, but we were finally forced to submit to the downward pull of entropy as our aggressive pointing gave way to shoulder shimmying, in turn degenerating to the head bob, until finally we found ourselves sitting in garden chairs out the back, speaking to a red-faced station hand of indeterminate age in a waxed leather hat and Blundstones.

The fact that he had somehow ended up entertaining both of the only two unaccounted-for women in the bar seemed to have aroused a great hilarity among the other regulars, who kept stopping by our table to slap him on the shoulder in congratulatory fashion, or to ask us if this man was bothering us. After a while the music was turned off and the main lights on, but rather than throw us out, the bar manager, DJ and doorman came to join us out back with drinks in hand.

'Where are all the Aboriginal people in Tamworth?' I asked. 'I haven't seen any.'

'They're here,' the doorman assured me. 'But they don't hang out in this bar.'

'Where do they hang out?'

They exchanged glances. 'Not bars that *you* want to go to,' the doorman said, eyeing my bare shoulders, following the line of my clavicles with an expression I wasn't entirely comfortable with. 'There's parts of town that they all live ... but not the nice parts.' A beat passed. 'Why do you want to know?'

I hesitated, then dived in. I was just passing through, I told them, on my way to Gippsland to investigate the massacres led by a relative of mine, generations ago. I wasn't sure what I thought about it yet. But I felt strangely guilty, as if some of the responsibility for the current poor state of the Australian Aboriginal population lay at my feet. And much more so, here in person, now that I realised how ghettoised that population really was.

It was late, and we were all drunk, and I wasn't really sure how well I was explaining myself. Partway through my speech I felt a surge of self-censure for ruining the mood. But after a pause for consideration, the doorman rose to the occasion.

'That's a really dangerous thing,' he said finally. 'Taking on that responsibility. I don't think that helps anything. Actually, it makes it worse. Accepting blame. The problem with the Aboriginals is that they're always blaming other people for the way it is now.'

I must have been frowning, because he held up an appeasing hand. 'Think about it. I don't care if your great-great-grandfather killed my great-great-grandfather because my great-grandfather speared one of your great-great-grandfather's sheep. It's not good that it happened, obviously. But that doesn't mean that *you* are in any way to blame for all the failures in *my* life now. It's nothing to do with you.'

It was an argument I had heard before – a simple refusal to accept collective debt. Not a denial of the past, but a shrugging of shoulders. Many contemporary Australians feel that being assigned responsibility for their forebears' actions is not only unjust, but could lead to costly reparations and a revival of ill-feeling that should have been laid to rest long ago. It is time to move on, not – as the controversial historian Keith Windschuttle has argued – to 'add fuel to the politics of permanent grievance on which the hard men of Aboriginal activism have long thrived'.

'But doesn't it make you feel bad?' I persisted, not willing to let it drop. 'To be a member of the group that's at such an advantage? An advantage gained at the expense of the others?'

'Yes, but ...' He thought about it. 'But that's life. Some people are born rich. Some people poor. We all have to work with what we've got.'

'It really fucks me off,' the DJ burst in, 'the way the Abos are always blaming white people for the shit that goes on in their community. As if it's our fault if they're drunk, or that their kids aren't going to school, or whatever. They're blaming us for their shit lives, their shit houses, their shitty behaviour. But that's not my fault. I didn't make it this way. And they can change it. No one's stopping them going to school. Nobody's stopping them getting jobs.'

He was swaying slightly. I wasn't sure how he'd managed to get quite so drunk in the short interval since the music stopped. Around us and above us the disco lights continued to spin and churn to an unheard beat, bringing a strange, hallucinatory tinge to the whole scene.

There was an awkward silence. I had the sense that although the other men agreed in principle, the drunk man had put it more bluntly than they were willing to.

'Hey,' he said suddenly, as if something completely wonderful and unexpected had just occurred to him. 'Do you want to have another drink?'

Mariánne and I looked at each other. She raised her eyebrows at me, shrugged.

'Sure,' I said. 'I'll have a gin and tonic.'

5

First In, Best Dressed

Jeannie Haughton was a playwright. I'd first come across her online, in an ABC segment on a play she'd written about Angus McMillan: *Salute the Man*. A scathing take-down of him, by all accounts. She was pictured looking rather stern on the verandah of his former homestead, which has now been relocated and reconstructed in an odd mixed-period 'heritage park' fifty miles away to the south-east.

I'd emailed a few months back, not knowing what I wanted from her. Just to make contact – as if McMillan was a friend we had in common. 'I'm thinking of coming to Gippsland,' I wrote. 'Perhaps we could meet up?' My mission had taken more concrete form even as I typed the words onto the page.

Her reply came like a gift. She'd always wanted to follow McMillan's trail herself, she said. Perhaps we could travel together, as a sort of investigative unit, and her husband could drive us from site to site. 'We have maps, a four-by-four, a caravan and a tent.' It was an offer I couldn't refuse.

Jeannie met me off the train at Drouin, on the eastern edge of Gippsland. She was a statuesque, bohemian-looking woman with a cloud of red corkscrew curls and a multicoloured coat. 'Haughts is delighted,' she said, meaning her husband, Ian. 'He's always looking for an excuse to get out in the caravan, and I'll never go with him.' Ian turned out to be a wiry, bald fellow, particular about order and systems, and quick to laugh. Jeannie was right, he *was* delighted, greeting me like an old friend.

'Make yourself at home,' said Jeannie. 'Sorry about the wall.' She gestured vaguely towards a gaping hole in the front of the house where an extension was being built, over which a tarpaulin flapped weakly.

'You can lock the door if you like,' cracked Ian, 'but there's not much point.'

I lingered in the house for a couple of days as Jeannie crammed in a last few appointments. The waiting was not unpleasant. I was patient, expectant. We were in 'the McMillan electorate', said Jeannie, and this relaxed me. I was already getting closer. I leafed dreamily through books, watched king parrots and rainbow parakeets bicker and preen in the garden, wandered the roads nearby.

It was greener here in Drouin than in New South Wales. I was captivated by the eucalypts: gum trees, the Australians call them, although they didn't look like any trees that I knew. They had lissome, flyaway branches that struck off at haphazard angles then curled in unexpected directions, silvery white and gleaming in the hazy morning light. Above, the delicate slips of the leaves – clouds of them, showers of them. They came down in the wind like confetti, or feathers discarded

Lower down, around their trunks, the bark grew in thicker layers that were shed to fall down like shadows made real, each species disrobing in its own style to reveal the slender white limbs underneath, fresh and clean, and as wrinkled as newborns. Long strands peeled off in streamers and gathered in bundles in the joints of branches below, hanging over the road like bead curtains. Or in small islands, leaving pale fresh patches behind, an impressionist painting made up of blotches of unexpected, overlapping colours: sage, dove grey, a pale primrose auburn. On others, layers upon layers of bark unfurled, old books falling open, their curling pages coming loose at the seams.

I began to read the second diary, McMillan's expedition journals from his exploratory years. In fact, there were several versions – I'd located the original copy in the state archives, ink on blue paper, browned and blotchy after all those years but still legible, the others written for assorted periodicals during his lifetime. Each gave slightly different insights. I read and cross-referenced them against each other.

Jeannie had printed out a nineteenth-century map that showed the routes of the early explorers. McMillan's path had been picked out in a lurid yellow. I pored over it, trying to match his journal entries against first this, then a modern road map. His party started somewhere called Currawong, which did not seem to correspond to anywhere on the present-day map, before looping somewhat haphazardly through the mountainous region north of the Snowy River, reasserting their purpose and finally charging south into Gippsland along a river called the Tambo.

It was this latter phase that Jeannie suggested we retread. 'A lot of this,' she said, waving her arm airily across the top half of my map, 'is still very rough country. Very remote. If you want to head into these mountains for bushwalking and other young-person stuff, you can do that later.'

As we prepared to leave, Ian gave me a tour of his four-wheel-drive, which was kitted out ready for the full Aussie off-road experience: safari snorkel, double-sized diesel canisters, a battery-powered fridge that slid into the boot like a drawer. I was amused by the prospect of heading out on a caravanning tour, but Ian advised me solemnly as he started the engine and rolled down the drive that the caravan scene was different in Australia from in Britain, more extreme.

'Have you heard of the grey nomads? There's a trend here for older couples to hit the road after their children have left home. Take early retirement. Sell the house, the furniture, the whole caboodle, then spend that money on a good motorhome, or a top-class caravan at the very least, and head out on the road – and they don't come back.

'This is a huge country, Cal. You can just get out on the road and drive and drive and drive and always be covering new ground. Up to the Kimberley for the dry season, down through Western Australia in time for the wildflowers. Just pull over whenever you're tired of driving, no worries about finding a campsite or anything – you've got your fridge, your cooker, your water tank, about a hundred litres of fuel ...'

I nodded, smiling. I understood his fervour. There is something thrilling about mammoth countries, the freedom of having nothing hemming you in for thousands of miles in any direction. The Americans have an equivalent name for itinerant pensioners like these, which I prefer: 'snowbirds'. These snowbirds migrate south in winter like geese taking flight on the bitter Arctic winds, picking their way south, seeking sun and a place to roost, usually in Florida or Arizona. Small desert towns find themselves dwarfed by the swathes of campervans that spring up on their outskirts in neat suburban rows, year after year.

Peck peck. Gobble gobble. They pass the winter picking bare the local stores. Come rainy season they pack up and drive back to where they came from, leaving only desert where once there was an endless white, plastic city.

'You could just drive and drive and drive,' Ian repeated. He glanced into the back seat hopefully, but Jeannie wasn't listening.

1839. With the colony of New South Wales racked by drought, ever more settlers flooded into the interior, looking for fresh land. It was the scramble for Australia: a race to annex the best pasture. Finders keepers – that was the rule. The settlers would occupy the land as 'squatters' and wait for the freehold to be formalised later, once they were too established to be removed. As they say locally: first in, best dressed.

By this time the dray track from Yass that stretched 350 miles to the 'huddle of huts' that comprised the newly founded Melbourne had transformed into a busy highway, where an estimated 20,000 cattle were so tightly crammed that 'great care [had to] be exercised to prevent the mixing of herds, and consequent annoyance and confusion', one drover recalled later. On arrival in this new portion of the colony the migrants would search for suitable 'vacant' pasture upon which they might graze their stock, but this was getting harder and harder.

It was a rushed game of hide and seek that they were joining late: everywhere they looked – under the bed, behind the curtain – someone had nestled themselves in before they got there. Their hunger for land was never-ending.

Gippsland, however, 14,000 square miles of fertile land tucked into the south-eastern corner of the continent, had so far survived the occupation unscathed. A few half-hearted attempts had been made to scale the Australian Alps to see what lay beyond them, but with no success. If there was grazing land to be found there, it was bounded by precipitous mountains to the north, steep gorges to the east, a tempestuous sea to the south, and an impenetrable forest of thorns to the west. It was a natural fortress, with no easy way in and no easy way back out.

But suspicions as to the region's potential were aroused when that winter the ship of James Macarthur, son of the pastoralist John, was blown off course while sailing in Bass Strait, and his party found themselves travelling parallel to the coast 'far to the west of Cape Howe'. Macarthur noted: 'Mr [George] Blaxland and I both observed that the mountains receded considerably inland towards Wilson's Promontory, and that it was likely a valuable grazing country existed between the mountains and the coast.'

They were so close, yet so far away. The beauty of the crescent beach, a scythe of white sand, belied the danger of their situation – uncharted rocks and reefs that lurked beneath the surface, unpredictable currents that whipped through the waves, the surf battering down upon the shore like so many slamming doors. Already this perilous stretch of water had claimed dozens of ships; there was no way to anchor and investigate. But they took note, made plans.

What lay in this hidden dell? It was a secret, held out like a promise.

Angus McMillan too had seen into the future, standing high upon the peaks to the north-east.

By February he had found himself manager on a station high up on the Monaro plateau, around a hundred miles to the south of where Canberra sits now. With a year of station work under his belt he had been tasked with seeking out fresh land by which his master Macalister's hungry stock might be spared, and his imagination began to drift south to the undiscovered land beyond the blue-tinged peaks.

Two months later, restless for action and fired with ambition, he climbed to the highest point of the Tingaringy ridge, *and to my great delight got a view of the sea.* He sat there for hours, comparing what he could see with Matthew Flinders' chart of the coast, and calculated that the mountain range he could see stretching off to the west must be set around thirty miles back from the beach. He knew at once, he wrote later, that he must one day penetrate this unknown region. *I looked to the S.W., and said here is a noble work for a bold and determined mountaineer, thinking all the time how I could accomplish the object in view.*

Seeking information, he visited a nearby Aboriginal camp. Its inhabitants – the Ngarico tribe of the Monaro – were the first indigenous people he had encountered at close quarters, and he found them helpful. *With a palpitating heart I listened until one of them, pointing to the S.W., cried out cabone benel which means a large plain. I then took both their hands in mine and expressed a wish to go there.*

But neither of the two Ngarico men who had seen the great lakes, plains and rivers of that hidden country with their own eyes were able to accompany him. They were old now, and too frail for the journey. Besides which, they were not keen to make contact with the natives of that land – the 'warrigals', as they called them: wild dogs. In Gippsland, they warned him, there were *plenty fish, plenty kangaroo, thousand duck, thousand swan, and thousand blackfellow, 'like it chumbug along o' plain'* – *meaning that they were as numerous as the sheep.* Nor would any of the white men in his party accompany him. He was too inexperienced a leader, the rumoured wild men too alarming.

But the Promised Land beyond the mountains became an obsession to McMillan. Finally, after many weeks of persuasion and a demonstration of his abilities with a shotgun, the elders consented to one of the younger members of the tribe accompanying him as a guide. The pair set off with four weeks' provisions on what turned out to be a bruising false start: a short-lived attempt to breach the fortress walls by way of the Snowy River gorge.

They were soon forced to turn back north, towards the high plains of Omeo, where McMillan's friend James MacFarlane had recently established a station at the furthest edge of white settlement. But not before he had clambered to the top of Mount Macleod for a bird's-eye view of what would become his kingdom. *To my unspeakable joy there was the low country at my feet – the lakes and plains extending to the W.S.W., as far as the eye could carry.*

*

We came into a huge, flat country where cattle grazed in vast yellowing meadows. It was flat as flat could be. Far off on the horizon to the north, the foothills of the Australian Alps could be seen, painted with the green-blue tinge of the eucalypts. They seemed so distant and out of keeping with our surroundings that they might have been sketched onto a backdrop and reeled across the skyline like the scenery for a play.

This was Gippsland. In 1839 it would have been lush, widely spaced woodland dotted with freshwater lagoons and punctuated with the curling smoke of the fires of innumerable Aboriginal encampments. Today it is a vast expanse of flat, fertile farmland, well occupied by contented herds of cattle that roam this grassland like wildebeest on the Serengeti, black as silhouettes and up to their bellies in flaxen grass heavy with seeds.

Irrigation channels offered the only contours, their existence proclaimed as proudly as latecomers to a ball – 'I announce the attendance of Boisdale Drainage Ditches nos. 1 and 2!' – and mobile sprinkler systems stretched motionless across the length of the fields, endless metal hoses lifted high in the air, snakes on skates.

The sun was almost directly overhead, the sky streaked through with cirrus harpstrings. I gazed out at the landscape as we flew by, reading the signs. They had a storybook ring – 'Cherry Tree Creek', 'Stringy Bark Cottages', 'Dirty Hollow'. Someone was selling wildflowers in bunches from a trolley at the side of the road. This *was* a huge country, I was realising afresh. From dot to dot on the map, barely a speck of the state, a distance I had rashly assumed too short to worry about – a short hop, nothing more – was apparently going to take us four hours' drive.

More signs, pleading now: 'Sore Eyes? Powernap Now', and 'The Only Cure for Tiredness is Sleep'. A campaign of persuasion aimed at all those cruise-control drivers speeding thousands of miles across the continent without a pause. As if on cue, I felt my eyelids flutter. Sleep roared up behind me, and overtook.

I woke up in the Wild West. Omeo had a dusty, frontier-land feel, like the set of a spaghetti western, the main street lined with clapboard shops with high, scroll-topped façades in an autumnal palette. Everything seemed to have closed early for the day, adding to the sense that there wasn't really anything behind the blinds except empty cardboard boxes and trestle tables bearing props. I half-expected John Wayne to come clattering out of a pair of saloon doors and whistle for his horse.

There was a butcher, a redbrick 'post and telegraph office' and a handful of old colonial-style boarding houses: Snug as a Bug (est. 1879) and Martin's Place, a cute wooden hut in peppermint green wearing a pretty copper windvane like a tiara. 'Survived Two Bush Fires', a sign out front boasted. The road continued north out of town past the Golden Age Motel towards Mount Bogong, where once Aboriginal groups would gather from miles around, every year, to feast on the fatty bogong moths during their spring migration. It is now a highly seasonal skiing destination; mismatched skis bleached in the window of the petrol station, while fluorescent orange snow-gates stood incongruously in the crisp dead grass by the petrol pumps.

We pitched our camp on the banks of Livingstone Creek, where sulphur-crested cockatoos were grazing like sheep in the shade of the trees. As we drove up they flew into the branches, noisily indignant, voices sharp and rasping and unexpectedly harsh, screeching criticism as I pitched my tent below. Jeannie and Ian unhitched their caravan and got the kettle on as I strolled back up the hill into town.

In some ways, the town and its surrounds had changed little since McMillan's days; the cattleman, or at least the legend of him, still reigns supreme. The placenames had a rough drovers' humour to them: a local paper informed me of a bushfire that had recently rushed through the valley between Terrible Hollow and Mount Buggery – Mount Buggery having apparently evaded the notice of the group of prudish surveyors who rechristened nearby Mount Arsehole as Mount Arthur in the 1930s. Posters in the windows advised that I had just missed a pioneer skills demonstration and 'late-night bush jam', but if I hung around for a few more weeks there would be whip-cracking, wood-chopping and the Great Australian Pack Horse Competition at the annual mountain cattlemen's festival.

Back in 1839, Omeo was in its most primitive state – no more than a few huts and shacks thrown together while the cattle wandered loose across the tablelands 'as wild as hares' – but to McMillan and his guide trekking up through the Cobberas range to the south-east it must have been a welcome sight. It was June, and bitterly cold in the mountains, hoarfrost clinging to the leaves of the snow gums, thick drifts high in the lee of the peaks. But lower down, where MacFarlane and his rivals were setting up shop, it was dry, brittle-grassed, a reminder of the droughts that still blighted the interior. It refocused McMillan upon his task. He didn't stay there long.

*

When I returned to the tent, feet wet from fording the creek, I found Jeannie and Ian itching to get back on the road. 'There's a viewpoint nearby called McMillan's Lookout,' said Jeannie, pointing it out on the map. 'I think you should see it.'

The view from the lookout, at 3,060 feet, was indeed spectacular. The land slid away from us down steep slopes choked with gnarled gums and tea trees that filled the air with their thick, medicinal aroma. Below us the plains radiated out from the dwindling waters of Lake Omeo, golden meadows carpeting a shallow, undulating basin hemmed in at the back by the three peaks of The Brothers. Here and there were the silver glimmers of the gums, slipping out of their clothes, pale bark falling to the ground like halos, their shadows lying long and lazy in the evening light.

The sky enormous above; the land enormous below. I could feel the curvature of the earth, and its endless possibility. Raw desire rose inside me, a yearning not only to read about this man, or even to read his words, but to see this brave new world through his eyes. I wanted his drive, his self-sufficiency. I wanted to star in my own epic.

This was just the starting point, I thought. This was only the beginning.

There was a low stone cairn raised on a plinth where an older couple were posing for photos. Ian ambled across to help out. 'Do you want a picture of you both together?'

They acquiesced, thanking him, the woman adding as an afterthought, 'You know, we're here visiting because my husband is a descendant of one of the original pioneers.'

We three laughed, unable to believe the coincidence. 'Really? Which one?'

'James MacFarlane. He set up the first cattle station,' said the man. He was a big, barrel-chested guy of around sixty-five, with silver hair and a kindly, academic air.

'But I know all about him!' I cried. 'I'm here to follow the trail of Angus McMillan, a relative of *mine*. He was one of the pioneers too – the explorer who opened up Gippsland.'

We regarded each other with pleasure. It was amusing to think that more than 150 years ago, our forebears could very well have been standing together in the same spot. This man and I were the same, drawn to a place we had never been, treading and retreading the paths of our fore-bears. Looking for significance, for recognition, for a sense of ourselves and of where we have come from. Of who we could be.

Finally, after a delay of months while he rushed back and forth to Currawong and Clifton to gather supplies and support from his employer, McMillan was ready to make a second attempt. First he established another run on behalf of Macalister, a jumping-off point twenty-five miles south of Omeo at a spot the local Ya-itma-thang people called Numbla Munjee, 'Blackfish Place'. Then he gathered his party of three men and his kit and they set off once more into the unknown.

The journey was tough going, through some of the worst country McMillan had ever seen: a hilly and broken landscape of rocky gullies and dense, thorny undergrowth. The party lost a packhorse early on when it slipped and fell on one of the steeper slopes, rolling until it was finally halted by a sturdy tree, *having staked itself in four or five places.* Eventually two Ya-itma-thang guides led the group to an ancient Aboriginal walking route along the river-banks – now reborn as the Great Alpine Road – where they saw the first evidence of the warrigals McMillan had been warned about: ashes from the *extinct fires of what must have been a numerous body of natives.*

At this point, little was known of the Gunai people except for the rumours retailed by the natives of the Monaro and at Omeo. They were a ferocious, warlike people, the guides warned them. Yet the first meeting did little to confirm that reputation. As McMillan rode on ahead, he was suddenly confronted by dozens of Gunai tribesmen who emerged noiselessly from the bush. They stopped a few yards away, and stared at him in open dismay. *When I dismounted, and moved my hands in friendly salutation they fled in all directions.* Not so fearless, then.

But they were not taken entirely by surprise by the arrival of the white man. They had heard reports of a new type of man, a pale-skinned man with the power of mlang-mri, 'lightning eye', flashing death to those who looked at him, and the ability to draw together the banks of a river so he might pass over it. Many other explorers and pioneer settlers had encountered remote tribes who seemed to be expecting them. The explorer and surveyor Thomas Mitchell, for example, reported in 1834 of how on encountering an unknown tribe in New South Wales his party were met by 'calls in various directions, and "white-fellow" pronounced very loudly and distinctly [which] appears to be their name for our race'.

For the Gunai, however, McMillan's horse came as a shock: *from the astonishment displayed at the circumstance of my dismounting from the horse, I fancied they took both man and horse to constitute one animal.*

The tribesmen were gone, disappeared back into the bush. But they had not gone far. *At a great distance we heard all day their cooeying, and the cries and wailing of women and children.* First contact: the Gunai had been found. Although, of course, they had never been lost.

Another cairn now marks the location of McMillan's Numbla Munjee homestead, a square base of rocks bound by rough mortar which rises to a blunt pyramid topped with shards of stone. I leapt out of the car to sniff around. Photos show me leaning chummily against the cairn, grinning inanely. I was getting into the swing of it now; the appeal of his celebrity was rubbing off on me.

This was the second in a series of cairns thrown up in his honour during a rush of nostalgic patriotism in the 1920s, like a trail of breadcrumbs that traces the route of the successful expedition from this spot south along the River Tambo and down into the shifting grasses of the alluvial plains. At Bruthen we came across another. A plaque on it read: 'Angus McMillan passed by here, 1839' – like schoolboy graffiti. This one was topped with a concrete pillar supporting a large stone ball. Cairns flew past like flags – one at Mossiface, at Sarsfield, at Lucknow. I was hot on his heels.

Down, down, we followed him. Into the flats. Into the deep rich earth of the floodplains. The word 'wide' could have been invented for this space. An enormous expanse, with everything open to the air. Long vistas to the Alps in the north, the ocean to the south.

Ceremony at a cairn commemorating McMillan's achievements, 1920s.

I had a copy of McMillan's expedition journal with me, and I read it aloud as we drove, trying to conjure what he had seen, then superimpose it upon the present day. *The country consists of beautiful open forest, and the grass was up to our stirrup-irons as we rode along, and was absolutely swarming with kangaroos and emus. The lake was alive with wild ducks, swans, and pelicans.*

To our right was the hill McMillan had climbed from which to survey his new domain. There he saw not only the magnificent body of water he called Lake Victoria, but the rivers that ran like arteries through the flesh of the land. To the Highlanders, struggling down from the parched, drought-stricken dustbowl of New South Wales, it must have seemed a land of milk and honey. It put him in mind, he wrote later, of another place entirely. Of Walter Scott's 'Land of the mountain and the flood'. A place he had been dreaming of and grieving for ever since he left its fair shores.

A vision came to McMillan as he looked out across this paradisiacal scene, something not unlike a religious experience. *It was then I keenly felt that I had a noble and glorious task to perform and that I was only an instrument in the hands of the Almighty to accomplish it. Here was a country capable of supporting all my starving countrymen lying dormant.*

I named it at that moment 'Caledonia Australis'.

No time to celebrate. Shortly after this, the party would turn back to prepare for the next phase, settlement – though not before another brief encounter with the Gunai. A hundred tribesmen fled into the scrub upon their approach, burning their camps as they went, but McMillan's party managed to catch up with an elderly man who trailed behind the rest of his tribe. They found him, chillingly, adorned by four dried human hands that hung from his neck like costume jewellery.

If they thought this a bad omen, they didn't say so. It was only onwards, ever onwards. Six weeks' backbreaking work cutting a road suitable for livestock. Next, another return to the Monaro to bring five hundred head of cattle down into the new country, this *Caledonia Australis*, to form a new station on a *delightful tract of country* by the Avon River as a base for further expansion.

It was a punishing lifestyle. The excitable young Matthew Macalister (nephew of Lachlan, and McMillan's assistant) kept a journal too, recording in more detail how they were constantly on the move through uneven terrain, fording rivers and slashing through thorny scrub. They slept in the open air or under roughly constructed bark shelters, and subsisted on rations and whatever could be scavenged. 'Emu eggs for breakfast (one each),' Macalister wrote one morning. 'Mr McMillan and I could not finish ours but Ross managed to get sight of the bottom of his.'

McMillan brushed over the strain in his own workman-like journals, save to note at one point that he had spent sixteen of the last twenty-four months sleeping on the ground *without even the luxury of a tent*. A letter by a contemporary, George Edward Mackay, who settled the Ovens River area around the same time, gives some insight into the physical travails: 'I may mention as a specimen of the fatigue undergone by the earlier squatters, that for six days and nights before I left the Ovens I never lay down,' he later recalled, 'being engaged all day in herding the cattle, and all night in walking round them.' He was alone all this time, he added, his men being either similarly employed with the sheep or in guarding the stores. 'As soon as the necessity for exertion ceased, I was seized with œdematous swelling of the legs and eyelids. I could neither see nor walk, and was carried back to the Hume on a dray.'

'Bushed on this trip,' admitted Macalister.

Angus McMillan would soon take his place among the notables of the district, but the following twelve months were a challenge. His patron was not as impressed as McMillan had hoped, telling him only that without a harbour to allow shipment of livestock to the markets in Hobart, all this beautiful pasturage might prove more trouble than it was worth.

McMillan was dispatched back to the south to find a suitable location for a port. In the meantime Macalister kept McMillan's discovery of this rich new land quiet, all the while applying more and more pressure. Months of false starts and failed missions culminated in a bad-tempered power struggle between McMillan and Lieutenant Ross, who had been dispatched by Macalister to replace him as leader, and had even – to McMillan's fury – mounted himself on McMillan's own grey horse, Clifton.

He was spitting mad. All his work, all these months of discomfort and labour seemed to count for little. When, finally, the instruction came through to abandon the country and sell the existing cattle in Melbourne, it was too much. Disobeying his orders, McMillan instead formed a party of five, took four weeks' provisions and set off with the intention *to do or die.*

On 11 February 1841, from a hill they named Tom's Cap, they at last got sight of the much-longed-for natural harbour of Corner Inlet. Three days later, on Valentine's Day, they struck the coast. The inlet was thickly lined with vegetation and heavy with the stink of the mangrove, but McMillan did not care. Its waters were sheltered and seven feet deep at low tide; finally they had found a safe harbour on this destructive stretch of coastline.

Triumph at last. The cautious Scot allowed himself a moment of unfettered joy, bathing his feet in the warm waters as he thanked his God. *This was a happy day. Having accomplished my object, I had great cause to be thankful to Him who guarded me and shielded me from many a danger.*

They called it Port Albert. Taking his axe to the bark of a fat gum near the water's edge, he cut his legend:

ANGUS MCMILLAN
14–2–1841

and turned back towards the interior. He had proven his worth as an explorer and as a man. Not only to his employer, but to himself.

This breakthrough could not have been more timely. Unknown to McMillan, Melbourne was already abuzz with the news of the glorious grazing land to the east. A second party financed by James Macarthur – he who had prophesied the existence of 'valuable grazing country' while swept off course in Bass Strait – had tailgated McMillan into the region, following his tracks for part of the way, before striking off and cutting west through dense forest towards Melbourne. It was led by the charming Polish adventurer 'Count' Paweł Strzelecki. Tales of his daring exploits and a near brush with death – the party had become disoriented in the near-impenetrable scrub, been forced to abandon their horses and only spared starvation thanks to the skills of their Aboriginal guide – were the talk of the town.

Then, coincidentally, the paddle steamer *Clonmel* had been stranded on a sandbar off the coast only a month previously, and those aboard had managed to row to Sealer's Cove, at the foot of Wilsons Promontory. Curious probing by boat around this region had already aroused some interest in the harbour in which McMillan now stood, carving his initials.

This constellation of events had primed the businessmen of Melbourne to the region's possibilities: news of Port Albert, and of McMillan's brand-new overland route from the north, spread quickly. All his faith in the project had been vindicated. But there was a small catch. As word of Strzelecki's expedition had got out first, many of the names suggested by the *foreign imposter* for prominent landmarks had already entered the local lexicon. This rankled with McMillan, who thought it little more than *piracy*; some of these names, like Lake King, he pointed out, could not be less appropriate for Queen Victoria's colony.

In the following years, as news of McMillan's primacy spread – and bitter proxy battles over the men's rival claims to the title of 'discoverer of Gippsland' were fought in the letters page of the *Port Phillip Herald* – some of Strzelecki's names were officially overturned in favour of McMillan's: Mount Gisborne reverted to Mount Welling-ton, the Macarthur River to the Mitchell, the River Riley to the Nicholson.

It was too late for the most significant, however: Strzelecki's name had stuck irrevocably. In honour of the governor of the day, Sir George Gipps – declared by the *Sydney Morning Herald* 'the worst Governor the colony has ever had' – *Caledonia Australis* and the grand vision it symbolised had been written over: it was Gipps' Land.

Port Albert's day in the sun is long over. Since the construction of the Princes Highway – from Sydney south-east along the coast through Melbourne and beyond – and the dimming of Hobart as a centre of commerce, there is no need of it as an agricultural port. Instead it is a pretty, somewhat overlooked little tourist town, a few yachts roped tightly to the jetty as their crews squint into the wind that batters in off the strait. We stopped by only briefly, listlessly perusing the models in the maritime museum then following a walking trail out of town to the spot where McMillan struck water, now known as McMillan Bay. The tree with its Valentine's carving was chopped down during his lifetime by the local commissioner Charles Tyers with the intention of preserving it as some kind of monument, but it is long lost. No matter.

We turned back north towards the site of the first station, that *delightful tract* on the banks of the Avon River, since grown into a town and renamed Stratford – thus becoming, incongruously, Stratford-upon-Avon. It makes the most of it: the local gallery displayed a jolly technicolour portrait of the Bard on the wall, copies of the collected works in the gift shop, and posters for the annual Shakespeare festival on the door, the result of what I could only presume to be an extended local in-joke taken root.

A few miles downriver was the site of McMillan's homestead, his much-beloved Bushy Park. It was here that he finally struck out alone in 1841, the quarrel with Macalister over the search for Corner Inlet having driven a wedge between them, and he found himself marking out land, laying claim in his own name for the first time.

Over the next twenty years McMillan amassed a steadily growing fortune, and from this new family seat oversaw a property empire that at its height extended to seven runs encompassing a total of 150,000 acres, an area ten times the size of Barra. Each run had its own accommodation, gardens and agricultural facilities. Bushy Park boasted a homestead, assorted outbuildings including stables and a 'ball room' where he held ceilidhs, a six-acre orchard and a further thirty acres under cultivation with wheat, oats and peas. Today such an estate would be worth many millions of dollars.

Von Guérard's *View of the Gippsland Alps, from Bushy Park on the River Avon.*

He had made the jump that his father had never managed, from tacksman to laird. As befitting a gentleman of his status he took to wearing tweed three-piece suits as well as his omnipresent tartan bonnet. He hosted visiting dignitaries, including the anthropologist Alfred Howitt, who would later diligently record the traditions of the vanishing Gunai, and the botanist Baron von Mueller. Eugene von Guérard, the most significant landscape artist of the period, stayed at Bushy Park too, and while there painted the panoramic view from the terrace: blue ranges skirting the horizon, horned bullocks lazing in the long grass, Aboriginal children playing on a fallen gum.

It was all McMillan's own. He was the Laird of Gippsland now. But he hadn't forgotten his roots. His brother Donald joined him at Bushy Park after a period in the West Indies. McMillan also arranged for newly emigrated Scots to stay at the Port Phillip Club in Melbourne at his expense until they had found suitable employment in the colony. He himself employed plenty of Highlanders; they flocked to him. He served the workers two drams of whisky a day. 'If hospitality be a virtue his was unbounded, and he exercised it continuously,' one contemporary recalled.

And his generosity was rewarded. He was made judge at the 'Green Wattle' races, highlight of the Gippsland social calendar, and was later elected by a landslide as Member of the Legislative Assembly for South Gippsland. The controversy over who had better claim to the discovery of the land – McMillan or Strzelecki – had died down: McMillan had stayed, while Strzelecki, attention-seeker that he was, had torn off in search of greater glory elsewhere. McMillan, everyone was agreed, was the true hero of Gippsland, and rightly deserved the title.

The first of a series of annual dinners in his honour was organised in 1856. Amid 'loud and repeated cheers' and toasts to the queen, McMillan was singled out for the highest of praise and prevailed upon to give a speech, the body of which was later reported in the Melbourne *Argus*:

Chairman and Gentlemen, – you have by your unexpected and unlooked for kindness this evening placed me in a position that nearly deprives me of the power of utterance. Little did I think when, in the performance of my duty to my employer, so many years ago, in forcing my way inch by inch through the wilds and fastnesses that bound this now fertile district, that my humble efforts would be thus so signally honoured by the inhabitants of this favoured territory ... It was a happy day to me when I found my way to the Old Port, but this indeed is the happiest hour of my life.

This version of the truth – the story of plucky Highlander made good – is what seems to have stuck, on the surface at least.

McMillan took to styling himself as a gentleman.

Near the site of his former homestead at Bushy Park we found the inevitable cairn, and a noticeboard outlining his achievements and legacy. No mention of any trouble. We drove the perimeter of the old estate along a long line of red gums that stood sentry on the verge – stained with dark clots where the trunks had been bruised, like blood on a grazed knee – and I hung my head out of the window, trying to identify the spot where von Guérard must have stood to paint his panorama.

This trip, I reflected, had so far been unexpectedly painless. I had come face to face with precisely no uncomfortable truths about the family legacy. It was almost as if no one had told anyone in Gippsland about all the ugly goings-on in their own history. Maybe, suggested a small voice, there's been some kind of misunderstanding. Maybe it wasn't as bad as all that. It's possible that I've got the wrong impression.

This growing suspicion – or was it hope? – did not abate when we visited McMillan's grave in Sale. The enormous graveyard was on the outskirts of town, 14,000 plots laid out in extravagant style in the form of a clover. At its centre, where the leaves branched off, a many-headed signpost directed each denomination to their own patch of sacred ground, like one of those humorous signs at tourist hotspots indicating that New York lies 3,796 miles in one direction and Moscow 1,435 in another.

We followed the 'PRESBYTERIAN >>>' arm to a decrepit section where rusted metal fences kept visitors from treading on the bare earth of the graves, the stones cracked and watermarked, their inscriptions barely legible. Some sat at drunken angles, set askew by rabbit holes dug directly underneath. The names I could make out were like the roll call at a Scottish school: Isabella and Archibald MacLachlan from Rothesay; Flora Macdonald Brown of Portree; Robert Alexander, native of Linlithgow; even a William Wallace ('loved husband of Bridget, RIP').

I searched fruitlessly for McMillan on all the headstones around a central obelisk that dwarfed them all, until finally I realised with a start that the obelisk was in fact the grave I was looking for. It too was fenced off, and a large sign bearing the logo of a local tourism initiative stood nearby, commemorating

THE DISCOVERY OF GIPPSLAND
by
ANGUS MCMILLAN
1810–1865

and bearing a blurb briefly outlining McMillan's achievements.

This grave, I learned later, had been the focus of an 'annual pilgrimage' of Sale residents from 1924 until the events of the Second World War overtook their nostalgic fervour. Local newspaper reports describe how dignitaries, well-wishers and schoolchildren gathered to commemorate the life of 'undoubtedly one of the greatest men Gippsland had ever known'. They gave speeches, recited poetry and sang songs written in his honour:

> Let Onward, Onward, be the cry
> Of each brave heart to-day.
> There's land and room for all
> Does not McMillan say.

(*Chorus*) Then come over the mountains,
 Come where the green wattles grow;
 Come where sweet birds are singing,
 Come where the rivers flow.

 Then Hurrah, Hurrah for the Pilot
 That first set foot in Gippsland.
 And three cheers for the boys that were with him
 With our glass, our heart, and hand ...

On the way back into town we passed a turn-off for
McMillan Street. A few blocks down, McMillan Park. The
local college, I knew, had a McMillan campus. Later,
totally lost and searching for a place to camp, I would
stumble across an abandoned, overgrown campsite; an
entrance arch labelled it the property of the McMillan
County Scouts. It was almost eerie, the way a sort of
personality cult had grown up around him. Nowhere was
there mention of any massacres. I had come here expecting hushed voices and recriminations, but instead I had
found him canonised, immortalised at every corner.

What did that mean? I was struggling to understand
where I stood, distracted by the heaving of my push-me-
pull-you emotions. In one sense, if Angus McMillan wasn't
the villain I had understood him to be, then my entire trip
was nothing more than a self-congratulatory lap of victory
around the sites of my relative's achievements. At the
same time, I still felt the warm glow of reflected fame. I
wanted it to be the truth. I *wanted* him to be every bit as
good as they said he was.

I wanted him to be a hero.

*

We were late, horribly late. Jeannie and I came barrelling in through the doors, blurting our apologies.

Two representatives of the Maffra Historical Society, based near Bushy Park, had agreed to meet us in what was once a beet factory, now a makeshift museum exhibiting what seemed, to my eyes, a collection of the most incredible mundanity. Much wall space had been awarded to the 'rise, success, and eventual end' of the sugar-beet industry in the district, closely followed by a series of exquisitely detailed pen portraits of all the local farms and their homesteads circa 1890.

Perhaps this is the purpose of these odd, hyperlocal societies: to catalogue the past in such painstaking detail that only the residents themselves would be interested in doing so. In Boisdale, a nearby village, an equivalent group had sunk much time and thought into a series of bronze plaques logging the birth and career of almost every building – the butcher's, the post office, the brick cottages 'built to house the cheese and butter factory workers' – as if they couldn't bear even a single detail to be forgotten.

Taking this into account, I was all the more staggered by the inexplicable lack of information about those supposed massacres, some of which were alleged to have been committed only a few miles from this spot. Wouldn't a group of such evident diligence and focus have alighted breathlessly on a thrilling historical scandal in their very district? This, I thought, was *real history*, a meaty saga of ambition and butchery and the struggle for power – a more fertile patch for study, surely, than lists of factory workers and municipal planning through the decades.

Still, it was generous of them to have agreed to meet me at all, and they were well informed. They were delighted to discuss the local area, and had come prepared with a list of references I should look up in the local archive; but they were oddly taciturn on the subject of Angus McMillan and the massacres.

'Well,' said one of them cautiously, under close questioning, 'I'm not sure we have very much on McMillan. Although I know of him, of course.' She was a mumsy woman, with wire-rimmed spectacles and mouse-coloured hair. She blinked at me, then gestured to a small patch of wall space where McMillan was pictured hand in hand with two unidentified Aboriginal men. 'I think he was ... very much a man of his time. I think he did what he thought was best. It was all they could do at the time.'

Angus McMillan sits hand in hand with two Gunai men.

Her companion, an older man, was more headstrong. 'When we learned about him at school, we never heard anything about this,' he said. 'All these claims originated from the research of one man,' he continued, opening his hands as if inviting me to reach my own conclusions. 'What some of these so-called historians come up with to sell their books!'

I knew who he was referring to: Peter Gardner, a local historian who had written a series of books in the 1980s in which he laid out much inflammatory evidence of bloodshed in the earliest years of settlement, causing quite a kerfuffle in the press and historical journals.

The woman chimed in again. 'Angus was a pioneer. He was doing a job, clearing the land of whatever it was full of. We wouldn't be here without him. Maybe it was nasty at the beginning, but it's history now, and you just have to get on with things. You know, when Aboriginal people go on about … Well. They're lucky it was the British, and not the Dutch or Germans. Then they'd *really* have been in trouble.'

That night we stayed with Cath and Mike, old friends of Jeannie and Ian's, retired teachers who lived in a low-slung, surprisingly spacious bungalow up a long, gum-lined drive on what was once the Boisdale run, Bushy Park's neighbour station, set up by McMillan on Macalister's behalf in 1840.

Cath welcomed me with a pile of books she had salvaged during a clear-out of her school library. 'Local history was on the curriculum, but it seems to have gone out of fashion,' she lamented. We sat on the terrace at the front of the house, where long tendrils of climbing plants stretched down to stroke our faces, kindly tentacles.

I was usually slightly deflated by Australian country homes, which even on the largest estates tend to make little impact on approach: almost inevitably single-storeyed, stretching off backwards like a maze. They are not grand, but it's the roof space that counts: almost everyone collects rainwater for their private supply, and many houses in the country are not attached to the mains supply at all. The gathering and filtration systems are a constant source of fascination, and at any rural gathering, as time goes on the probability of any two Australian men turning to the subject of water collection approaches one.

The house lay in a 'rain shadow', Mike informed me broodily at dinner. 'It looks great, good farmland, until there's a ten-year drought … then it feels like it's never going to rain again.' On the wall was a frame holding a series of photos of their daughter bouncing on a trampoline, one a year, every year, for ten or fifteen years, as she grew through infancy and girlhood into her awkward teens. In the background the photographs unintentionally charted the state of the climate, the yearly rainfall tracked and coded by colour. In the early pictures the grass was green-yellow, then strawlike. A few years later, shorn short and so blond it was almost white.

'Our son got married here that summer,' said Cath, following my eyes. 'We had to lay a red carpet to make it a bit more presentable. The grass just turned to dust under your feet.'

'What about you, Cal?' Jeannie changed the subject. 'What about your partner? Doesn't he mind you disappearing off to the other side of the world for weeks at a time?'

I felt the eyes of the table on me. 'Not really!' I chirruped. 'He's off doing something else. Trekking in the desert. Counting leopards.'

'Oh. Then you understand each other.'

'Yes,' I said, at first pleased and then uneasy. Recently we seemed to have been misunderstanding each other more often than understanding. Or we had been, at least, until he went to the desert.

He'd emailed from a border town: 'I won't be able to message much after this.'

'That's fine,' I'd lied. 'I understand.' I hadn't heard from him since.

I smiled, falsely, breezily, around the table, and changed the subject again.

After dinner, head swimming, I excused myself and walked down the track in the dusk towards Maffra, the nearest town. An earlier squall of rain had soaked immediately into the thirsty earth, and the sky had opened up again above me, now awash with stars, the sweep of the Milky Way a veil drawn fast across its naked breast. The sliver of new moon hung hooklike, a bright satellite-star at its foot.

The air was still, but the night was alive with sound, which grew in pitch and volume as I veered off through the thick grass towards a shallow pool that reverberated with the rasping of frogs – some deep and percussive, others melodic, singsong, all falling quiet as I approached then resuming behind me when I moved on, in a bubble of silence.

I ran my hands along the smooth trunk of a fallen gum, tracing the silky folds where the limbs joined the trunk. They were sensual somehow. I'd been aching to touch them for days, slipping my fingers into the puckers in the bark that brought to mind thoughts of warm flesh, of wrists and ankles, of the creases between thumb and forefinger, the no-man's land between the curve of a jaw and the neck.

A flock of black birds sat massed in the bare branches of a dead tree above, watching and catcalling, dark menaces with long curving beaks and the hunched wings of vultures. Their shrieks were guttural, penetrating.

The dark drew in like a cloak, the wall of sound closing tight around me. I could imagine, now, the long, slow summer nights on the runs. The soundscape, the landscape, the pull on the heart of these wide-open spaces. The catch of breath in the back of the throat at the sheer scale of the place.

Imagine tumbling off the boat with your bag of belongings and finding all this endless land stretching out before you, when at home they were being pushed from their tiny cliffside toeholds.

6

Black War

But of course it hadn't been lying there empty. The Gunai people were already there, had been there for tens of thousands of years.

McMillan may have taken umbrage at Strzelecki's renaming, his 'piracy', but the Gunai too had names for everything, long before his arrival. The disputed Lake King – or was it Lake Victoria? – had always been, to its residents, known as Narran, meaning 'moon'. To them, the river by which McMillan constructed his homestead was not the Avon, but the Dooyedang. And they did not see the land as McMillan saw it, in acres and yields, in heads of cattle, but through the prism of a complex system of mythology and tradition.

The deep waters of Corner Inlet and its surrounds – the mangroves and wetlands, the scattering of islands in the bay – were not a natural harbour at all, but a souvenir from the events of the Dreamtime. Long ago, legend had it, this region had been part of a land bridge connecting Gippsland to far-off Tasmania, but one day the frog spirit Tiddilik had drunk all of the water in the land and carried it around in his gut until finally, at Tarra Warackel (Port Albert), he spewed it all out in a great flood that washed away the land and left only islands and the perilous stretch of water of Bass Strait. These wetlands became the home of Boorun the pelican and Tuk the musk duck, the father and mother of all the Gunai peoples.

Further east, at Bung Yarnda (Lake Tyers), the sea-being Narkabungdha found himself tired from rushing over rocks and rolling back and forth across the sand, and came inland to rest. He found a quiet place among the shady gum trees where he fell asleep, creating those magnificent freshwater lakes that irrigate the fertile grasslands. To the north, the limestone caves that riddle the hillsides of Bukkanmunjie (Buchan) were home to the mischievous nyols, who stole the memory of those who visited them, and at Ngrung a Narguna (Den of Nargun) a huge living rock from the beginning of time sheltered behind a water-fall, waiting for stray children to snatch away.

These stories and beliefs were unique to Gunai culture, one of several hundred distinct Aboriginal nations that patchworked the Australian continent at the time of the arrival of the First Fleet. Together, these nations – who, in the southeast, refer to themselves collectively as Koories – comprised a total population estimated at between 700,000 and a million. Within what is now the state of Victoria alone there were dozens of Aboriginal nations – as many as thirty-nine, according to one estimate – each of which had its own language, culture and beliefs, and constantly shifting relations with its neighbours, as alliances formed and dissolved, territory was disputed and blood feuds fought.

Five linguistically similar groups around the Port Phillip area to the east, for example, had joined together to form the 'Kulin alliance'; they hated and despised the Gunai, who in turn terrorised the Ya-itma-thang and Ngarico peoples to their north and west. These bitter conflicts had played out over centuries, as each made incursions into the other's land to wage war in night-time raids – black-skinned men painted with ochre and clay emerging like phantoms from the darkness to kill or to steal away women. This was the backdrop of the warrigals' fearful reputation.

Alfred Howitt's map of Gippsland describing the territories held by each clan.

All of these nations were subdivided into smaller 'clan groups', each with a specific dialect and variants of tradition, and in turn these clans were divvied further into smaller family groups of perhaps a couple of dozen members each, who would come together for special ceremonial occasions. The Gunai nation was made up of five clans: the Brabawooloong, of the high country and central lowlands;

the Bratowooloong, who lived in the south; the Brayak-ooloong of the west; the Krowathunkooloong to the east; and the Tatungooloong of the coast and the lakes.

All lived a nomadic existence, moving with the seasons between a number of different sites, following the fluctuating sources of food and water, constructing their temporary shelters as they went from leaves or bark or branches, or simply commandeering caves among the rocks. As the hunter-gatherer lifestyle had proven sufficient for nutrition and shelter – tasks required for survival taking up only four or five hours of the day – there had been no need for agriculture or pastoralism. There were no fences then, or permanent structures; no marked boundaries between each clan's territory.

The first European arrivals in Australia were baffled by these eccentric natives, who had no yen for personal possessions nor any obvious leaders or hierarchy. Political power and land ownership had little relevance to them; as Captain Cook observed on his arrival in Botany Bay in 1770, 'all they seem'd to want was us to be gone'.

And it was the intangibility of the Aboriginal presence that initially lulled the colonists into the false sense that they were settling an unoccupied land. Cook, in fact, had originally been issued with instructions from the Admiralty that he should take possession of 'convenient situations' in the new country in the name of the king, 'with the consent of the natives'. But such agreements were never made concrete, unlike in New Zealand, where representatives of the Crown negotiated directly with Maori chiefs and recognised traditional ownership; put simply, the British could not identify any Aboriginal leaders with authority to negotiate, and so did not negotiate at all.

In later years, in misguided attempts to gain a foothold in the shifting sands of indigenous society, the settlers would crown Aboriginal 'kings', picking out the most cooperative elders and presenting them with curved copper breastplates, their names engraved upon them like a plaque for a wall, and the title 'KING OF THE ———' underneath. They were intended to act as handy name tags so other colonists might court these new, recognisable powers, but the policy met with mixed success. The recipients would sometimes trade away these 'king plates' to others, or as the Gippsland missionary John Bulmer later wrote, "These fellows who have been given a brass plate wait at every steamer landing ... asking for sixpence to get grog with.'

Gunai encampment, 1870. The man on the right wears a king plate.

The only documented attempt to bargain directly with an Aboriginal group for ownership of the land took place many decades later, in 1835, when the explorer and pastoralist John Batman negotiated the 'purchase' of 600,000 acres of land in the Melbourne area from Kulin leaders, in return for an annual tribute of blankets, axes, knives, scissors, mirrors and assorted clothing. There have been a number of questions over the validity of the resulting document, not least because the Aboriginal 'translators' brought by Batman's party shared no common language with the Kulin – it is now thought that the Kulin leaders believed they were being offered gifts in exchange for safe passage through their land – but nevertheless this 'treaty' was perceived as enough of a threat to the Crown, which assumed ownership of all Australian land, for Governor Sir Richard Bourke to issue a proclamation declaring it null:

> every such treaty, bargain, and contract with the
> Aboriginal Natives ... for the possession, title, or
> claim to any Lands lying and being within the limits
> of the Government of the Colony of New South
> Wales ... is void and of no effect against the rights
> of the Crown ...

Any persons found in possession of such land 'will be considered as trespassers', he added. Thus Bourke made explicit the principle that had underpinned the actions of the British colonists up to this point, and that would become the explicit doctrine of the administration for more than 150 years: the concept of Australia as *terra nullius*, no-man's land. An empty place, belonging to no one. The Aboriginal people who wandered its tracks, picking its fruit, catching its fish, but not tilling the soil or grazing the plains, were considered as wild animals; they came with the territory, but could not be considered its owners. Without an owner, the land was there for the taking. And take it they did.

Driven first by drought, and then by the depression that hit Melbourne in the early 1840s, new settlers rushed for the new land. Those coming from the west were largely following the siren call of Strzelecki, who had very successfully spread word of the pleasures that awaited them in Gippsland, even going so far as to produce a (horribly inaccurate) map suggesting the most direct route into the region from Melbourne. Whether any of the incomers thought twice about taking directions from a man who had almost starved to death whilst undertaking the same journey I don't know, but certainly many of them ran immediately into trouble.

The area through which they must travel to reach the pastureland – a primeval forest of eucalypt, bonewood and towering mountain ash – was notoriously difficult going. William Odell Raymond, an English magistrate who would become McMillan's neighbour when he took up the Stratford run in 1842, found himself and his party caught in the dense, prickly undergrowth like flies in a web, 'suffering severely from the cuts we got getting through the scrub[,] our clothes and boots being completely torn off of us'.

The Gunai generally avoided the area, considering it subject to an ancient curse. They called it *Wea-wuk*: the bad country. Both the Gunai and the neighbouring Bun Wurrung clan of the Kulin believed that strangers who walked upon this cursed land were at risk of harm. To travel safely, it was thought, visitors had to travel in the company of the traditional owners (the Brayakooloong or

Bratowooloong clans of the Gunai), sleep on a layer of leaves so as to keep from touching the ground, and eat only what morsels their host brought them, pulling them from a skewer using their teeth.

Of course, the incoming European settlers knew none of this, only the extreme difficulties that many of their number suffered in their attempts to breach the 'fortress' of Gippsland. Henry Colden Harrison, 'the father of Australian Rules Football' and the son of a grazier, wrote many years later of his family's unsuccessful attempt to settle in Gippsland. Having set out with five hundred cattle and 'five or six thousand sheep', they managed to lose most of the former in the scrub. As for the latter, they were so thirsty that 'the poor animals, on seeing the sea, rushed into it, and many of them were attacked and killed by the sharks'. By the time the Harrisons finally got to their destination with the sad remnants of their livestock, they were out of luck: the choicest cuts of land had already been snapped up. At the Tarwin River, on the edge of Gippsland, they met future Victorian governor Charles La Trobe, who advised them to turn back, assuring them 'that there was not a yard of country left'.

From first discovery to 'not a yard left' took less than five years. It was a sea change, a transformation far too rapid in nature for colonial infrastructure to keep up with. With a scattered, autonomous and largely undocumented population came a total lack of governance: this was very much the Australian frontier – the Wild East, perhaps.

In the early years there was no state presence whatsoever. The first government representative, Commissioner Charles Tyers, arrived by boat in 1843 – following three failed attempts to enter overland, repulsed each time by the viciousness of the Bad Country – to find total chaos. The region was 'infested' with 'runaway convicts and other bad characters', he complained in a note to his superiors, adding an appeal to be provided with a unit of mounted police to help him keep order. The first resident minister, Reverend Willoughby Bean, found things little improved by 1848, when he reported on the 'disreputable and immoral class of persons' who continued to reside in the area, and quoted a local judge's pronouncement that the outskirts of Port Albert had become a 'pandemonium upon earth'.

It is hard, perhaps, for someone who has grown up in the security of a developed country to comprehend the vertigo felt by those who launched themselves out into this new land, only to find themselves floating in a stateless vacuum. As an unsupervised classroom will morph in minutes from quiet concentration into a seething mass of feral children, any community without effective government oversight is at risk of speedy descent into chaos and injustice. Henry Meyrick, a young English settler who travelled with his brother to the region in 1846, wrote home, overwhelmed by the experience. 'We have learned some wisdom in Gippsland,' he told his mother. 'It is a current saying that a man who has lived here can match the devil himself. It is certainly the most lawless place I have ever heard of.'

The sheer pace of change could be difficult for some of the earliest pioneers to come to terms with; the very first arrivals often reflected with mixed feelings upon the role they had played as harbingers of this change. Evelyn Sturt, an early settler in the Ovens River area, looked back two decades later with some nostalgia, remembering how on his arrival the country had been 'most beautiful – miles of it untrodden by stock, and indeed unseen by Europeans. Every creek abounded with wild fowl, and the quail sprang from the long kangaroo grass which waved to the very flaps of the saddle. It has often been a source of regret to me,' he added, 'that all the charms attending the travers- ing of a new country must give way to the march of civilization; the camp on the grassy sward is now super- seded by the noisy road-side inn; the quart pot of tea by the bottle of ale. All the quiet serenity of an Australian bush, as we have known it, has yielded to the demands of population ... I look back to those days as some joyous scene of school-boy holidays.'

Theirs were not the only sets of eyes looking upon the evolving landscape in horror. The explorers had, at least, seen Western civilisation before; they recognised it, and had made it their lives' work to advance its interests. But imagine the same through the eyes of the Gunai. Imagine the shock of seeing your country, through which you had wandered unfettered all your life, re-form and mutate before your eyes: the ground left stubbled and raw as acres of bush were cleared; fences erected to contain hordes of alien beasts, those slack-jawed masticators; wooden shacks popping up like fungus in all the best camping spots by the rivers and waterholes, appearing one day and never moving off. And everywhere, now, these white-faced men.

The Gunai had a close relationship with the dead. They believed their departed kindred passed through the solid vault of the sky to live in the spirit-country, a land like their own, of tall eucalypts and fast-flowing rivers, but that they could send down ropes and revisit the land of the living. And so they stayed on, ever present but not always visible. They wandered among the sleeping bodies at night, conversed with the Gunai in dreams – counselled them, warned them, brought them offerings of song and charms to protect them from evil.

They were often friendly, but not always – evil spirits sometimes cursed or physically attacked the living – and the appearance of even the benevolent dead could be a portent of doom. The anthropologist Alfred Howitt relayed a story of an elderly Koorie man who reported that 'in the night, his father, his father's friend and a female spirit he could not recognize, had come to him and said that he would die next day, and that they would wait for him'. Howitt added that he could give many similar instances, 'and, strange to say, the dying man in all these cases kept his appointment with the ghosts to the very day'.

The Gunai therefore treated their dead with a respect bordering on veneration. As McMillan had already seen, they had a propensity to wear the hands of the deceased slung around their necks as a token of affection. 'They are beautifully preserved,' noted a later arrival, 'nails and flesh, with veins all perfect. Their mode of preserving them is by a curious process of stewing with hot stones.'

It was traditional to carry around the bodies of the dead for weeks or months, in a very literal interpretation of the grieving process. The corpse would be wrapped in a curl of bark as it decomposed, flesh liquefying, hair and teeth loosening. Every so often the bark would be unpeeled to reveal what was left of the body, and the grease exuding from the corpse applied to the mourners' skin. Finally, when the body had truly decayed, the fingers and other appendages were broken off and stuffed into a possum-skin bag for use as a pillow.

The Gunai too, under certain circumstances, would eat the flesh of warriors they had killed in combat — not for sustenance, but in a ceremonial act of conquest. They believed that by consuming the flesh of their enemies, particularly the fat from around the kidneys, they would gain the strength of the dead man. 'They said the flesh tasted better than beef,' reported Howitt. To roast human meat, they would cut sections from the corpse and pass a burning firestick over them. During this process the scorched outer layer of skin peeled off and the blood drained away, leaving the chunks of carcass an eerie white hue.

When the bushmen first encountered McMillan on the banks of the Tambo, they recognised the colour of his skin as the pallor of death. 'Mrart', they called the white man. Ghost.

It was an obvious assumption to make. Elsewhere in Victoria, the escaped convict William Buckley had been taken in by the Wathaurung Kulin, who thought him the returned spirit of a dead tribesman. The widow of the dead man had found Buckley wandering the bush holding a spear that had been used to mark the grave. She took him to be her husband and he was welcomed into the clan, with whom he lived for over thirty years.

But now, in Gippsland, the mrart's own people had come en masse to settle this country. All of them men, all of them white-faced, all of them speaking in tongues and spraying violence from the rods they raised to their lightning eyes. An invasion of ghosts, each with the power to strike a Gunai man down dead at a hundred paces with that sudden crack and a great fountain of blood.

The initial encounters between the two groups – notably McMillan's encounter with the elderly man bedecked with hands, who after receiving gifts of a knife and trousers from the party, shook hands with all its members then turned to the horses and *shook the bridles very heartily* – were fairly innocuous. But when the Gunai realised that their white visitors planned to set up home, they reacted strongly and negatively, and moved to repulse them.

In October 1840, after establishing the first station on the banks of the Avon, McMillan and five men made a third, failed attempt to fight their way to Corner Inlet. Foiled by a succession of marshes, thickets and torrential rivers, they were forced to admit defeat not twenty miles from the anticipated harbour, the existence of which they still had to confirm and locate before settlement of the region could begin in earnest. In ill spirits, and by this stage barely speaking to one another, the party turned towards home, with the uncomfortable sense that they were being watched.

The tribesmen kept their distance, flitting away through the bush faster than the heavily laden visitors and their horses could follow, but the group grew uneasy. At night they took it in turns to keep watch, eyes searching the formless dark beyond the circle of light cast by the fire, ears pricked for the sound of footsteps in the dark.

Finally, as they struggled across Clifton Morass – a mire where McMillan's *gallant grey* had once been so badly

bogged they were obliged to parbuckle him to solid ground
– their shadows revealed themselves. The party were
suddenly surrounded on all sides by around eighty Gunai
men, each brandishing a quartz-tipped spear and a carved
wooden shield. Vastly outnumbered, and feeling his party
in danger, McMillan *fired both barrels, but did not kill any of
them.* It was enough: the Gunai took fright, and fled back
into the scrub.

This was the first sign that all was not well.

Those dark faces, which had formerly seemed so innocent – fleeing the explorers' approach with such urgency
that they would leave their belongings behind – now
appeared threatening and unknowable. They had allowed
their ghostly visitors to pass unscathed as they watched
from the shadow of the bush, but now McMillan recalled
the warnings of those infamous warriors conjured up by
the Omeo blacks.

Leaving his men to their work, he hurried back along
his old tracks to the Monaro and civilisation, where the
nearest commissioner of Crown lands might be found.
They needed assistance, fast, he told officials when he
arrived. Could the commissioner spare men and firearms
for the protection of settlers in the new district?

The appeal fell on deaf ears. Any settlers heading so far
beyond the limits of the colony, the commissioner told
him, were doing so at their own risk. McMillan's and his
men's safety was entirely in their own hands.

Dejected, McMillan turned back once more, only to
find on his return to Gippsland that his fears had been
realised. While he had been away, wrangling with bureau-
crats in the Monaro, the station on the Avon had been
attacked. His men had escaped with their lives, but barely

— they had fled to Numbla Munjee with the Gunai in hot
pursuit for the first twenty-five miles. The cattle, they
said, had all been speared or dispersed.

It was a major setback, but McMillan was damned if he
would give up now. Steeling himself for combat, he
formed a party of eight men, armed them well and
returned to Bushy Park, to find a hellish scene: the remains
of their dead animals scattered all around, the one-roomed
hut where once they'd slept reduced to ruins. They rebuilt
it, further back from the creek this time, and hunkered
down.

Each day they lit fresh fires to advertise their presence
to the Gunai, then returned to the hut to wait it out.
Time passed slowly. The sun rose, plateaued and fell
again. Flies settled on faces and forearms, buzzing lazily
away whenever the men raised a hand to shoo them, then
setting down again as soon as the coast was clear. The
nights were endless and oppressively hot. Finally, on the
night of 22 December, the men were disturbed by noises
from outside. McMillan's horse, Clifton, had come up
close to the hut, showing the whites of his eyes; he had
been spooked by movements in the dark. The men knew
then that they must prepare for attack.

Dr Alexander Arbuckle, the first doctor to practise in
Gippsland and a close friend of McMillan's, had been
injured during the journey to the station, so they installed
him in the fireplace, where he was told to load the spare
guns in between volleys. The others cut loopholes in the
hut's thin walls and waited for sunrise.

The day faded in. Birdsong; the sigh of the wind through
the tall grass. Light crept through the valley, illuminating
the figures of the Gunai men who circled the hut like a

bad dream. An army, five or six hundred strong, all of them watching, waiting. The tension was unbearable. Then – movement, as the men crouched, fixed spears to their woomeras and prepared to let loose upon the hut. A voice sounded, low and urgent, in the dark interior: McMillan's. He told his men to prepare to fire. They were not to waste a bullet.

'There was a desperate fight,' the *Gippsland Times* reported later, 'but history is silent as to the casualties among the natives. The whites came through all right.'

*

I do hereby strictly forbid any of His Majesty's Subjects, resident or stationary in this Colony, from using any act of Injustice or wanton Cruelty towards the Natives, on pain of being dealt with in the same manner as if such act of Injustice or wanton Cruelty should be committed against the Persons and Estates of any of His Majesty's Subjects.

Proclamation by Governor King, 30 June 1802

The rules were clear enough. Thou shalt not kill. Thou shalt not torture. Thou shalt not inflict wanton cruelty. But the Sydney government's moralising grew further and further out of step with the reality of the frontier.

The Gunai were growing more troublesome as the settlers dug in. The white men, it seemed, were in infinite supply, and as their population began to multiply they were carving up every scrap of grazing land between them. The Gunai found their traditional campsites and hunting grounds occupied, and their prey animals – kangaroos, wallabies, emus – driven to the margins of the country

and replaced by those strange swarms of four-legged creatures. Resentment grew on both sides.

With no concept of pastoralism or the 'ownership' of
animals, the Gunai turned to hunting the settlers' stock,
spearing the slow-moving cattle and eating what they could
before the huge carcasses rotted. They drove flocks of
sheep to remote spots, then broke their legs to restrain
them, and thus keep their meat fresh. 'It is absurd to blame
the aborigines for killing sheep and cattle,' the Gippsland
court clerk George Dunderdale reflected. 'You might as
well say it is immoral for a cat to catch mice.' Still, it
drove the squatters, who had painstakingly driven the
animals hundreds of miles, to distraction. Edward Bell, a
pioneer in the Wimmera region during the period, remembered: 'I recollect a cow being brought into the stockyard
stuck all over with spears, like a porcupine ... In tracking
cattle I came upon a place where the blacks had within a
few days camped some stolen sheep in bough-yards, and
where the torn fleeces and broken legs and joints, since
gnawed by wild dogs, told a tale of wasteful destruction.'

Many facing financial ruin turned, as McMillan had, to
the government for support, and found none forthcoming.
'It was scarcely to be wondered at,' Bell wrote, 'that the
settlers took the law into their own hands on such occasions.' So it proved in Gippsland. McMillan's 'defence of
Bushy Park', as it came to be known, had set the tone for
future encounters between the two peoples. The settlers
were hardening their hearts.

New arrivals were confronted with a simple choice: beat
a retreat, and seek out a less fertile location in some unex-
ploited cranny in a less conflicted area of the colony; or
face the Aboriginal threat and attempt to neutralise it. To

most of them, the choice was simple. Within a very short space of time, they began to kill without compunction.

The second clash – perhaps more accurately, the second *known* clash – took place shortly after, when McMillan's same party is thought to have ridden down a group of Gunai to the marshy confluence of the Avon and Perry Rivers, where they were trapped and shot down in their dozens.

Later, George Augustus Robinson, Chief Protector of Aborigines for Port Phillip with the duty to 'protect and civilize' the besieged indigenes of Victoria, to which Gippsland had latterly been added, would – after a jolly evening's entertainment at Bushy Park – stumble upon 'many human bones and skulls' in the area, which lay bleaching in the grass for years to come. No doubt this was the source of the spot's macabre name: Boney Point.

Pastoral scene on banks of Lake Wellington. Boney Point, scene of the second clash, is not far away.

Most often the flashpoint would be the spearing of sheep or cattle; the squatters would retaliate by shooting dead the first Gunai they came across, usually with no evidence that the victims had been the culprits. Patrick Coady Buckley, one of McMillan's contemporaries, described such a scene in his journal: 'Walked out ... to scrub below House where blacks had taken some sheep evening before. On our way out saw five Blackfellows about one hundred and fifty yards ahead[.] Marshall and I fired at them and chased them but they got into the scrub ... Marshall and I had double barreled guns.'

The wronged Gunai would then wait for an opportunity to take their revenge. In a straight fight against an armed militia they stood little chance, but they were skilled practitioners of guerrilla warfare. For this *was* war. Unofficial and undeclared it may have been, but for a period of around a decade the two groups were in a state of total hostility.

It became unsafe to travel alone or unarmed in Gippsland. Wandering shepherds and lonely drovers were picked off in sudden raids or by carefully laid ambush. 'Unfair!' cried the settlers, without irony, and prepared their response. And thus was the bitter cycle inflamed.

It was a reprisal killing like this that led to by far the fiercest confrontation of the period, the massacre at Warrigal Creek. In July 1843 Lachlan Macalister's nephew Ronald was killed while out riding near Alberton, the fifth in a spate of recent black-on-white murders. Investigating later, Protector Robinson suggested that Macalister had been killed in retribution for an earlier incident, when 'some depraved white men had in a fit of drunkenness shot at and killed some friendly natives'.

When the corpse was discovered, all hell broke loose. Whether they had known it or not, by killing Ronald Macalister the culprits had landed a solid punch at the core of Gippsland society. The settlers united in a single, furious body with McMillan at its head, ready to strike down the next black face they saw. The nearest Gunai target lay a few miles along the coast, a long-standing encampment in a picturesque curve of the creek. They charged down there, waving pistols and crying obscenities, and let loose upon the unsuspecting tribesmen.

They were like madmen, these men of the 'Highland Brigade'. When the carnage at Warrigal Creek was not enough to quench their blood-thirst they rode on, marching an orphaned child guide ahead of them at gunpoint. They stalked the flats searching for quarry, even as the wails of the dying rang in their ears and the stink of blood-spatter hung in their noses.

The Bratowooloong clan targeted at Warrigal Creek and in subsequent attacks had once numbered between 330 and five hundred members. When they were next counted, in 1869, there were only seventeen. Afterwards there was no great outpouring of grief, for there was nearly no one left to grieve. The memory of those who had been killed was snuffed out and buried along with them, as an entire clan group collapsed in on itself like a black hole.

As race relations grew ever more antagonistic, the attacks became more one-sided, taking on an element of sport: the killing of the Gunai had become something like a culturally acceptable hobby. Letters of the time take on the air of match reports, thrumming with the rallying cries of the huntsmen – Hark forrard! Hark forrard! – as they call ever more hounds to the hunt. Even Crown Commissioner Tyers took part. 'A.M. – rain[,] P.M. – fine,' began one 1845 entry in his journal. 'In pursuit of blacks.'

The next year, Patrick Buckley recorded a tortuous episode when, after a series of cattle-spearings, he stumbled upon a young Gunai couple walking along the beach. He waited behind a dune until they drew near, then rode them down and forced them into the water at gunpoint. 'I had pistols with me and fired Blank Shots to keep them in the Sea which I did for about four hours,' he wrote later. The male fared worse; he seemed nearly drowned in the breakers. Buckley rode down into the surf, got a rein around his neck and pulled him up onto the sand. 'He pretended to be dead.'

What struck me most on reading these journals is how rarely their authors appear to be implicated in any actual killing. There are many, many accounts of 'shots fired' and 'pursuits' or 'chases', of storming Aboriginal encampments to 'take the natives by surprise'. Very few record the specifics of any actual deaths. But killing was certainly taking place; the young settler Henry Meyrick had been watching, wide-eyed, from the sidelines. 'The blacks are quiet here now poor wretches,' he wrote in 1846. 'No wild beast of the forest was ever hunted down with such unsparing perseverance as they are. Men, women and children are shot whenever they can be met with ... No consideration on earth would induce me to ride into a camp and fire on them indiscriminately, as is the custom whenever the smoke is seen.'

One does not have to look far for an explanation of the diarists' coyness. 'These things are kept very secret,' continued Meyrick, 'as the penalty would certainly be hanging.' Of course: the Myall Creek executions had shown that this was no empty threat. No further prosecutions had yet taken place, but who was to say they would not?

The culprits were educated men: landowners, justices of the peace, even the Crown Commissioner himself. They knew what could and could not be put down on paper. The clues are in what remains unsaid, the gaps in the accounts, the turning-away of heads.

A new vocabulary came into use. The Gunai did not commit 'crimes' or 'theft'. They perpetrated 'outrages', 'depredations' and 'barbarities'. By contrast, Aborigines were not 'killed' or 'murdered', they were 'dispersed'. Sometimes, following an 'outrage', they would be 'punished', or 'chastised'. Shots might be fired. It was never made clear where they landed.

The purpose of this new vocabulary was to obfuscate, and it did the job well. Meyrick reported what he knew of the massacres to William Thomas, the Assistant Protector, who recorded this 'most awful statement of doings', but noted the 'utter impossibility of bringing forward valid evidence to convict in a court of law'. His hands were tied, he said, 'yet the awful spectacle of human skeletons & packs of bones & reports of doings within the last 3 yrs, shows that the Aborigines have been cut off in awful numbers, & the residue left almost totally destitute'. And so the two men watched through their fingers as the Gunai were picked off like ducks in a shooting gallery.

If the written accounts of the period fail us in terms of objectivity, perhaps a set of figures tells the story more accurately, without the need for words. Commissioner Tyers, writing to Governor La Trobe in 1854, laid down his best estimates for the Gunai population at the time of his arrival (four years after McMillan) and at the present day:

GIPPSLAND: NUMBER OF ABORIGINES.
1843 – 1,800
1853 – 131
1854 (February) – 126

One of the oldest cultures in the world was being abruptly extinguished.

But secrets like this are very difficult to keep secret. It was far from the perfect crime. There are rumours, of course, and remains. Scraps of evidence that, when put together, form a convincing case for the prosecution.

To Bairnsdale. It was a low-slung town whose suburbs of wood-slat bungalows stretched out in a maze in all directions. The streets bore the names of early settlers: Pearson, Anderson, Nicholson, Wallace.

We had an appointment to meet Peter Gardner, the historian so disliked by my friend at the Maffra Historical Society. I knew his writing from a series of shocking exposés in historical journals of the massacres, but I had struggled to get hold of his three books, which had been published by a tiny local press with a minimal web presence.

He was, as he himself would admit, a subscriber to what is described by the Australian right wing as the 'black armband' school of thought. The term has emerged during the so-called 'history wars' which have drawn much public debate in Australia over recent decades, as academics and politicians of all stripes clash over what should be the proper interpretation of colonial history. Is it a daring tale of pioneers and plucky underdogs? Or is the truth to be found in the hidden lining, the dark recesses, that secret history that for the most part went unrecorded?

The most contentious area of debate centres on the dispossession of the Aboriginal population, and the significance that should be afforded to reports of violence on the frontier during this period. For many years, indigenous groups were simply not considered part of the grand narrative – writing in 1959, the historian John La Nauze observed that Aboriginal Australians had been little more than a 'melancholy anthropological footnote' to Australian history – but for some, the pendulum has now swung too far the other way.

Revisionist historians like Bill Stanner and Henry Reynolds did much to bring the Aboriginal experience of colonisation to light in the 1970s and 1980s, and their work has been very influential. Critics claim that this new school of thought paints an unnecessarily jaundiced picture, and achieves little other than creating a 'guilt industry' that has skewed modern politics and feeds the political correctness that ties it in knots. These criticisms have been levelled at Gardner too, as he waged what has been, a lot of the time, a one-man battle to get at the truth of the 'Black War' of Gippsland.

But he has persevered. 'The charge of "political correctness" has always been laughable,' he has written in response to his detractors. 'I first commenced my studies and writing in the early seventies. It wasn't until the mid-1980s ... that the question of frontier violence was even generally considered in Gippsland. Far from being politically correct, this work was new, somewhat controversial and challenged the status quo.'

Gardner moved to the region in 1973, initially working as a high-school teacher, and found his curiosity aroused by the paucity of information on the original inhabitants of the area. Some locals went so far as to deny the prior existence of any Aboriginal group – another claim he found 'laughable'. He immersed himself in Gippsland's history, fossicking in the archives, and began to piece together the uncomfortable reality. His earliest papers were published to a sometimes hostile audience – one local columnist dubbed the events Gardner described as the 'might-have-been' massacres – yet he stood resolute.

On paper I knew him to be bullish and self-assured, unafraid of controversy. His shocking conclusions were always backed up by quotes and figures, the veracity of which he had weighed and measured with clear-eyed exactitude. Conflicting voices were given short shrift: he declared Keith Windschuttle's claims that historians had falsified evidence to exaggerate the scale of frontier violence 'so much garbage'.

So it was with some surprise that I greeted the man who answered the door to us. He seemed quiet and non-confrontational, even shy. Tall and broad-shouldered, he was casually dressed, beard and ponytail grown long and slightly grey. He ushered us through to the kitchen table and put the kettle on, apparently discomfited by the attention. His gaze skittered away to the window behind me whenever we made eye contact.

'It's a pleasure to meet you,' gushed Jeannie. 'You changed the way we think about history in Gippsland.'

'Oh,' he said, looking away. 'No. Not just me. Don Watson, of course —' the author of *Caledonia Australis* — 'and others.'

'You do seem to have done a lot of the heavy lifting,' I said, eliciting a rather awkward smile. 'So what next? Will you publish again?'

A shake of his head. 'I don't have the energy for it any more.' He gestured around the modest bungalow: its old-fashioned wallpaper, the squat bookcases full to overflowing. 'This place was my daughter's retirement plan for us. It has … come to fruition a bit earlier than expected.' He sighed. 'I've handed over the copyright of the books to the local Aboriginal corporation. They can do what they want with them now. Reprint them. Sell them, if they can.'

He got up from the table without explanation, and disappeared into a back room. There was a pause while we waited. My eyes and Jeannie's met. We'd come expecting a firebrand, but instead we had found a tired man, a moderate who had fought hard and met a great deal of resistance. He reappeared holding a stack of his books. The publishing house *was* small, he agreed — it was his own. Struggling to find a publisher, he had decided to print them himself. He handed over the books I had been unable to locate. The topmost title made me wince: *Our Founding Murdering Father*. Underneath was the same picture of Angus McMillan I'd seen in the old beet factory at Maffra, hand in hand with two black men, one of whom seemed to be holding a spear.

'What I would say,' Gardner said, catching my dismay, 'is that this is one side of a debate.' He seemed to feel uncomfortable that his allegations might upset me.

'No, no,' I said, flicking the book open. 'I want to know.'

The books were forensic, yet at the same time tub-thumpingly polemical, carefully argued and backed with evidence filleted from early settlers' diaries and letters. His main sources — the cast of characters in a murky pastoral drama — were outlined with deftly drawn character sketches: the naïve Meyrick, the hapless protector Robinson, the gun-happy Buckley. The massacres themselves were neatly dissected: dates, locations, names of known participants, estimated death tolls. Asterisks marked the most likely locations on inky hand-drawn maps.

These were only a few of the known instances, Gardner was at pains to explain. Elsewhere he attempted a rough estimate of total Gunai deaths by white violence:

Warrigal Creek: range 60–150. My estimate 100.
Associated massacres (clashes following): range
    30–80. My estimate 50.
Boney Point: range 40–80. My estimate 60.
Butchers Creek: range 30–80. My estimate 50.
Slaughterhouse Gully: range 20–40. My estimate 30.
Milly Creek: range 20–40. My estimate 30.
Tambo Crossing: 'upwards of 70'. My estimate 70.
Estimated 20 further massacres (5 deaths or more):
    range 100–140. My estimate 120.
Estimated 30 other clashes (fewer than 5 deaths):
    range 60–140. My estimate 100.

Result —
Bottom estimate 430.
My estimate 610.
Top estimate 820.

This calculation roughly tied in with that made by Meyrick in a letter to his parents in 1846: 'I am convinced that not less than 450 have been murdered altogether.' Written several years before the conflict came to a close, it is not improbable that this figure would have grown to six hundred, or more.

And at the heart of it all: Angus McMillan, the Butcher of Gippsland.

McMillan's heroism was a myth of his own invention, wrote Gardner. At best, he can be seen as 'a fanatic – misguided in his beliefs, and more than slightly dishonest in his methods. At worst he can be considered a rogue of some stature ... If today McMillan is to be admired as a local hero, at the very least it should be known why this is so; that his popularity was originally, in large part, directly attributable to his brutal and violent suppression of the original inhabitants of the region.'

I came away chilled and unhappy. Essentially, Gardner's books seemed a character assassination. Every one of McMillan's achievements, so lauded in the annals of Gippsland, was called into doubt, every facet of his character redrawn in less flattering lines. 'Our Founding Murdering Father'. I repeated the phrase in my mind, again and again.

This fresh avalanche of criticism had hit me like a body-shock. It was strange. I had known that there were questions over McMillan's conduct, and more; that he had been implicated in a string of mass murders. And yet somehow, over the last few weeks I'd allowed myself to grow close to him. What with all the celebrity and celebration I'd become – what? – proud of him, I supposed, and the enormity of his fall from grace hit me afresh. I was now completely tied up in it all, I realised, emotionally speaking. But I didn't feel any closer to understanding what had happened.

For reasons that were unclear, I felt I wanted to go there, to the sites of the massacres, as if the places themselves might summon some homicidal insanity I might tap into and comprehend.

Boney Point was the closest. Jeannie, Ian and I made a short, poorly conceived trip down the long track that led to a carpark on the banks of the Perry River. The road stopped short several hundred yards from the site, an impassable mass of marshy scrub in between. Two men sat at the water's edge fishing, not speaking, empty tinnies littering the sandy soil behind them. No go.

I came back later, equipped with a borrowed kayak, and pushed down between the mangroves that crowded the edges of the river, trying to imagine the action unfolding in front of my eyes. But it was difficult. The view was obscured, the land hard to picture under all this growth. Did they ride along there? Did they shoot from here? Was that where they stumbled upon the bones? It was no use. After a few minutes I gave up and just sat alone on the water, the soft breath of the wind on my face as I let myself be slowly towed downstream. Pelicans swept by overhead, coming down in a graceful loop to land somewhere flat beyond the scrub.

The site of the Warrigal Creek massacre was on private land, but Peter Gardner had given me the phone number of the current owner, Elizabeth Balderstone. After a few hours I'd summoned up the courage to call her, but there had been no answer. I left a garbled message on her answer-phone, something along the lines of 'Hello! Do you have a massacre site on your land? Can I see it?!', then hung up, flustered. I could have kicked myself. The reporter in me knew that the best thing to do would have been to leave a cryptic message with my number, then get her talking when she called back. I had probably blown it. Why would she want her property to be known as a place of slaughter? Why would she open her doors to massacre tourists like us?

Hours ticked by, with no response. Jeannie and Ian were restless. They needed to get back home, so we began to make plans to return to Drouin. Yet we were reluctant to give up hope.

We drove to the area, holding Gardner's line map up to the GPS to get our bearings, and stopped at the closest point to the site that we could reach on public land. It was a bird reserve now, on the edge of Ninety Mile Beach. The wind was up, but we staggered out over the dunes and picked our way along the tideline. The beach was littered with hundreds of dead birds, half buried by sand.

'Butcher birds,' said Ian, nudging one with his foot. 'A mass death. It keeps happening. No one knows why.'

I wandered off alone, feeling sick to the core, and climbed high on the dunes to search for the mouth of the creek, where once the blood would have run down into the sea. Sand stretched off to either side as far as I could see. It was beautiful but bleak, the sky hazy and as heavy as my heart.

My phone rang. Elizabeth.

'I got your message. Come tomorrow.'

The next day dawned like a gospel. The sun was out, a light breeze ruffling the grass. We drove the three-mile driveway with the windows down. Sheep were scattered across enormous flat fields like marbles on a tabletop. A few twisted old gums stood guard along the track, warped by the wind. Closer to the house, freshly clipped sheep picked their way back from cream-gloss shearing sheds, bare and surprised-looking, woollen trackmarks circling their torsos, tufts of missed-a-bits poking as if through loosely wrapped bandages. The buzzing of the busy production line drifted through the open doors as we trundled past.

The homestead was at the far end, surrounded by mature gardens. It was a glorious two storey house with a big terrace and a round brick well. Roses climbed the walls, branding irons sat in wooden barrels like lilies in a vase, mismatched cowbells hung from pegs by the door, as if carefully prepped for a lifestyle magazine shoot. It was stylish in a *European* way, I thought vaguely.

Elizabeth strode out to meet us with a nervous, alert smile. She was a fine-boned woman with a neat blonde bob, wearing a purple rugby shirt over jeans and work boots. She must have been in her fifties, but looked younger, glamorous somehow. 'Call me Libby,' she said.

She led us into the kitchen, where the high ceiling was ornamented with hammered tin tiles, the shelves stacked with bottles and jars of home-made preserves: plum sauce and Seville-orange marmalade. A blocky old-fashioned fridge was collaged with family photos: long-limbed daughters who laughed and rode horses, a handsome smiling man I tentatively identified as her late husband. After his early death she had kept the farm, she said, and now ran it on her own.

'The site you're looking for,' she said, locking eyes with me, 'is just beyond the house, in a bend of the creek.'

'Does it not feel strange, to live so close?'

She sighed. 'The way I always think about it is that I've taken on the role of a guardian. We fenced it off, you see, to keep people from walking on it. And if anyone wants to visit, to see it for themselves – well, of course they're welcome. There was some discussion that perhaps there should be a marker, or a memorial of some kind, but that's not a decision I feel I can take alone, and it's difficult to know exactly who needs to be asked. Would you like to see it?'

I nodded keenly, and we all trooped out through the garden. Two fat Labradors wrestling in the garden leapt to greet us, while spook-eyed kelpies, working dogs, watched us jealously from their kennels out the back.

'Here,' said Libby, gesturing beyond a thin-strand fence enclosing a flat area that had grown thick with brush and prickly grass.

I felt as if I'd been hollowed out. The others left me to it.

By now I'd read the accounts of the massacre so often I could play them like a film reel that unfolded over the pleasant pastoral scene in front of me. Yes, I thought, I can see it now. It was a beautiful spot for an encampment. A slope led down to a babbling brook feeding into a deep waterhole, where ducks swam in tight formation. I imagined children playing in the shallows, women digging for roots and weaving baskets, men sharpening their spearheads.

The gunmen would have stood *here*, I thought, pacing it out. Along this line. Then they would have advanced – I stepped forward, determined the necessary distance – and fired from *here*.

Crack, crack. The shots came like punches. The pause to reload, the rattle of shaky hands. The screams and the howls. The shuddering last breaths. The cries of children jerked awake, of tiny newborns dropped from lifeless hands. For the wounded, the final thud of the rifle butt to bash in their heads. The blow of mercy, or mercilessness.

The Highlanders were driven by rage and retribution. Their hearts were hardened by anger and grief. But oh — the things they must have seen that day. They must have known that this was wrong. They must have known it was wrong when they fished out that one surviving child, bleeding from the eye, and marched him on and on, in search of his people, so that they might kill them in front of him. They must have known this was wrong.

Later, the cover-up would begin. They came back, loaded the bodies into bullock drays, dumped them and burned them amid the dunes on the beach. Now they truly were a band of brothers, bonded together by their secret. They kicked the evidence over with sand, and tried to forget the whole thing. But how could they?

That night, when the bloodlust had subsided and they slunk home to their shabby bark huts, pulled their itchy wool blankets around them, the sights of the day must have played and replayed before their eyes. Such sights could not be shrugged off easily. Colin Maclaren, one of the participants, was asked years later by a young stockman whether he had 'shot plenty of blacks in his time', but Maclaren 'merely shut one eye and, screwing his features to that particular side, remained silent'. In his later years he retreated to an island in Lake Victoria where he lived as a hermit, alone with his remembrances.

To Angus McMillan the ringleader, lying awake as the kookaburras bounced their maniacal laugh between each other outside, it must have seemed a sort of madness. He must have seen the blood swirling, the water churning. The women turned flesh, the children turned meat. The crowding of the flies upon the bodies.

I'd been reading a lot about massacres lately. Phrases and images began to lurk in the shadowy parts at the back of my brain, slipping in and out at inappropriate moments. Shrink-wrapped meat in the supermarket took on a gruesome aspect; puddled footprints at the poolside were recast as trails of gore; visits to the toilet block at night became suffused with the psychological tension of a thriller. I had opened myself to the horrors of the past, and now its skeletons were taking up residence in my mind.

Perhaps this explained the dreams that had begun to interrupt my sleep. I would wake with a shock, having dreamed I was being chased by unknown, faceless men with guns. In these dreams, made dumb by fear, I would make pathetic attempts to hide, pulling leaves or blankets over myself like a child and waiting, heart hammering – *If I can't see you* ... – or I would run, fast, from the attackers, but they were faster, and they caught me they caught me they caught me.

Sometimes, if I was really deeply asleep, I would feel the bullets pass right through my body. And then I woke up.

7

The White Woman

A rumour was born. At first thin and insubstantial, it rose into the atmosphere like a ribbon of smoke from the tip of a cigarette. It emerged in the form of a letter to the editor of the *Sydney Herald*: a white woman had been spotted in Gippsland, lost in the bush. Held captive, reportedly, by a group of Gunai tribesmen.

Angus McMillan, as usual, was at the centre of it. It was his letter; his exploratory party, tramping through the unknown *fastnesses* of Gippsland, who came upon an Aboriginal encampment which, deserted by its panicked inhabitants on their approach, was found to be stocked with a vast assortment of European objects: checked shirts, moleskin trousers, shoemakers' awls, a lock of brown hair, coins, several English-language newspapers and a bible printed in Edinburgh two years previously. Out of context, many days' travel from the nearest station, the men found the hoard unsettling.

There was more to come. 'Enclosed in three kangaroo skin bags we found the dead body of a male child about two years old,' he wrote. 'Dr Arbuckle carefully examined [it] professionally, and discovered beyond doubt its being of European parents; parts of the skin were perfectly white not being in the least discoloured.'

In light of the dead child, the cache of incongruous belongings seemed altogether more ominous. The obvious conclusion, McMillan's men felt, was that tribesmen had attacked a party of Europeans nearby – perhaps a group of shipwreck survivors – and killed them all. The trinkets and the infant's body seemed to have been kept as souvenirs of some sort. With this grim notion in mind, the party reconsidered the events of the moments before as they approached the encampment, and agreed that they must have seen a survivor of this *melancholy catastrophe*:

> [As they fled] we observed the men with shipped
> spears driving before them the women, one of
> whom we noticed constantly looking behind her, at
> us, a circumstance which did not strike us much at
> the time, but on examining the marks and figures
> about the largest of the native huts we were
> immediately impressed with the belief that the
> unfortunate female is a European – a captive of
> these ruthless savages.

The letter was published in the *Herald* on 28 December 1840, six weeks after the event, and caused a minor stir among its readership. Not everyone was convinced; a few sceptics poured cold water over McMillan's interpretations of events, perhaps best demonstrated by a scathing editor's comment in the *Port Phillip Patriot*, added when it reproduced the letter a few days later:

> The clue to the foregoing mystery is doubtless to
> be found in the robbery of Mr. Jamieson's station
> at Western Port, which must have occurred very

shortly before the date of Mr. McMillan's
excursion. The European dead child and living
woman, are we suspect mere creatures of the
imagination. – Ed.

And yet, something about these creatures of the
imagination caught the public's attention. Their spectral
forms rose up like smoke, eddied, and dissipated, but at
their feet the source still burned. Cast aside in the dark
undergrowth, the flames caught in the dry grass and began
to spread. The fallout from this letter would cascade
down through the next seven years, gathering pace as it
went.

The mysterious white woman found sustenance in the
social and political climate of the time. Fed by a dozen
different agendas and motivations, she took on a life of her
own. Interest rose to fever pitch; soon she had taken solid
enough form in the minds of the public that rescue parties
would tear off into the bush in a desperate bid to find and
retrieve her, fuelled by the self-righteous fervour of the
wronged.

That first glimpse of her, of that departing, insubstantial
figure, would be reiterated endlessly over the coming
years. Always fleeing, always fleeting, always almost out
of sight.

Steve had chosen the bar. It was a trendy, gentrified sort
of place in Fitzroy, an artfully dishevelled suburb of
Melbourne where the buildings had been left to decay in
a picturesque manner: paint peeled from the lacy filigree
of the terraces, old posters from yesteryear slowly

unhitched themselves, leaving only their traces, a spray of bright graffiti colours collaged in every alley.

I got there early and found a table, reflecting while I waited that I did not know precisely what I hoped to achieve with this meeting, nor what to expect; merely that Steve Paton, a young artist of Gunai descent, would be the first Aboriginal person I had met – or at least, the first who had identified himself as such.

In fact, there was scant evidence on what Australian television I had seen, or in the newspapers I had read, that a contemporary Aboriginal population even existed. Nor had I noticed obviously Aboriginal people 'around' – in the streets, in the bars, in the shops. It was strange, I felt: although I knew the Aboriginal community was a small minority, at roughly 3 per cent of the population nationally, that still worked out at one in every thirty or so individuals, or around 670,000 people – not an insignificant number. Their invisibility perplexed me.

Steve turned out to be my age, well-groomed, well-educated, and dressed as if he might be on his way to a pop-up tiki bar – which, incidentally, was exactly where he was planning to go later. He wore Ray-Bans and an ironic Hawaiian shirt, on which coiling lilies were picked out in muted shades. He had striking features – molasses-brown eyes set beneath a heavy brow, and a fairish complexion, more olive than black – with a hipster beard and shoulder-length hair pulled up into a bun at the back of his head.

We sipped our drinks tensely for a while as I fluttered around the issues of race and identity without landing. 'Look,' I started afresh, finally hitting solid ground. 'I suppose what I'm trying to get at is that it's not very clear to anyone outside Australia how current all of these issues I'm reading about are. Are there still two cultures, running alongside each other in parallel? Is one still in the process of being choked off by the other? I mean ...' I gestured vaguely at his shirt. 'I guess I can tell you're not really living a traditional lifestyle.'

No, he agreed. There *were* Aboriginal groups in Australia, he said, mainly in the remote north and west, living something closer in nature to the old ways — isolated from outside influences but combining elements of modern life such as cars, shopping and so on with hunting, foraging for 'bush tucker' and maintaining ancient beliefs and customs. But to him Aboriginal identity was now more about passing on what cultural knowledge was left, and ensuring that it was sufficiently acknowledged and respected.

As a youngster he'd had little interest in the past, but by the time he reached his mid- to late twenties he suddenly found himself passionate about researching his family's history and cultural heritage. I nodded in recognition.

Steve's family has been at the heart of Aboriginal affairs in Gippsland for decades. His grandfather, Uncle Albert Mullett, a respected elder, spearheaded the campaign to have the Gunai people's right to their traditional lands officially recognised (via a specialist field of Australian law known as 'native title'); other relatives have played prominent roles in furthering Gunai culture, including Steve's mother Doris, who had worked for many years to revive the Gunai language, and his aunt Jenny, a painter and ceramicist whose work is often inspired by Aboriginal history and folklore.

As part of an art project in 2012, Steve asked Uncle Albert to teach him and his cousins to build a bark canoe in the traditional style: cut from the tree in an enormous sheet, smoked, rolled up at the ends and sealed with clay. Then they brought the whole family together by the riverside and floated it on the water. Traditionally, knowledge of how to create a canoe like this – as well as a thousand other necessities for survival – would have been passed down to every young man during a period of initiation called the *jeraeil*. The canoe was a symbol, explained Steve, not only of the old lifestyle and values, but of the ancient origins of his people.

In Gunai folklore, Boorun, the first man, came down from the mountains in the form of a pelican, carrying his bark canoe on his head. As he came to the shores of Corner Inlet, he heard a tap-tap-tap coming from inside the canoe. Lowering it to the water, he found that he had carried a woman with him all that time. She was Tuk, the musk duck. Together they became the mother and the father of all the Gunai people.

Steve called his project 'Boorun's canoe'. It was the first time a bark canoe had been floated on the waters of Gippsland for a hundred years. To attempt it was a risk, he said – right up until the last second they feared that it might sink, and unwittingly become a terrible symbol of all the lost Gunai knowledge – but he didn't like the idea of it becoming yet another dusty old artefact sitting behind glass, unused, another aid for anthropologists, with which to teach *them* about the way their people had once lived, but then forgot. The canoe, and a series of photographs documenting the process taken by an old schoolfriend, Cameron Cope, were now on display in the Melbourne Museum.

I'd been to the museum already, and seen the canoe there. But something about the display had confused me.

Elsewhere I'd seen the name of Steve's people spelt a number of ways – 'Gunai', 'Ganai', 'Kurnai', 'Kurnay' – which I had loosely assumed to be due to some issue in rendering the language in the Latin alphabet. But in any official context, as in the museum's display, it was given instead as a weird double-barrelled name, 'Gunaikurnai'.

Steve pursed his lips when I mentioned this. 'Gunai,' he said. Then, 'Kurnai.' Almost indistinguishable. 'Say it with a guttural sound at the beginning ... To me, they're one and the same. But saying that, it's all tied up with an issue of identity.' Some families described themselves as Gunai, others as Kurnai. He sighed. 'It was a detail that became *political*.'

During Uncle Albert's land-rights campaign in the 1990s and 2000s, the faction identifying themselves as the Kurnai broke off to file a counter-claim, disputing the right of any others to the land. Their claim, later rejected by the courts after an exhaustive six-day hearing, was that due to a combination of tribal rules, only the descendants of a single, named Gunai (or rather, Kurnai) woman might be rightly considered heirs to the traditional lands.

It was an unpleasant episode of infighting which, among such a small community, could not help but become personal, and it was one too that sent its combatants spinning endlessly back into the past, only to return bearing more evidence of birthrights and superior bloodlines. This was not the first time such small differences in spelling have come to represent wider divisions within an ethnic group: in Canberra, for example, a bitter feud raged for many years between two groups which identified themselves as the Ngunnawal and the Ngunawal respectively, each disputing the other's claim to better represent the region's traditional custodians; similarly, in Melbourne, rival groups representing the Boon Wurrung/Bunurong people, each utilising a different spelling, have vied for recognition as the 'official' cultural body.

'This was a disagreement that arose after the process of Anglicisation, rather than an existing rift that pre-dated settlement,' explained Steve. In any case, it was an issue that had only been settled recently, and the compromise – running both names together: Gunaikurnai – was intended to provide a united identity through which to state their case.

'I suppose it's a bit like ...' He paused, and looked at me appraisingly. 'Do you know there are five subgroups, language groups, within the Gunai nation?'

I nodded, flicking through my notes and pointing to my list:

Bratowooloong
Brayakooloong
Tatungooloong
Krowathunkooloong
Brabawooloong

'Yes, exactly. Strictly speaking, I'm from this group – Tatungooloong – but really, there are so few of us left and it's all gotten so mixed up that we all just identify now as one group, the Gunai, or the Gunaikurnai.'

I'd been put in touch with Steve by his photographer schoolfriend Cam, with whom I had made plans to travel through the more remote sections of Gippsland – Jeannie's 'young-person stuff' – as we retraced Angus McMillan's journey back to its source in the Monaro plains.

'I thought I might come along with you for a bit,' said Steve. 'I've been thinking for a while about doing some artwork based on the Aboriginal experience of settlement.'

'If you like,' I replied, pleased. It would be useful to travel through Gunai country with someone with knowledge and an intuitive understanding of its traditional culture. 'The more the merrier.'

A band struck up on a small stage in the corner, in front of a backdrop painted with a kitsch frontier scene. Three men were silhouetted, on horseback, in ten-gallon hats, rifles slung across their backs. A sunset had been rendered behind them in broad brushstrokes of orange and magenta and gold. Cowboys and Aborigines.

Cam picked me up for our road trip at Jeannie's house. He came straight from a work event in Melbourne; tall, fresh-faced, clean-cut in a suit and tie but driving a dusty old ute. We went to his mother's house, an airy, high-ceilinged bungalow filled with treasures brought home by her sons from their foreign travels, like cats bringing offerings of mice to the doorstep. I laid my maps out across the kitchen table and we pored over them, plotting our way up into the high country, following McMillan's route as closely as possible, focusing on his initial failed attempt to enter the region from the Monaro. As we worked, Cam reeled off a list of books I should read, prefaced with a warning.

'Aboriginal folk won't always be impressed with what you've read or heard about from the "experts",' he said. 'They'll like that you take an interest, but they won't all have read the same books as you, necessarily, and what you've read might not tally with their own experience. People won't be pleased if *you* try to tell *them* about their own culture or history, if you see what I mean.'

I nodded.

'Just listen.'

We met Steve the next day, and drove slowly east through the Latrobe Valley towards Traralgon, first through the coalfields, the forest of cloud-height chimneys belching thick white smoke into the atmosphere. The columns themselves wore a certain leggy elegance, but the structures and machinery at their feet had a nasty look in their eyes. A retired coal-harvesting machine was parked up on the roadside, its mean metal teeth on a rotating device at the end of a long, crane-like neck, ludicrously outsized, something from science fiction or a real-life alien invasion.

'DREDGER 21' read a label at its base, like a name-tag at a mixer, above a list of its vital statistics: 'Manufactured 1952. Weight: 725 tonnes. Height: 23 metres.' The bucket-wheel dredgers in use today were much bigger in size and capacity, the sign continued, and had now grown too large to fit inside the Melbourne Cricket Ground. I imagined one trying and failing, scattering stadium seats, a scene of Armageddon unfolding behind.

The lookout point nearby offered the dispiriting vista of an enormous flooded crater: the Yallourn open-cut coal-mine. 'This was the site of the township Yallourn,' announced a sign cheerily, offering up a scale outline of the crater superimposed over a map of a 1920s model village – hospital, railway station, golf course, neat wooden houses with terracotta roofs – all carefully planned and purpose-built for energy workers and their families, before it was dismantled in the eighties so these sawtoothed monsters might get at the heavy, coal-rich ground beneath.

'Today the town no longer exists,' continued the sign, unnecessarily, indicating the scene of devastation behind. The sides of the mine were roughly terraced, hewn from the earth, its base flooded with mud and filthy water. The mud was scarred with trackmarks and silty, rust-like tide-lines. Somewhere there, now many feet above ground level, was Yallourn.

I was fascinated by this phantom town, whose access roads still led up to and off the edge of the cut. Of course, its inhabitants still exist somewhere – they were rehoused, 'rationalised' among a number of nearby towns – but even so, something, some collective identity, was lost. However humane, this dispossession must have had a profound psychological impact that left its people clawing for purchase on their former selves. The historian Peter Read has described how the town's citizens were haunted by the memory of their old home:

> Yallourn people bought their houses and re-erected
> them elsewhere, or hunted for them in nearby
> towns and photographed them. They dug out
> plants, they souvenired bits of their houses and
> public buildings, they bought the building supplies
> and laid their [new] paths with Yallourn bricks.

That identity, that Yallourn-ness that had gone, was something residents are still trying to keep alive, decades on. Later I stumbled across a version of Yallourn that lived on online. Setting the year to 1959, I strolled between computer-generated houses and wandered the main square. A database contained details of the sort that would never be recorded in any history book: the technical-school badge (a pylon and a book, the motto 'Knowledge is Power'), the recipe for Poulos' famous spaghetti bolognaise, a book of numbers for phones that no longer ring.

It was a virtual town built by rootless people, endlessly dreaming up an afterlife for their home. But no matter what they do, the experience of how this all fitted together to make Yallourn Yallourn – the smell of the theatre auditorium at night, the sound of voices echoing in the school canteen, the way the trees' long shadows would striate the empty streets in the low sun of the late afternoon – all that will die with their generation, and there is no way to keep it alive.

I wondered, disloyally, whether the Yallourn residents' attempts to keep their town alive might act too as some kind of parable for the Mullett family's own crusade to keep alive a culture that preceded them. Steve building a canoe that was no longer needed for fishing, his mother reviving a language that is no longer spoken. What drove their attempts to sustain a way of life that would otherwise disappear? How valid were the results of such efforts, if the participants had not lived that culture themselves? I didn't know the answers yet.

'That was the ugly bit of Gippsland,' the boys assured me as we roared on. 'We'll be past it soon.'

Golden Beach at dusk: an odd, empty seaside hamlet with a time-warp feel, like the set of a *Carry On* film. A spare Norfolk pine stood in the square, decked out in fairy lights that traced its trunk and branches, a child's drawing of a tree. A squat building offered hot showers for two dollars. Overhead an unlit revolving sign advertised GOLDEN BEACH FOODARAMA.

We drove on, and turned off down a track to a clearing between the trees, tucked in behind an enormous sand dune. It was so close to the shore that we could feel each incoming wave booming loudly down and then sighing in relief as it slunk back through the sand. I felt as if we were standing in an enormous pair of lungs, the sea's salty breath on the backs of our necks, ruffling the dry leaves above our heads.

A pit was still charred by the remains of the previous occupants' fire. Steve and Cam lit it afresh, using the dry seedpods of the banksia to get it going. They were woody toilet-brush heads, each harbouring dozens of horrid muppet mouths that gaped open like castanets to scatter their seeds when they came into contact with the flames. The straw-like fronds and wooden beaks caught quickly, and as the fire took hold their fat bodies gave off a red-hot glow like coals.

We erected our tents then sat on a tartan rug by the fire, drinking beer and wine from a cask, swatting at sand flies, squinting against the smoke. It was a nice spot, and we savoured it for a moment for what it was, talking lazily about inconsequential things, skirting the subject of what had brought us together.

At last Steve cleared his throat. He had an idea, he said, that he wanted my help with: a collaborative project that would explore settlement by reinterpreting the events of a key period of early Gippsland history from an Aboriginal point of view. 'I'm interested in exploring the myth of the

White Woman of Gippsland,' he said. 'Have you heard about this?'

The author and Steve around the campfire at Golden Beach.

I had, of course. It was a strange episode, one so rife with misinformation and misinterpretations that I did not know what to think of it. On the face of it, it seemed a simple story: the tale of a damsel in distress and her would-be rescuers. But the truth of her, and what she symbolised, was more complex. She may have been an unfortunate soul; she may have been merely a figment of the collective imagination. Either way, her arising, and the significance she was accorded, exposed the most vulnerable parts of the colonial mind to the air.

In the end it was this white woman, whose very existence has never been fully confirmed, who would bring black–white hostilities in Gippsland to a climax. The hunt for her would result in a renewal of the climate of fear, and a squall of Aboriginal deaths from which the Gunai would never truly recover.

For several years after her initial sighting, the trail had gone cold as the settlers turned their attention to more pressing matters: the building and the burning, the construction of the huts and the homesteads, the growing conflict with the Gunai.

The white woman made occasional cameo appearances, popping up in the footnotes of the period; unconfirmed sightings mentioned in the journals as she dipped and dived, ducking out of sight before rearing up again, her story told and retold in the Chinese whispers of frontier society.

But in May 1846, with the 'Black War' at its height, she made a glorious comeback, the ubiquitous Angus McMillan at her back. He reappeared in the newspaper, stirring the pot: he had 'captured the child of a young lady, whom the blacks stole away some years since, and for whom there is a reward of £1,000'. Proof! Or proof of sorts – the child was never mentioned again – but it was enough to catch the attention of a community that had by now become well primed to the dangers of the Gunai.

This mysterious creature who lurked in the darkest shadows of the bush soon became something of a *cause célèbre*. News of her tragic plight raced through the home-steads of the district and the smoking rooms of Melbourne, the fledgling city now thriving to the west. As hunger for action grew, so came a rallying call from the editor of the *Port Phillip Herald*: 'Will *no one* come forward and put the

Government to the blush by leading a party in search of this truly unfortunate lady?'

She formed a focus not only for the flexing of masculine bravado, but also for the increasing dissatisfaction with the colonial government. Melbourne was growing restless; soon it would strike off from New South Wales, taking the entire Port Phillip district with it, and establish itself as the capital of a new colony, Victoria. The white woman 'cause' formed a convenient rallying point for influential Melbourne figures, a symbolic crusade through which they might show up the Sydney administration as both apathetic and out of touch. If the government would not save this woman, they said, then they would do it themselves.

Press coverage, steered by calculating editors, began to heat up. Details from every sighting were endlessly rehashed as letters pages hosted a furious debate over every aspect of the tale: Who was she? Where had she come from? Why had they taken her? What were they doing to her?

This last question was the one that aroused the most lingering interest. With concern for her well-being as justification, the erotic imagination of the papers' over-whelmingly male readership was permitted to run riot. She was not only a captive, it was soon agreed, but was being held as a sexual slave, 'compelled to yield to the disgusting passions and desires of a set of black cannibals'. Deflowered at spearpoint, she was now concubine to a chief, and mother to his half-blood children. Pulses rose. Heavy-breathing conjecture was published uncritically under the heading of 'news'.

White men were enraptured by the plight and the penury of the white woman. They debated and deliberated over her best means of rescue. They fundraised and planned, prepared for action, all the while their minds whirring with horror and arousal and longing.

It is an episode which, to modern eyes, is distasteful in a number of ways.

To Steve, the entire basis of the outcry, specifically the assumptions behind it, was deeply offensive. The lost woman, of unknown character, was widely assumed to be whiter than white, a virginal *naif*; her unidentified Aboriginal 'captor' instinctively characterised as the most monstrous of fairytale villains.

These attitudes are clearly manifested in the language of the articles and letters about the white woman's disappearance. A poem written in her honour and published in the Melbourne *Argus* typifies the vocabulary and tone employed:

Unhappiest of the fairer kind;
Who knows the misery of thy mind?
Compell'd to breathe the pois'nous breath
Of a rank scented black;
To yield to his abhorr'd embrace,
To kiss his staring, ugly face,
And listen to his clack.

'It's just so *vicious*,' said Steve. 'As if we [the Gunai] were a pack of rabid animals.'

To my eyes, the affair also threw the double standards to which women and men were then held into sharp relief. White society was clearly scandalised by the prospect of one of its women having sexual contact with an

Aboriginal man, despite implicitly acknowledging that its own men were regularly fornicating with Aboriginal women whenever they might be convinced or coerced to do so.

Sometimes, in Gunai society, sex with a wife or young female relative had been offered to visitors as a gesture of hospitality. Perhaps misinterpreting this generosity as indifference to the fate of their women, early settlers soon began to pass these 'gins' and 'lubras' between themselves. Some Aboriginal women rode as 'boys' among the cattlemen, keeping them warm at night, but they were not considered on a level with either the cattlemen themselves or European women, who were expected to adhere to higher moral standards. These women were sex objects, yes, but low-status ones, and when they returned to their own people they often took unwelcome gifts back with them in the form of sexually transmitted infections.

As a result, venereal disease rampaged through the frontier. Complications arising from gonorrhoea alone are estimated to have cut Aboriginal reproductive capacity by 40 per cent nationally between 1815 and 1855, while in Gippsland notes kept by a local physician between 1849 and 1852 show syphilis to be the most common ailment among his largely white, male, unmarried patients, who numbered among the most esteemed members of the community. Such infection rates went unremarked in the popular press.

Thus the settler men were free to mop up their lust with the native 'gins' without criticism, while the missing white woman, a placeholder for all of her fair-skinned peers, was winched by many hands up to a pedestal so high as to give the girl vertigo.

For the white woman stood for far more than her single lost soul. She was an icon for the life the settlers had left behind. She was a delicacy, an innocent who cringed from the horrors that lay in the no-man's land beyond the last station. By saving her they had a chance of redeeming themselves, of casting themselves as the heroes in a tale that had theretofore been lacking in moral character.

She was not the first of her kind. In fact, the idea of a white woman taken captive by 'primitives' was a well-worn trope in colonial societies. In America, a rich literature had already grown up around these women — 'captivity narratives', as they are known — loosely based on a number of real-life cases, including those of Mary Rowlandson the minister's wife; Eunice Williams, taken by the Mohawks aged seven; Mary Jemison, sold on by the Shawnee to the Seneca.

These unfortunates spawned a genre that fascinated the American public. Survivors' accounts of their captivity became bestsellers. Songs were written and dedicated 'to the white woman'. She would be drawn sometimes: stripped naked, roped roughly up against a tree, squirming as the light of the flames danced over her skin and the painted savages whirled and ululated around her helpless figure, leering, victorious, hungry.

In Gippsland they saw her similarly subjugated: unclothed, herded ahead of her captors at the point of their spears. If she slowed, one report claimed, they would plunge the spears into her ripe flesh. The commentariat outdid themselves in their florid portrayals of the carnal existence in which she now found herself. She was 'wandering about the bush in a state of nudity', they panted, 'a slave of savage lust and barbarous violence'.

The recurrence of the white woman motif – for it is better understood as a motif than as an isolated incident – shows us something of the psychological undercurrents in colonial culture. The settlers' task had been to civilise and make safe this new land for their future wives and children. Now, the loss of one of their own to the bush was an existential threat to their life and work. The real-life captives of America had acted as a lightning rod for the colonists' deepest fears; in Australia, the same terrors echoed.

To understand the fascination that she held, it helps to recall how scarce women were in the colony at this time. On his arrival in Melbourne in 1842, the settler Edward Curr commented upon the 'total absence of women from the streets'; the few who were there dodged harassment by avoiding the rabble of the town. Out on the frontier the numbers were thinner still, with hardly a white woman – wife or maid – to be found during the earliest years of settlement.

This was largely because the rough and ready work of pioneering was not seen as a suitable life for a woman – or at least a woman of refinement. Living in a bark hut in a troubled district was no place for a 'young lady', or a girl who had been 'well bro' up', as Gippsland settler John Pettit explained in his letters home. But the lack of women posed a palpable threat to the colony's future. During the following decades there would be a great push to bring unmarried women to the colony, poor Irish and Scotswomen for the most part – many of them speaking only the odd, heavily accented word of English – their fares covered by the government in the name of the continued existence of the colonial project.

Boatloads of them would disgorge upon the dockside, and men dressed in their Sunday best – ties uncomfortable around thick workmen's necks, belts pulled tight round scrawny waists, ragged fingernails scrubbed clean – worked the crowds of women, enquiring politely whether any in search of a husband might take them. Others simply allowed their employers to pick one out on their behalf. Soon, Pettit wrote, these women had disappeared 'like smoke'.

One of their number was Christina McNaughton, a farmer's daughter from Argyllshire who arrived in New South Wales in 1849 as one of a shipload of migrant women. She was barely literate, undoubtedly poor, certainly not one of Pettit's 'well bro' up' young ladies. Little is known of her in the first three years after her arrival; like smoke, she drifted through the colony without trace, until she popped up in Gippsland as housekeeper at Angus McMillan's Bushy Park homestead in 1852.

He had not propositioned her with marriage on the dockside. McMillan would have had his sights set on a more accomplished, refined woman, a wife befitting his status as landowner and respectable figure of Gippsland society. Perhaps even his *dear Miss Margaret* back on Barra, with whom he had continued to correspond for some years after his emigration. Nevertheless, two children followed, Ewen in 1858 and Angus in 1861.

Back in 1846, when the white woman made her re-appearance, all this was far in the future. Like so many other men in the colony, McMillan was starved of female company. More and more, his mind was taken up with the fragrant, ethereal figure of the lost woman. She lurked on the edge of the bush, on the edge of consciousness, like a siren, luring men in, haunting their dreams.

But who was she? That, no one could agree upon.

Each community put forward its own preferred candidate. The Irish suspected her of being a Mrs Capel. The English preferred Miss Lord. The Scots thought her Anne – or perhaps Anna – Macpherson. She was no one and anyone. She was an everywoman, a figure every settler could relate to, upon whose anonymous, unsullied face they might project their own particular brand of virtue.

The theory was that she had been the lone survivor of a shipwreck, that she had fetched up on Ninety Mile Beach, not far from where we were camping, either alone or as one of a party that was attacked and slaughtered by the hostile Gunai. The idea was not unfeasible: any number of ships had found themselves in difficulties in the treacherous waters of Bass Strait. The *Britannia*, for example, wrecked off the coast in 1839 en route to Sydney. And the *Britomart* a month later, bound for Hobart.

Either wreck could plausibly have left a white female survivor marooned in Gippsland in time for her first sighting in November 1840. A young Aboriginal boy known as Jackie Warren (sometimes Tackewarren), somewhat *too* coincidentally now living with McMillan at Bushy Park, attested to a shipwreck survivor having lived with a neighbouring tribe near the coast.

Once feasibility was established, certainty began to grow, and details of her identity embroidered. She was young, beautiful, educated – that was a given. She was the wife of a brewer, the daughter of a respectable Sydney merchant, the employee of a prominent Melbourne hotelier. She was all of these and none of them.

Jackie Warren/Tackewarren as a grown man in 1866.

But she was a true victim – that they could all agree upon. Anyone who dared suggest anything different was soon shouted down. The mayor of Melbourne, who suggested that, if she did exist, the white woman might have formed over her six years' captivity 'connections and ties with the blacks which she might not wish to dissever' (a reasonable argument, given the reactions of some American captives following 'rescue': Cynthia Ann Parker, for example, would reportedly die of heartbreak after her 'rescue' from the Comanches after twenty-four years) found himself 'denounced in forcible terms' at a public meeting. The continuing inaction of the government drew fervent criticism, targeted now at the superintendent specifically:

> If Mr. La Trobe had a daughter situated as this
> friendless woman is, what would he not do to
> rescue her? ... Would not every energy be brought
> into play to relieve her? Would not the services of
> a dozen – aye, a hundred – parties be engaged in
> the pursuit of this savage tribe?

The controversy rose to a fever pitch. Public meetings were held, donations flooded in. By October 1846 two search parties had been dispatched, one state-sponsored, the other privately funded.

The private expedition, led by Christian de Villiers, consisted of five white and ten Aboriginal men, carrying provisions for four months and a great many white handkerchiefs printed with a message to the woman in both English and Gaelic, to be distributed among the tribes:

> WHITE WOMAN! – There are fourteen [sic]
> armed men, partly White and partly Black, in
> search of you. Be cautious; and rush to them when
> you see them near you. Be particularly on the look
> out every dawn of morning, for it is then that the
> party are in hope of rescuing you. The white
> settlement is towards the setting sun.

The state-funded expedition, by contrast, consisted of twenty-five men, comprising twenty-three 'native police' (Aboriginal officers of the Wurundjeri and Bunurong Kulin)

Both sides of the printed handkerchiefs distributed by de Villiers' party.

led by two white officers, William Dana and William Walsh. This was the first of three native police forces in Australia, all of which would become notorious for their heavy-handedness and cavalier use of violence as their indigenous members wielded new state-sanctioned power over their traditional tribal enemies. Dana's force tore off into the bush wielding firearms, the ghostly presence of the white woman enticing them ever onward, like a beacon on the horizon. They would cut down all in their path.

Later, Commissioner Tyers would estimate the official expedition to have been responsible for 'at least fifty' Gunai deaths during the hunt for the white woman, as they confronted ever more remote and hostile tribes. In one instance, they rushed upon an Aboriginal encampment on the banks of the Snowy River at night, a brutal incident that continued to be discussed among the Gunai in hushed undertones for years to come. De Villiers' party – whose leaders were of a more humanitarian bent, writing fascinated commentaries on the tribes they encountered for the *Port Phillip Herald* – inadvertently became witnesses to the aftermath of this attack when de Villiers and his deputy James Warman stumbled upon piles of black bodies riddled with bullets and a pair of escapees stumbling around shackled together at the ankle.

They reported these horrors, first to the authorities and then to the newspapers, denouncing the 'wanton barbarity' shown by 'those harpies of hell, *misnamed police*'. 'So long as such persons as Messrs W. Dana and Walsh are in command of the native police, nothing can stop [the Gunai's] extermination,' wrote Warman, adding, 'I should not wonder if we are subpoenaed to give evidence in the wholesale butchery at the Snowy River.'

Their allegations were published in January 1847, prompting the government to recall the native police to account for their behaviour. Dana denied everything. Nevertheless, he received a dressing-down from Governor FitzRoy, who deemed him to 'have acted with a great want of discretion, to say the least', and substituted a Sergeant Windridge in his place.

The hunt continued. Rumours of the woman were constantly reported by the Gunai they came across. She was the wife of a chief, the mother of two children. She 'cry plenty', and 'ask why did not the white men come and take her away'. Perhaps some of these reports were true, perhaps all of them. She danced ahead, tantalising her pursuers, always ever so slightly out of reach.

But they were gaining on her. They could taste her on the air.

By midsummer, the search parties had narrowed her abductors down to a single clan, of whom the warrior Bungelene was reputed to have taken her as a wife. De Villiers' party gathered titbits in every tribe they came across: she was 'tall, with a considerable stoop'. She was unable to suckle her children. She was very sick, others warned them, since Bungelene had been 'beating her about the head with a waddy'.

There was always some ambiguity when dealing with remote tribesmen. Due to the language barrier, much of the tracking depended upon a mime involving two paper cut-outs – both women, one shaded black – and asking the tribesmen to point to the figure who represented Bungelene's wife. This was not a failsafe method. One of de Villiers' party reported how a source 'shouted with delight, as much to say "I know what you want"', before racing off to his camp. He returned to the breathless party 'with a brace of sylvan nymphs, and presented one to me and one to Mr A.B.'.

Nevertheless, with a name for her captor, and a chase under way, the white woman's existence seemed more concrete. Any lingering doubts were forcefully countered by her supporters, not least by McMillan, who took to the pages of the *Herald* again in February 1847. 'As a proof,' he wrote, 'I am now willing to give my services to assist in her recovery.' The *Herald* judged this submission ('the decisive letter of Mr. McMillan – an old and most respectable settler') as itself another plank in a 'body of evidence [that] has now been established to prove the existence of the white woman among the blacks, as perfectly irresistible'.

Superintendent La Trobe disagreed: the evidence, he said, remained 'far from conclusive'. But the public believed it. What could La Trobe do? He authorised the search to continue 'without regard to expense'.

A few days later the *Port Phillip Patriot* waded in. 'FORCE MUST BE USED, AND OUGHT TO BE USED,' it thundered. 'There appears to exist a degree of sensitive apprehension for the safety of the savages,' yet 'the matter comes to this – the blacks declare that the woman shall not be given up unless captured by force ... Is then the woman to remain in their brutalizing dominion, until the *ultima ratio* be adopted?'

Force, then.

Bungelene and his two (Aboriginal) wives were rounded up by the obedient Windridge and his party, and taken into custody at the native police base in Narre Warren. His wives remaining there as security, Bungelene was then marched into the bush, charged with obtaining the white woman's release.

If she did exist, he did not lead them to her; the party was growing thoroughly frustrated by endless wandering and the spiral of lies and uncertainties that seemed to lie at the heart of the Bungelene theory. They 'upbraided him with his duplicity', and threatened to shoot him 'for leading us astray'.

But at last, in April 1847, the search party seemed on the edge of a breakthrough. They found themselves in the scrub on the edge of the beach, waiting breathlessly for the white woman to be brought out. After several days' wait and repeated false promises, she arrived with great ceremony, carried by her captors as if upon a sedan.

The white men gasped. She was bare-breasted, her body painted with the harsh rust-red of ochre. She was battered indeed; both arms had been cut off at the elbows.

She was the figurehead of a ship.

Imagine their dismay. Thousands of pounds had been squandered on the search, both state funds and public donations. Weeks of their lives had been lost out in the bush, sleeping rough and remonstrating with unfriendly tribes.

They had been like greyhounds, racing pell-mell around the track, jostling for position. And when finally they had grabbed the lure with their teeth, torn it roughly down, they had found it was not a rabbit at all, but an empty glove. And all around the voices of the spectators still rang out, yelling, screeching, cursing, crying out for a win.

Was this her? The fabled white woman, the angel of the south? There seemed no clear explanation.

Bungelene took the brunt of their disappointment, being returned to Narre Warren in disgrace and 'brutally chained to a gum tree for many days and nights', according to

Assistant Protector William Thomas. 'The old man is very uneasy,' noted Donald Mcleod, a member of both the private and the state expeditions. 'We have been telling him that the White people are Coming from Melbourne to Shoot the blacks on the Islands and the Mountains and that we are to bring him to Melbourne there to be hanged[,] all which he believes which makes him rather Down hearted and frightened.'

They did not shoot him, but nor did they set him free. He continued to be held without charge. By July, the day book records him as 'very menancolly being detained so long'. In November he died. 'Of grief', said the papers.

None of this grim business achieved anything in terms of clearing up the confusion surrounding the white woman. All that was obvious was that the whole affair was getting out of hand. Further, unofficial, parties made up of maverick young men had joined the hunt; anarchy and disorder loomed.

Finally, Commissioner Tyers prevailed upon Angus McMillan to stop the madness. And so, having been present at the birth of the white woman, he became witness to her death. He was inextricably tangled up in the affair from first to last.

An extraordinary edition of the *Herald* was published, headlined 'Murder of the Captive White Woman at Gipps Land', reporting intelligence conveyed 'from the station of Mr. McMillan'. A woman's body had been located, alongside that of what appeared to be a mixed-race child. Bungelene's brother was blamed for the deaths; he was supposed to have killed them in a revenge attack. Tyers had called McMillan and the good Dr Arbuckle to the inquest, at which it was determined that 'there could not be an atom of doubt of one of [the bodies] being that of a white female'. Thus the white woman was finally laid to rest.

What was McMillan's motivation in creating the myth? Was she a cynical ploy with which to stir up hatred of the Gunai? Did he think her resurrection a tactical strike? Or had it been based on an honest belief in the existence of a suffering woman in need of salvation?

Whatever the truth, it seems he had been convinced to back down. The white woman was dead.

There is something tragic in the observation that a woman who may or may not ever have existed, with no confirmed name or identity, became the most significant woman in the history of Gippsland. Hard-done-by wives, mistresses and housekeepers would continue with their home-making, spreading civilisation one household at a time, and raising children in often extraordinarily difficult circumstances, while in the newspapers, for decades to come, discussion continued to rage over the fate of the phantom woman and how she might have been saved.

In Angus McMillan's own homestead, Christina would bear two children before this pious man would deign to marry her, and only then after the local preacher prevailed upon him to stop living in sin. He signed the marriage certificate with a loose, careless autograph; his wife's signature, however, gives much away. In a laborious hand, Christina both reclaimed her place in polite society and misspelt her own name.

'C h r i s t i o n', she wrote.

*

Steve's idea for his project was simple. He envisaged a series of photographs depicting a modern-day re-enactment of the white woman affair. But, he suggested, told from an Aboriginal point of view, these events might be seen in a different light. He had in mind something like a love story, an outback *Romeo and Juliet*. 'What if she really did exist,' he floated, 'but she went of her own accord?'

I nodded along, not entirely following his train of thought. But a runaway bride, I later learned, would not seem so surprising to a person looking through Gunai eyes. The disappearance of the woman, the subsequent pursuit, the constant dodging – all of this bore a marked resemblance to the traditional courtship customs of the Gunai.

As the anthropologist Alfred Howitt explained: 'The young Kŭrnai man ... could acquire a wife in one way only, namely, by running off with her secretly and with her own consent.' Under cover of darkness, a young couple would make a break for it. 'Stealing round to the back of her parents' camp, in which she was sitting, he touched her with a long stick, and she being ready to run off pulled the end as a signal. He then left, and the girl, having her bag (*batung*) packed up, in fact, having her trousseau ready, flitted after him.'

After their departure, a sort of ritualised outrage would unfold. The young woman's father would beat his breast, gather a hunting party and set off in the couple's wake. If found quickly, they would be soundly beaten then packed off back to their separate homes, only to run off again at the next chance they got. And so it went on, again and again, until the outrage grew stale and the union was finally accepted by the clan. Better-prepared couples might successfully evade capture, sometimes staying away long enough for the woman to bear a child before they returned home (the pair attacked by Patrick Coady Buckley on Ninety Mile Beach were in all likelihood on such a 'honeymoon'). In these cases the match would be accepted more quickly, although a ceremonial fight between the groom and the bride's family would still take place upon their eventual return.

Though blood was drawn on these occasions, 'there can be no doubt that the old people of the Kŭrnai winked at this practice of marriage by elopement. In by far the greater number of cases, they themselves had obtained a wife or husband in this manner, and yet when their daughter married in the same way they were furious at it, and punished her with severity.'

And so, as the white woman made her break into the bush, hand in hand with her Gunai lover, an angry mob in hot pursuit, she could be confident in the knowledge that her mate was well-versed in the quick getaway, that they were following a well-trodden tradition of forbidden love in his culture.

This was the backstory that Steve imagined when he heard about the white woman. This was the story he wanted to tell, one that resolved not only his reservations about the traditional interpretation of the incident, but also mine. He planned a series of images portraying her flight, casting me in the role of the white woman – not as the damsel in distress, but a decision-making woman – and he as my Aboriginal captor, or rather companion, taking me by the hand.

Who knows what really happened? Perhaps she existed, perhaps she didn't. Perhaps she was stolen, perhaps she went willingly. Each scenario seemed to me as unlikely as any other. Increasingly, I was coming to the conclusion that whatever most had the appearance of truth tended to turn out to be the furthest from it.

We stood together knee-deep in the surf, squinting against the light. Ninety Mile Beach stretched off to either side like a smear of paint, silver sand bleached white as bone under an insistent sun. And behind us the ocean, enormous, restless, tugging at the hem of my dress, sucking at my feet, sand shifting with each stroke of the waves.

Cam was a hundred yards up the beach, staring intently through his lens as he tried to fit in the full sweep of the landscape: the endless ocean, the infinite sky. And us, two antlike figures, staging our own small drama in the bottom eighth of the frame. I shut my eyes, felt my hair lift

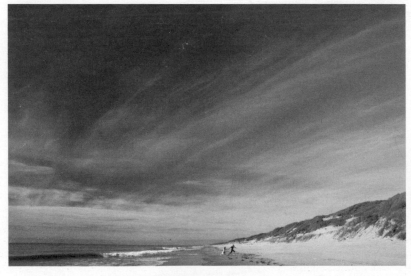

Steve and the author run from the waves on Ninety Mile Beach.

upwards on the breeze, like a seabird riding the thermals. I lifted my arms from my sides. Wings, I thought. Like wings.

'Stand closer!' Cam called, yelling to be heard over the surf. 'Can you face each other? Look at each other!'

I swivelled awkwardly and stepped forward, self-conscious now, keeping my face level with Steve's chest. After a moment I forced my eyes to dart up to his, and found him regarding me with what seemed to be barely suppressed amusement.

We chatted awkwardly as we stood arm's distance apart, like two dancers waiting for the music to begin, trying not to move our lips. 'Hands down!' ordered Cam. 'Shoulders square! Heads up!'

We subsided into silence, regarding each other obediently, humour slipping away. We were standing too close now to maintain eye contact. I let my eyes wander along Steve's jawline, keeping my expression neutral. I could feel the salt water soaking through my skirts, rising up from surface level towards its high tide.

'Okay?' Cam's voice was reedy, trembling in the wind. He raised an arm to signal.

'Okay?' asked Steve, turning to look at me. I nodded. He grasped my hand in his and we ran, careering through the shallows, leaving perfect footprints across the wet sand, which gleamed momentarily as the water retreated towards the withdrawing wave. When we crossed the tideline I stumbled as my feet flailed in the soft sand, but Steve's hand was clamped tight on mine and he pulled me upright, towed me along behind him. I was flying now, running faster than I had ever run, bare feet pedalling, hardly touching the ground. Reaching the foot of the dunes we scrambled up, powered by momentum, scrabbling at the ropelike roots of the spinifex with our free hands. We clambered and climbed, making our escape, we were away ...

Finally we came to rest, laughing, chests heaving, in the lee of the dunes.

Below us on the sand, Cam was already hollering more instructions.

'Come back down!' he yelled. 'Again. Try and run in step. Try to go when the wave has swept all the way back out.'

'Okay,' we called back. 'Okay.'

And we padded back along the wet sand, into the surf. My wet dress was sandy now, and sticking to my legs. We took each other's hands and waited for the signal to go.

8

Slaughterhouse Gully

It was time to take stock. I'd been on the trail of Angus McMillan for weeks now, amassing facts and stats and theories in my notepad: the what, the where and the how. I had attempted to crack open the mythology of the man to get at the truth of him, and at his less admirable achievements. I had mapped the course of his life from fresh-off-the-boat emigrant to landed laird, from sea level to highest peak. But though I now felt in possession of the facts, I still had not resolved my core question. I did not understand what could have pushed a man to such extreme behaviour, caused him to slip his moral moorings so completely.

I knew that he had started out a good man, if somewhat self-righteous. And I also knew that he seemed to come good again in the end: well-liked, well-respected, generous to a fault. And in the middle – what? A complete mental break?

Certainly the speed of his transformation was remarkable. In 1839 McMillan was railing against the mistreatment of the convicts at Camden; by 1841 he had taken up 'hunting blacks' as a favoured pastime. What could possibly have happened between his departure from the Monaro and setting up in Gippsland that could have hardened him so?

It seemed so incredibly out of character that to attribute it to some inherent evilness seemed a get-out somehow. Even Peter Gardner, McMillan's greatest critic, had backed away from such a conclusion.

I no longer knew what to feel. McMillan had become a sort of logic problem, and I didn't have enough information to solve it. Or rather, I had the answer, but I didn't understand the process by which it had been reached.

But this equation was common enough. Angus McMillan, I knew, was not the only man to have made such a transition. The same metamorphosis had taken place in homesteads across Gippsland, across Australia, across the colonial world. All these respectable men; all these cold-blooded killers.

I was mulling this over as we drove north, leaving the swell of the ocean far behind, heading into the hills, up into the Snowy gorge, towards Currawong and the Monaro plains. We were following McMillan's tracks upstream, back to the source.

Junction of the Buchan and Snowy Rivers, painted by
Eugene von Guérard in 1867.

The three of us were packed in the car along with our tents, water, fishing rods, a crossbow, sleeping bags, stoves and other outdoors paraphernalia. I sat wedged in the back, my feet resting on a pile of kindling and a small sheathed axe, listening to the boys talk, occasionally chiming in with a bit of information I'd read somewhere. Past Buchan – neat town square, the brilliant lavender-blue blossom of the jacarandas bursting over lawns like confetti – we lapsed into a companionable silence which Cam occasionally interrupted to read us passages from Peter Gardner's books.

'Listen to this,' he said. '"Some settlers gladly hailed the proposal of one who said, 'Let's take our guns, and go into the bush, and shoot a lot of blackfellows for a lark.' And they did it."'

He turned to look at me with an unreadable expression. It was unspeakably horrid. But also inexplicable, impossible to relate to. I screwed up my face, trying to think of a suitable response. But I had only questions. What on earth could have been going through those men's heads?

Perhaps, as Steve suggested, they simply didn't think of Aboriginal men as human. They did, after all, talk about them as if they were pests. Like kangaroos grazing wild upon the pasture, perhaps, or dingoes picking off the lambs at night. Even Henry Meyrick, the conscientious objector, admitted that 'if I caught a black actually killing my sheep I would shoot him with as little remorse as I would a wild dog'.

But it was more than that: killing was so normalised it had become a sort of entertainment. The journals of squatters of the time are peppered with episodes of such senseless violence that they beggar belief: buckets of burning embers thrown onto tribesmen's bare feet; bags of flour laced with arsenic handed out to hungry women. What was the *point*? They were like little boys pulling the legs off butterflies, incinerating ants with a magnifying glass.

'Hang on,' Cam said suddenly. 'We're about to pass pretty close to Slaughterhouse Gully, one of the last massacres before the Gunai were effectively defeated. Not by McMillan and his men, but ... friends of his.' He read another passage aloud:

> The blacks who were living in a wild state had been spearing cattle. [The local settlers] organized a party well armed and mounted, and according to my information cornered the Abos on a flat close to the Murrindale river and shot them down without mercy. Some escaped but many did not and for many years their bones lay bleaching on the ground, some of the victims I have been told were thrown into the river at a spot where the river flows under the hill.

There was a pause.

'Well,' said Steve. 'Shall we go there and see it for ourselves?'

To find Slaughterhouse Paddock we left the car on a verge and shinned over a gate marked 'Private', following a rough track down between a limestone quarry and a muddle of wooded hills. The cattle grazing there scattered, herding their calves before them, then stopped to look back at us, lowing, warning us off. We followed in their wake through the waves of long grass, crickets flying up in clouds with every step; the grass was moving with them, reactive.

The pitch of the land was wrinkled by dusty tracks where the cows had worn in the ground like an old pair of shoes. The karst landscape had left jagged grey stones protruding from the hillside like broken teeth in their gums. Ahead and above, the ground gradually rose to the Pyramids, a conspicuous limestone outcrop crowned with a tiara of stony needles.

I frowned, folding my copy of Gardner's *Gippsland Massacres* open at the hand-drawn map and holding it up to compare it to the scene in front of us. We were looking for a gully that was supposed to be nearby. According to Gardner it would be an 'appropriate site for a large number of Aboriginals to be trapped against the rugged bluff'. Somewhere between a dozen and two dozen of the Krowathunkooloong clan had been shot down as they cowered there, with no means of escape.

The boys frowned, distracted from the human tragedy for a moment by the difficulty of piecing together the historical accounts, of linking Gardner's line map to the place we stood in. We split up to cover more ground, me cursing my white dress – still stiff with salt from the waves at Ninety Mile Beach – which caught on the barbed-wire grass with every step. I had paused to pull the prickles from my hem, teasing them carefully with my fingers, when I spotted a wombat moving at great speed ahead of me, waddling a quick escape as Steve obliviously clambered up the slope above.

I grinned, ticking off another box in my mental list of quintessential Australian wildlife, and made to follow him. His fat little legs whirred as he rounded a bend and hopped down some terrace-like steps trodden in the hillside by sheep or cattle. I sped up, trying not to lose sight of him, quickly cornered a couple of thorny shrubs, then had to skid to a halt to stop myself from slipping into a deep fissure in the earth.

My mouth formed an 'O'. 'Come here!'

The wombat flinched at my voice but kept running, skipping down and into the hillside where the ground had been torn open to expose its layers of rocks: red-raw but delicate as *millefeuille*, the earth's coats of paint.

Steve and Cam came up behind me wordlessly, and peered down into the abyss. I read aloud from the book I still clutched in one hand: '"No bones have been found and not surprisingly as some of the cave holes in the area drop down to a great depth to underground streams."' I couldn't see the bottom, nor to the back of the chasm where it pierced deep into the hill – a natural mausoleum. We had to be close.

'We need to get higher,' ordered Steve. 'Get a bird's-eye view.'

We headed up the rocky slope, gravitating towards the natural crenellations at the peak: 'the Citadel', as some of the locals called it, and I liked that better. The land spread out below us, its hairshirt of matted gums clinging to every curve. Blowflies buzzed around noisily.

I flicked back through the pages, looking for descriptive passages. '"The avenging party came upon the aborigines who were feasting on the banks of a lagoon behind The Pyramids,"' I read aloud. '"Confronted by the white men and all chance of escape cut off by the steep cliffs of the Murrindal River, the tribe had no chance of escape and was annihilated by the bullets of the enraged whites."'

'There,' said Steve. He was craning over the edge to look down at a flat green pasture in the hook of the river, neatly hoed and streaked with perfect dotted lines of green leaves. It was directly below us, stopping at the edge of the water, before the rocks jutted straight up to where we were crowded at the top of the precipice.

'Right there. It has to be.'

'Is that the right road? Shaws Gully Road?' Cam craned around in his seat. 'Stop. Go back.'

We slewed sideways, made a clumsy three-point turn and pulled onto the rough track. A five-bar gate blocked the way. A sign hanging from the top bar read 'Locals only'.

As we considered, a red saloon car trundled across a cattle grid on the other side of the gate and pulled up. The driver got out, opened the gate, got back in, drove through and came to a halt alongside us. He eyed us suspiciously and wound down his window.

'Can I help you?'

'Uh ...' Steve started uncertainly. 'Can we get down to the Pyramids this way?'

The driver sucked through his teeth. We could try, he said, but he didn't fancy our chances. He reeled off a list of gates that we would find blocking our path, as if it were a gauntlet we would have to run. 'Why do you want to go there?'

'You know,' Cam piped up, avoiding the question, 'we've got a relation of Angus McMillan in the back.'

'Oh, *Angus*?' The man glanced at me, interested now. I flashed an awkward grin back. 'Well, there's an old lady down there that lives in the original homestead from the pioneer days. Still got the gun loops cut in the walls. You'll want to see that.' He was warming to his subject now. 'I probably shouldn't say this' – he lowered his voice and leaned out of the window – 'but there's a spot down there where the Aborigines were all chased down and killed.'

We feigned ignorance, making little noises of shock and sympathy. 'Gosh,' I said, though he couldn't hear me through the window. 'Really?'

'Although, you know,' he said, brightening, 'it's a real beautiful spot. Well – try, why don't you? If you see anyone, just say Jack said it was all right to look around.' He lifted a hand in farewell and drove off.

We nosed through the gate and headed the way he'd come, past the old homestead – a broad building whose corrugated-iron roof rose to a high peak, climbing plants choking the columns of the terrace – and down. The track wound on through the deep blue of the evening, past collapsing agricultural sheds and through a milling flock of sheep badly in need of shearing, wool hanging down behind them in filthy dreadlocks, tangling in the undergrowth.

The bush closed in around us. After four more gates and a fifteen-minute drive, the track came to an abrupt halt at a padlocked driveway. We stopped again, unsure, then got out of the car. 'No Trespassing', read another sign. 'No Shooting'.

My eyes began to adjust to the lowering dusk. The track led down to some polytunnels, a row of stakes, tidy lines of neat vegetables. Close by on our left, the ground banked up to what looked like an old drover's hut perched on a grassy mound. We got out of the car and stood by the gate, hemming and hawing, finally deciding that we'd come too far to turn back. We climbed over the fence.

Up close, it was clearly a cattleman's hut that had been renovated to make a small homestead: a stocky little shed with a steeply pitched roof, a crude corrugated-iron chimney, and a stubby verandah tacked onto the front, where waxed coats hung in rows like bats. I stepped forward and rapped on the door. No answer. There was a dog bowl on the mat, but no bark. Three pairs of boots sat coupled up along the wall. The place had the air of the *Mary Celeste*, as if the inhabitants had walked out halfway through dinner, pausing only to shut the door behind them.

'Look,' said Steve, his back to us. We turned.

From higher up we could see the curve of the paddock's edge, the arced path of the river. The muscled back of the rock rose beyond, silhouetted against the darkening sky, its three-pronged crown. An 'appropriate site for a large number of Aboriginals to be trapped against the rugged bluff'.

Another fragment from Gardner's book came unbidden to my mind: 'Here the offending tribe was so badly defeated that its power was definitely broken, and never after did any of its members molest the whites.'

'Yeah,' I said finally. I didn't have anything else left to say.

*

As the night came in, so came the fear.

We drove back the way we had come, before turning off at a side track in search of a camping spot. It was properly dark now, our headlights picking out little but the branches that closed in around us and the insects that flitted, disorientated, through the beams, flecking our view with chaotic light trails like a meteor shower. The track seemed long disused, grass grown up between the ruts. No one had driven here for some time.

The trees opened out into a small clearing. We pulled up in a square, flat spot that looked as if it had been cleared for a house that had never been built. To our left, an old shepherd's cabin squatted in the shadows. Planks had been nailed over its windows and doors at crazed angles, a rush job. I felt the hairs rise on the back of my neck.

I thought about McMillan and his men fighting 'the defence of Bushy Park', and other desperate night-time struggles from huts like this. Firing through the gun loops at unknown attackers. Battening down, blocking the doors, bracing themselves for the inevitable attack. It made me think of those militant Zionist settlers in the West Bank, hiding away in their fortified homes – shuttered windows, reinforced doors – alternately terrorising or terrorised by their neighbours. What sort of life was that?

Here the settlers had sat, locked inside their tiny, flimsy pockets of safety, heads bent in silent prayer, hands clasped around the shaft of a rifle, ears pricked for the signal that outside all hell was about to break loose. Why did they stay?

Oblivious to my growing unease, Cam got out and went to search for firewood at the edge of the clearing. I opened my mouth to call him back, but couldn't think of any protest that wouldn't sound ridiculous. The door slammed, leaving Steve and me alone in the car. We sat in silence for a moment.

'I get the feeling we're not welcome here,' said Steve finally. 'I just want to get as far away from this place as possible.'

His words hung in the air. It was the sort of statement I'd normally shoot down in flames, denounce as superstitious nonsense. But this time I couldn't find the words. I felt it too. A rising panic. An unidentifiable fear of the clearing, the hut, the woods, the faceless shadows between the trees. I turned to stare out of the window into the dark, the rational part of my brain struggling to maintain calm.

After a moment Steve spoke again. 'Aboriginal people believe that the spirits of the dead continue to communicate with the living long after death. Some people have got a special sensitivity to it.' He had it, he said, or he thought he did. While working on his canoe project his dreams had become filled with spirits, seeking him out from beyond the sky to whisper secrets in his ears. When, finally, the boat had been launched, he had paddled out alone into the gloaming. Wisps of mist had spun up from the lake's glassy surface. They walked towards him like ghosts, dawdled alongside, then blew straight through him.

As he spoke, two lights appeared on the hill opposite, like a torch reflecting off the backs of a pair of eyes. Well-spaced car headlamps facing us straight on. 'If we can see them,' I thought, madly, 'they can see us.'

'Switch off the lights,' I commanded. Steve did so without hesitation.

Darkness. Silence, except for the sound of our breath.

Suddenly the passenger door opened, flung open angrily. The interior lamp flicked on with it, flooding the car with light again.

'What are you doing?' Cam had an armful of sticks. 'I can't see a thing.'

Steve cleared his throat. 'I think we should camp somewhere else.'

Cam looked at Steve, then at me. Outnumbered, he sighed. 'Okay. Let's go.'

Fear is irrational, illogical, inexorable. It is more force of nature than fleeting emotion. It is a survival method, hardwired into our bodies by millions of years of evolution. It bubbles up, more often than not at night, when one is tired and alone. Night is when the large predators come out, under the cover of darkness, creeping unnoticed behind their prey until it is too late. Are you scared of the dark? Of course you are. We're programmed to be.

In situations that your brain perceives to be high-risk, a single unexpected sight or sound is enough to trigger a physiological response, sending the body into high alert. Senses become sharpened, scanning in every direction for threats unknown. The creaking of a house contracting at night becomes the footsteps of an intruder. Wardrobes and cupboards appear as lairs, for humans or otherwise. Faces and figures materialise from the gloom, out of falling water or drifting smoke. *Pareidolia*, they call this: finding form in the formless. Knowing what it's called doesn't blunt its power to frighten.

To me, those headlights in the dark appeared as eyes looking directly at me. For Steve, out in his bark canoe, those whirling columns of air and spray that had blown up from the water's surface had appeared as figures – 'willy willies', he'd called them. In Aboriginal mythology, willy willies are spirits that have taken earthly form: the dead elders, said Steve.

Aboriginal people, of course, are not alone in turning to the supernatural to explain natural phenomena. For the white settlers, too, there was much that they did not understand, and this uncertainty was frightening. Maps of the region from this time resemble preparatory sketches for some unfinished work: Port Albert a speckling on the southern edge; cart tracks like snail trails across expanses otherwise barren of detail; blank spaces labelled with Brechtian simplicity – 'unsurveyed country', 'indifferent land'.

The only thing they knew for certain about this emptiness was that nothing was impossible. All sorts of weird creatures had crawled out of the earth: beavers with beaks, spiders the size of saucepans – pioneers in the 'bad lands' of west Gippsland complained of earthworms that grew to six feet in length. The black swans that swam unruffled on the tides of Corner Inlet were symbol enough, were they not, of Old World assumptions that had been all too easily disproven?

Thus they took seriously the Aboriginal lore that told of 'bunyips', hulking, hairy creatures with 'eyes like live coals and tusks like a walrus' that lurked in billabongs waiting for unsuspecting passers-by. In Ararat, two hundred miles to the west, the natives had once supposedly caught one; they pulled it up onto the bank and traced its form in the mud, this record drawn and redrawn for generations as an incontrovertible proof. The Gunai spoke of 'dooligahs', yeti-type figures that haunted the forests of the high country. The white men joked about them, but hunted them too, and they and the risk they posed took up a strange semi-existence in the world of the settlers.

The danger posed by the Gunai, however, was not entirely imagined. It would be disingenuous to paint them as hapless victims, as they so often are in present-day tellings of the frontier clashes. Henry Reynolds' groundbreaking book *The Other Side of the Frontier*, first published in 1981, was the first to present the settlement of Australia as a white 'invasion' which faced a sustained Aboriginal resistance, rather than the traditional narrative of the peaceful settlement of a formerly 'wild' country.

It would be inaccurate to describe the resistance as being so organised as to comprise a single, united movement, but certainly many tribes – including the Gunai – put up decades-long struggles, during which groups of what might best be described as freedom fighters engaged in a range of anti-white tactics, including massed attacks (as seen at the defence of Bushy Park), surveillance and the purposeful destruction of stock, horses and property in a form of economic warfare. Guerrilla tactics were at the core of the resistance. 'Their whole art of war', as one Tasmanian pioneer concluded, was 'a concealed, silent and treacherous attack'.

In pre-contact times, the Aboriginal methods characterised by early settlers as 'treachery' were an integral part of intertribal warfare. Sneaking up on a rival tribe in the middle of the night was a valid tactic; ruthless revenge might be taken months or years after an original slight. Warriors were revered for their displays of cunning and deceit. Now, disadvantaged in terms of firepower, this bent towards stealth and surprise was the Aboriginal warriors' only hope of success. They gathered in the dark and descended in force upon isolated homesteads; they ambushed lonely travellers. By necessity they were opportunistic, seeking out weakness and preying upon the vulnerable.

Correspondence of the time details an array of horrifying incidents. Shepherds were set upon while sleeping, their mutilated bodies discovered days later. Men in remote huts were found with pipes in their mouths, hands in their pockets, and an axe in the back of their heads. This is high-tension, horror-movie fare. So while it is certainly true that the white settlers had the upper hand, we must also accept that in the earliest years of settlement, despite the shows of bravado, much of the time they were scared out of their wits.

Alfred Thompson, writing about his time as a pioneer in the Mount Battery region around the same period, explained well how these terrors might worm their way into the heads of the squatters:

The effect of these atrocities upon the minds of the men, perpetrated in a lonely, isolated spot, remote from assistance, and where nothing distracted their ideas or prevented their brooding upon the one subject, was great. Their fears magnified the danger to such an extent that they lived in a continual state of anxiety, apprehension and alarm. The huts were loopholed to enfilade each other. They neither dined nor slept without their arms being within reach; the barking of a dog was a signal of danger which sent every man to his post; we had to place two shepherds with every flock, and when the hut-keeper went to the creek for water, a man was posted on the bank with a double-barrelled gun to guard him from the waddy of the ubiquitous aboriginal, who was supposed to lurk behind every gum-tree and to peer from every bush.

Facing this constant strain, and a shapeshifting opposition whose members seemed one day amiable, the next blood-thirsty, instilled in the settlers a hardened attitude as they ceased to regard the Gunai as individuals, but rather as a duplicitous mass. All Aboriginal people who had not yet come in from the cold to work as station hands or servants were seen as a potential threat, and viewed with a suspicion tinged with fear. They had ceased to be people, and were instead nameless, numberless members of the 'other side'.

A former British cavalry officer, a veteran of two tours of Afghanistan, once described a similar process to me. 'It wasn't soldiers versus soldiers out there,' he told me. 'That was the problem. Any Afghan walking around had the potential to be the enemy in hiding. Anyone who wasn't white, wasn't in uniform, was a threat. We were living in constant fear of suicide attack.' After a moment he spoke again. 'It gets to you, after a while, that kind of paranoia. So you hole up in your bases, you lock the gates, and you point your guns to the outside.'

The growing alienation between the groups – in socio-logical terms, the 'othering' of the Gunai – was reflected in descriptions of tribesmen of the time, which focused on characteristics the settlers found repulsive. A dispatch from James Warman, of de Villiers' white woman search party, is a good example. The tribesmen he met were all 'exceedingly dirty in their habits', he wrote, 'and the smell from their bodies is very disgusting; in their diet nothing goes amiss, they even eat the ant eggs, in short vermin of every description serves them for their meals; they are also cannibals, eating even the bodies of their own women'. They were naked, he added, 'strangers to shame', and what's more, 'their hair is suffered to grow long, and is matted together with grease'.

They made, in other words, a good bogeyman for the unoccupied mind to brood upon at night. It must have seemed a frightening world indeed, as bunyips lurked in every waterhole and stinking cannibals behind every bush. And fear can do funny things to a person.

Late afternoon. We rose into the mountains, weaving through the shining gums, tall, willowy women throwing their arms in the air, green-fronded fingers tickling the wind, brown fronds discarded, carpeting the floor. Dogwoods thrust their cream bouquets at the road like stallholders. Through Butchers Ridge, a one-horse town with a tumbledown metal shack and a goat on its front lawn. More gory names, more lost, unknowable stories.

Down into the thick undergrowth, red sand blowing across the road. Seldom Seen Creek. And up again. Wide, high country plains with blue mountains rising behind, layered upon each other like a watercolour, blue upon blue. Powder, periwinkle, cornflower, cobalt. The road snaked up between the trees, the tarmac came to an end and we shot on along a stony track. The trees were sparser here, silvery snow gums, splitting low, at ground level, and sending their slender limbs up where they gently parted to intermingle with their neighbours. The ground was rockier, the shrubs stunted and struggling.

High up the air was dense and humid, thick with the hazy antiseptic perfume of the eucalypt. Little River Gorge opened up like a crevasse to our right. Steve pulled over and we scrambled out to stare down into its depths – the rock tumbling away below us, the thin trickle of muddy water at its foot, thermals rushing up the rocky face like hot breath on our faces.

Difficult country, then, for an exploratory expedition.

It was down this way that Angus McMillan had made his first, failed attempt to reach Gippsland from the Monaro in 1839, and it was many years after that before a route through this region was found – before then, travellers had been forced to take McMillan's hundred-mile detour via Omeo. All attempts to find a way through this 'precipitous and broken country', wrote Tyers five years later, had failed 'in consequence of their horses being too jaded to proceed'.

McMillan had not helped his cause much by setting off in winter. In the highest mountain sections the horses waded through snow three feet deep, and the expedition was woefully ill-equipped. Jemmy Gibber, the Ngarico black who accompanied him as a guide, came barefoot and possibly bare-chested, and McMillan was travelling too light to be able to assist him much. He gave one half of his blanket to Gibber, but found he could not spare any clothes.

Alone with his Ngarico guide, who with every step into the unknown seemed to grow more distant, McMillan turned to his journal to pass the time. *Last night was bitter cold, having only one blanket, an old moulskin trouser and a blue shirt, and of course the luxury of a tent was never thought of. I felt cold indeed, and my companion, once he placed his strong body on the ground, could not be prevailed upon to put a piece of wood on the fire to warm his own frozen carcase. Very little riding today, hills rather steep, my friend grumbling all day.*

It wasn't the *fearful rough country* or the thorns of the scrub that curtailed McMillan's earliest attempt, but a hair-raising episode that left him fearing for his life.

It had taken weeks to secure Gibber's assistance. The Monaro tribe had scoffed when McMillan had first revealed his plan to explore Gippsland. One sceptical elder asked him if he wanted to be killed. The warrigals, the old man said, were much stronger men than they were. Such Ngarico scaremongering had unsettled the local settlers too, who were equally reluctant to join an expedition. *I again tried to get a European to accompany me but with no success; they were not to risk their lives in a country where the natives were reported as real giants, with red eyes and long red hair.*

Finally, after weeks of deliberation and a promise from McMillan to conquer the wild blacks so the Monaro tribe might live *in peace and quietness*, Gibber, a noted warrior, was dispatched to guide him, having been briefed by the few elderly Ngarico men who had seen this promised land.

Thus the pair, one keen and one reluctant, struck off south, but after only three days' travel Gibber's fear of the warrigal got the better of him. Growing steadily more spooked and unpredictable, he attempted to abandon McMillan in the bush, but was foiled. *He told me he was alarmed that the wild natives would come upon us, and that he would not be able to get away from them, as they could run faster than we could ride.*

Something about Gibber's panicked behaviour had the hair on the back of McMillan's neck prickling. That night he prepared himself to watch his companion, a pistol at each hand, *but being tired I soon dropped off asleep.* Later, a movement in the dark woke him with a start: *to my horror I saw my companion quietly picking up his waddy.* Both sprang to their feet at once, Gibber with his club in his hand. *In an instant my pistol was at his heart.*

A deadlock. Gibber attempted to deny that his intention had been to hurt McMillan, but the Scot did not believe him. He took possession of Gibber's club and axe, telling him that if anything happened to him while he was in the bush *he and all his tribe would suffer.*

McMillan would merrily recall this episode when relating tales of his daring exploits for the rest of his life. But, lying alone in the mountains with a hostile stranger, struggling to stay awake with a pistol under his pillow, must have been a formative experience for the young man. Not only had Gibber displayed that notorious Aboriginal bent for 'treachery' by his thwarted night-time attack, he had also demonstrated such a deep and deranging fear of the warrigals that, disregard it though he appeared to at the time, must have preyed on McMillan's mind during his earliest months and years in Gippsland.

*

Birdsong drifted from the gorge, the delicate strains of so many flautists practising their trills and scales. The sun was dipping quietly behind the distant mountains, taking with it the warmth of the day, and we stood gazing out into the depths, eyes straining as the light faded, until there was nothing more to be seen.

As the dusk rolled in, the wildlife emerged. Going was slow as Steve inched along the road, ready to brake if a kangaroo or wallaby leapt out in front of us. At the foot of a steep descent, a large deer stepped out of the shadows into the indigo twilight. It stared wide-eyed at the oncoming car, and froze, lit up like a stage performer. We slowed to a crawl, then stopped. There was a moment of respectful silence as we – humans and cervid – regarded each other with solemnity.

Steve slipped one hand back between the seats towards me. To touch my arm, I assumed, overcome by the wonder and beauty of the moment; but instead he stretched past me and closed his fingers on the empty air. Twisting, frowning, he looked back and located the barrel of the crossbow. I watched, horrified, as slowly, silently, he pulled it free from a tangle of fishing rods and slipped it through the gap between the seats, slotted in a bladed bolt and leaned out of the window to take aim. Slowly. Slowly.

Something in the movement must have spelled danger, for the deer took sudden fright and bounded out of the light and into the dark tangle of vegetation. 'Fuck,' said Steve. 'Fuck. I thought I had it.'

Cam scoffed. 'Good thing you didn't. What did you think we were going to do with a whole deer? We'd have been up all night gutting it. We'd have had to tie it to the *roof*.'

Steve was still cursing when he turned back to me, passing me the weapon and the bolt separately. I inspected the arrowhead – four mean metal blades, as on a kitchen knife, the sort of knife you need to keep in a guard – before wordlessly replacing it in a box on top of a heap of equipment.

We'd bought a carton of these bolts earlier, in a shop whose walls were lined with camouflage hunting suits, each printed with foliage as richly detailed as William Morris wallpaper, and glass display cases of weaponry worthy of *The Hunger Games*. I had dawdled, awkward as a husband in a lingerie department, looking sideways, out of the corners of my eyes, but not touching, reading the labels on the boxes. 'Dual side-by-side cutting blades and 6 razor-sharp cutting edges create up to a 250 per cent greater wound opening than traditional broadheads,' said one, before helpfully explaining: 'This means significantly greater blood loss, a better blood trail and ultimately, a faster kill.'

I frowned, contemplating the significance of 'a better blood trail'.

'Can I help you?'

I looked up to find a tall, tanned shop assistant smiling at me blandly from behind the counter. He dropped his eyes pointedly to the box, then raised them back to mine.

'Me?' I asked stupidly. 'Oh, no. No. No, thank you.'

We turned off at McKillop's Bridge to a camping spot far beneath its broad-shouldered span. The track was stony, steep, but as it levelled out the Snowy River came into view, huge and silver and calm in the moonlight.

We stopped repeatedly to allow more wildlife off the road: a fox, a large grey kangaroo, two dark-eyed wallabies, a fluffy possum that refused to be hurried. Several rabbits too, but Steve accelerated towards those, steering directly for them, trying to catch them under the wheels without taking us all over the precipice. But no such luck. Steve cursed again, Cam laughed.

The fire took quickly. Too tired to think, I listened to the boys talk as I lay back on my rucksack to look up at the stars, scattered across the night sky in their unfamiliar constellations. Cam had shown me how to find the Southern Cross, by joining the bright dots of Alpha Centauri and Beta Centauri and extending the line north, like a tail on the kite of Crux, its four bright points drawing the crossbars, its fainter fifth point, Epsilon Crucis, sitting on the edge of its sail. And beyond that, Carina, the keel of the great ship Argo that sailed the southern sky through the wash of the Milky Way, brighter here, shining with the lavender blue of a bruise.

My eyes, searching for a familiar handhold, alighted on my old friend Orion. Inverted from his usual posture, standing on his hands, but still reassuring in a sky that seemed so strangely foreign. Indigenous Australians saw him too, of course, but they interpreted him differently – some thought him not man but kayak, the three studs of his belt three hungry brothers, his sword not a sword but a fishing line, a kingfish on the end with a hook in its mouth.

Likewise, while Europeans saw Crux as the crucifix upon which hung the son of their god, the Gunai saw it as the head of an enormous emu, Ngooran, hunted nightly by Narran, the moon. Other Aboriginal groups saw the open talons of an eagle, or the prongs of a trident. The Maoris, across the Tasman Sea to the east, thought it a great aperture in the sky, through which wild winds would rush from another world.

A yowl broke the air, a melodic, haunting siren call. Then another, and another.

I sat up, eyes flitting nervously to the shadows that danced on the edge of our clearing, shadows that leapt and retreated in step with the flames.

Cam and Steve's eyes were wide, excited. 'Dingoes!'

The call came again, lupine voices joining together as one, then colliding and parting, rough, discordant, a dissonant choir. I lay back down to listen, pulled my jacket tighter around me, thoughts turning uneasily to the mysteries of the night beyond the clearing, beyond our circle of light. To bunyips, and doolagahs, and footsteps in the dark.

That night I dreamed about the massacres again. I heard those same shrill screams, the bloody thuds of spears hitting their targets. The crack of the guns, the rising panic of the reload, the blood spilling thick and wet across the ground, the animal groans of the wounded. It was the same scenario, the same sick thrill of fear and adrenaline. But this time they weren't killing me. I was killing them.

When I awoke I lay still, watching the light play across the sides of my tent. The leaves shifted in the breeze like kelp in a current. Birds called out and fell silent: rosellas, honeyeaters, the computerlike scramble of the magpie. Cockatoos gathered in a tree to complain, swearing and cursing, drunken revellers flashing their crests, then moved on as quickly as they had come. Bellbirds sounded their eerie sonar pulse, clear piercing tones, fingers drawn smoothly round the rim of a glass.

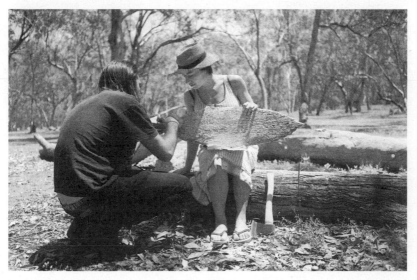

Steve cuts a shield from the bark of a gum tree, McKillop's Bridge.

I left Cam reading by the tents and wandered down through the straggly tail ends of the bush to the sand at the river's bank. Steve was fishing, bare-chested, his back to me. He didn't turn, but kept his eyes fixed on the point where his line met the water.

I shrugged off my clothes and waded into the river to bathe, the cold water hitting me like a slap in the chill morning air, making me gasp. Fresh air in my lungs. Clean white light on my skin. I dipped my head under like a baptism.

*

It was late by the time we left the Snowy, the early-morning clouds long burned off. By this time we were completely unanchored by anything so humdrum as schedules or obligations; we'd told Jeannie and Steve's parents to expect us back on Friday, and it was Sunday now, but it didn't seem to matter. Our phones had died days ago, and none of us had thought to bring an alarm. I didn't want to speak to anyone else, or know the date, or the time.

If anything, it was as though we were moving backwards in time. Not long after we crossed the border into New South Wales we came across an early settler's hut, restored, by the side of the road. It was the first permanent dwelling in the area, a sign said. It had been constructed in the 1840s. The smoke-blackened roof shingles were visible from the inside; on the walls flowery wallpaper peeled back to reveal newspaper print underneath, pasted there as a sort of plaster.

The bush here was dry, and made untidy by roots and the dry dropped limbs of the gums. Delegate, the nearest modern-day town to Currawong, was an old-style frontier settlement with false-fronted shopfronts of weathered clapboard and cracked tile terraces. Two old-fashioned petrol pumps sat beside the road, gleaming silver in the sunshine. A service station, or 'servo', as Australians call them. Long shut.

We stopped off at a bar before our last push up to Currawong, parking by an open-roofed horse trailer. As we got out of the car, three utes swerved off the road, windows down, music blaring, and their rugby-shirted drivers pushed in ahead of us, leaving their keys in the ignition and their windows open.

Inside it was dark, cool. A surly barmaid with frizzy hair was reading a newspaper behind the bar. 'NO CREDIT DON'T ASK' read a sign, not far from the 'BIRD SHIT TROPHY' and a list of its previous winners. Elsewhere, a flea-eaten dingo skin was mounted on the wall. 'Trapped May 1983 by John Coman,' read a plaque beneath it. 'Three legged yellow bitch with six yellow pups inside. Killed at the bottom of Tingiringi Mountain at the foot of a ribbony gum tree.'

I felt the eyes of the rugby-shirted men on us. Me in my white dress, ragged now, my skin drawn with sharp raw lines where the sun had caught my forehead and cheekbones, my collarbones picked out by scarlet brush-strokes, my hair loose and tangled; Steve with his topknot and ironic T-shirt; Cam with a fancy camera around his neck, zoom lens jutting obscenely. City kids, I could hear them thinking.

I steered the boys to a table outside so we could speak freely. I was in low spirits, still uneasy from the night before, but Steve and Cam were fired up by our travels. As soon as we sat down they turned again to the events at the gully. Steve did most of the talking, his face set with righteous anger. Cam nodded fiercely along, and I did too, but emptily.

I recognised Steve's tone. It was one I'd used myself in pub discussions, when I hit my stride explaining to English friends and colleagues how messed-up my country was, *thanks to them*. It was the tone I used when I spoke about the battle at Culloden, where *the soil ran with blood*, and about the Clearances, when my countrymen were *pulled screaming from their houses*, those same houses sent up in flames behind them. The tone when I lectured strangers in bars on the massacre at Glencoe, when visiting loyalists killed their hosts in their beds for refusing to swear allegiance to their new English king. And, and, and ... I had more where those came from: my people, your people. The balance of payments.

And it was all true, or close enough. The English were the perpetrators, if not directly then indirectly, through their agents among the Scots. But I was more comfortable in those conversations when I was assuming the role of victim; now, here I was feeling defensive on behalf of my own people.

I didn't doubt what Steve was saying. God knows, I'd been on the same trail for weeks now, and uncovering the same narrative. But I was unhappy and uneasy with my new role as the representative of the aggressors, and I watched their conversation from the other side of the glass.

We had coasted high into rolling plains, our car now a tiny dot in a vast open expanse. Huge round rocks poked through the earth, fluorescent with lichen against the yellowing grass. Far to our left a man was herding sheep, broad-brimmed hat pulled low, silhouetted in the dust-cloud kicked up by his flock. He was the only figure in an enormous landscape that stretched out endlessly before us, baking in the sun. Straight-lined plantation forest tiled the valley sides in great flat blocks of bottle-green and tired, straggling brown. This was the Monaro, the starting point from which McMillan first struck off into the unknown.

We got out at a small redbrick church that stood alone on the plain. All the names in the tiny graveyard were

Irish. O'Hares, Tiernans. The grass had been cut recently, and had dried in clumps like hair in the prongs of the fence, but the windowpanes were dusty, and behind them we could see that the pews inside had been pulled together at the centre of the building. No numbers on the psalm board. Out back a timber outhouse listed at a steep angle, its corrugated-iron roof measled with oxidation, plank door hanging from a single rusted hinge.

The wind ramped up over the fells and blew through the long dry grass. The sound of the ocean. An incredible sense of *scale*.

James Atkinson, a settler arriving in the area in 1826, found it unbearable. 'The silence and solitude that reign in these wide spreading untenanted wastes, are indescribable,' he wrote. 'Nothing meets the eye of the traveller, with the exception of a few solitary Emus, to enliven the monotony of the dreary expanse. From the contemplation of this vacancy and solitude the mind recoils with weariness.'

Still, in 1840 this was comparative civilisation. This was where McMillan had ridden to seek assistance right at the start of the pioneer days of Gippsland, when he had first realised that the Gunai might be dangerous, and had been spurned. He had nowhere else to turn. With no help or support forthcoming from the state, he had little option but to return to his seedling Bushy Park and his terrified men. With orders from Macalister to carry out and his own ambition to attend to, he had no intention of backing down. They'd take care of the matter themselves, then.

George Faithfull, a squatter in Wangaratta, a hundred miles north of Gippsland, had a similar experience. In 1838, as McMillan was finding his feet at Camden, a party of Faithfull's men were attacked and eight of their number killed. After this, white–black relations deteriorated sharply. 'The government during all this time gave no help, no assistance of any kind, and at last threatened to hang anyone who dared to shoot a black, even in protection of his property,' he wrote later. 'This, instead of doing good, did much evil. People formed themselves into bands of alliance and allegiance to each other, and then it was the destruction of the natives really did take place.'

What would I have done in the same situation? I had to admit, I didn't know.

Such thoughts set bells ringing. Looking at things through McMillan's eyes had unsettled me; the ease with which I had found myself sympathising with the predicament the settlers found themselves in was unnerving. It was a problem all of their own making, of course. But what was the alternative? Give up on the dream of land? Give up on the mission they had sunk their money and the best years of their lives into? Abandon the whole project and go back to where they had come from, back to the established colony, and put the darker side of settlement from their minds?

I don't think I would have done that. The thought fluttered around in my head, a plastic bag caught by the wind.

Some did, of course, and in time they, with the other innocents, would move into the newly cleared country and condemn those who had come before them, and the wild work that had taken place in their absence.

And all the while, George Faithfull and his ilk watched from the sidelines with bitterness. 'No sooner was all fear of the blacks dissipated than the whites became almost as great a nuisance,' he wrote in 1853. 'Unfortunately the

Government gave too willing an ear to them as we were all branded as murderers of the blacks. They readily deprived us of portions of our runs to give them to the other squatters, who were considered peaceful men, as well they might be after the war was ended.'

'Ours was the danger,' he lamented. 'Theirs the reward.'

9

In Search of Elders

By the time the state of Victoria split off from New South Wales in 1851, the 'Black War' of Gippsland was, to all intents and purposes, over. The white man had won.

The surviving Gunai had either fled to the inaccessible, bush-fringed mountains, or gathered in shanty towns on the edges of white townships or cattle stations seeking employment or handouts. In a single decade the colonists had overseen the total collapse of a culture that had survived in its existing form for more than 30,000 years.

In this way, the events of Gippsland typify the collapse of Aboriginal culture across the continent, as tribe after tribe was extinguished in the face of the expansion of the British colony. The 'Omeo tribe' mentioned in McMillan's diaries, for example – more accurately, the Theddora-mittung branch of the Ya-itma-thang nation – saw their region settled around 1838. They survived this initial occupation in relatively rude health, but when gold was discovered in the region in 1852 the ensuing rush ensured that the once-populous tribe numbered a mere 'four or five' members only a decade later.

The original inhabitants of the land were falling at the hands of the newcomers, not only directly through open warfare, but indirectly by more stealthy killers. Men bearing arms may have been the most obvious of the invaders, but in many ways they were not the most insidious. What they carried with them – viruses – would prove far more destructive. Syphilis and influenza ran riot, but the most devastating of all was smallpox, a vicious, disfiguring disease that ripped through the vulnerable tribes without mercy.

Within a single year of the First Fleet's arrival, it had already cut swathes through the Eora people indigenous to the Sydney area. Watkin Tench described how their bodies piled up in every cove, 'thickly spread' with pustules. And the deaths did not stop. The whole country became one enormous petri dish where, dripped into a vast population without immunity, diseases morphed and massacred. The destructiveness of the epidemics multiplied the psychological effects of the more open warfare – the demoralising effect of seeing white men impervious to these invisible killers, as Aboriginal people succumbed in their hundreds of thousands.

Men like Angus McMillan – heading out into virgin territory, mingling with unknown tribes – were wreaking death upon their new companions even as they smiled and shook their hands. Today, 'first contact' interactions with new tribes across the world are very strictly controlled for exactly this reason, but in the 1840s there was little understanding of the transmission of disease; it was still widely thought that sickness was caused by odours and 'bad air'. The resulting plunge in the Aboriginal population echoed similar catastrophes that had tailed European conquest around the globe, notably the plagues of smallpox that so devastated the Native Americans and precipitated the downfall of the Aztec empire.

The damage was not confined to the human population: native plants and animals suffered too, as invasive species struggled for supremacy. Brambles and scotch thistles now flourish in their thickets, uncontested in temperate regions. Camels originally brought from India and Afghanistan for use as bulk transport in the desert regions roam feral in their hundreds of thousands. The wild brumbies, descended from those few horses shipped in across oceans, are now so numerous that the population must be managed by sharpshooters in helicopters. The whim of one Victorian settler who introduced twenty-four rabbits 'so as to provide a touch of home, in addition to a spot of hunting' in 1859 led inevitably to a nationwide explosion, and the notorious 'rabbit-proof fence' that stretches 1,100 unbroken miles across Western Australia.

Jeannie had told me about all this. Her latest play had been inspired by the real-life experiences of a friend, a man of hippyish disposition who had moved deep into the bush with his family. They wanted to get close to nature, but found themselves at close quarters with a far more ferocious environment than they had been prepared for. Wild dogs – an unholy hybrid of domestic dog and the native dingo – roamed the bush in packs, and as summer turned to drought, the soil to dust, and food dwindled, they skulked closer and closer to the house, eyeing first the chickens, then the family dogs – and finally, his children.

Not knowing what else to do, he bought a rifle, and went to a nearby shooting range to practise. When the dogs next appeared, rabid with hunger, he walked out onto the front step and, to the horror of his wife, gunned them down. Soon there came panicked calls from neighbours, and the lifelong pacifist found himself reinvented as the district dingo-hunter.

I had listened to this tale with an air of disbelief, but in the hills above Omeo we had stumbled across the evidence. As we slalomed down through the bush a grisly sight materialised at the side of the road. An aged gum stood with its boughs hanging heavy with the bodies of dead dogs, dozens of them, their hind legs trussed, forelegs and heads dangling lifelessly. We stopped for a closer inspection; the buzzing of the flies and the stench of putrid flesh hit us in a wall like humidity as we opened the car doors. I pulled my shirt up over my nose and mouth and advanced, searching for the cause of death. The corpses hung close together like pheasants for the pot, tan or dun-coloured, most of them, the shades of dried grass, but the occasional dark-brown, and one lucky white.

Gum tree hung with dead dogs, Omeo.

They'd been scalped. A long strip of fur, including the ears, had been peeled down the spine from each forehead. The tails were gone too. 'For the bounty,' explained Jeannie. The state of Victoria paid $100 per scalp. We were looking at thousands of dollars' worth of dead dog.

Ian exclaimed behind us – another tree, another haul. These ones were long-dead. Bones showed through the fur, tobacco-stain ribcages and interlocking vertebrae. Of some, whose joints had given way, only the feet were left, hanging from long ribbons of blue and purple baler twine, oddly festive.

Seeing all these corpses left hanging up on the roadside like trophies for all to see gave me an uneasy thrill. I didn't have to ask the reason: the dogs were vermin, they killed the sheep, they roamed wild and unconstrained across the countryside. I understood the concept easily enough. I'd heard the same arguments before, in a different context. It brought to mind an anecdote I'd read in the letters page of the *Sydney Gazette* dated 1841, an image I had since tried and failed to repress:

> I see by the Gazette of this day, that the blacks
> have again been spearing some white people to the
> southward, which we take amiss and call it an
> outrage; but, Sir, at this present moment while I
> am writing this to you, [name deleted] has forty-
> two human heads, stuck upon poles around his
> house, and nailed to his door posts. Pray, Sir,
> would you call this an outrage committed by us?

The state of the Aboriginal population soon grew so parlous – and things so comparatively comfortable for the newly respectable settlers – that public feeling shifted away from overt aggression towards something more closely resembling ridicule, or even pity.

By the mid-1850s, as the remaining Gunai emerged from the bush and appeared at the stations in greater and greater numbers, in search of employment or handouts, the very men who had masterminded their demise were at the vanguard of the movement to 'save' them, or at least to make their passage into the history books as painless as possible.

Tarra Bobby, a Gunai man assisted by McMillan
when wrongly accused of murder.

Perhaps it was the manifestation of a guilty conscience, but Angus McMillan was considered a particularly charitable bleeding heart. As dozens of Gunai gathered in a humpy village by McMillan's homestead, the *Gippsland Guardian* wrote that 'his station at Bushy Park might well be called the Benevolent Asylum of Gippsland'. In 1858 he accompanied two Gunai men accused of murder – William Login and Tarra Bobby – to Melbourne, where he translated on their behalf. Soon enough he was appointed as an honorary protector for the region, and later as a member of a select committee tasked with the 'protection of Aborigines' – apparently with no irony intended.

And so they struggled on, until in 1859 a group of Gunai appealed to Assistant Protector William Thomas for a grant of land to be set aside for them, like that which had been granted to the Wurundjeri people of Goulburn the previous year. 'I tell them Mr McMillan will see & secure it,' Thomas wrote.

It took four years, but finally 2,300 acres were set aside for the remaining Gunai, in the form of a Christian mission where the struggling blacks could be fed and clothed and generally civilised. It was located at a site even McMillan had protested was singularly inappropriate: on a hillside overlooking Lake Wellington, close to Boney Point. It would be an unpopular choice, he said, as 'a great many Aborigines were killed [there] and as the bones lay about it got its gruesome name'. He made no mention of his involvement in their deaths.

His concerns went unheeded, and responsibility for the future of the surviving Gunai was taken out of his hands. The Ramahyuck mission station was established, led by the Reverend Friedrich Hagenauer, a German missionary. It

was one of four such missions in Victoria, run by the
Anglican or – like Ramahyuck – Moravian Churches. The
station was located in what had traditionally been
Tatungooloong country, but its residents were drawn from
far and wide, resulting in an unhappy broth of tribal rivalries and miscommunication between dialect groups. Its
organisers, however, were not concerned with the nuances
of Aboriginal lifestyle; they planned to obliterate it.

The Ramahyuck mission station near Lake Wellington.

On arrival, the Reverend Hagenauer assembled his new
Aboriginal charges and instructed them to place their
traditional weapons and tools – waddies, boomerangs and

so on – in a pile at the camp's centre, before setting fire to it. Corroborees, the traditional gatherings and festivals, were banned, and European dress made compulsory. To enable religious conversion, a basic education – 'reading, writing, singing and scripture' – was provided, and all tribal habits strictly forbidden. Aboriginal names were replaced with more appropriate Christian monikers; black, sun-ravaged faces bore names that could have been torn from the pages of a Jane Austen novel: Sophia Darby, Georgiana King, William Login, Percy Phillip, Mary Arnott. Hagenauer planned to record over the people like cassette tapes, and leave nothing of their original character.

The young Alfred Howitt, who moved to Gippsland in 1866, saw this, and realised that within a generation all the Gunai's age-old customs and knowledge would be lost. He began to invite the men to come and work on his hop farm on the Mitchell River, where he logged all they told him of the old ways. He did this, he wrote later, 'without definite aim', but these observations would form the foundation of his two pioneering works of ethnography, *Kamilaroi and Kurnai* (1880) and *The Tribes of South East Asia* (1904). These remarkable books detail the traditions and customs of the Aboriginal groups of Victoria and New South Wales, many of which have long since fallen into disuse. The sections concerning the Gunai are particularly fascinating, not least because they are the only written record ever made of many of their fantastical and other-worldly beliefs.

They believed that a great being, Mungan, had taught the Gunai everything they knew, and instituted the *jeraeil* (initiation) so that these secrets might be passed down, father to son, through the generations. Once, after the secrets of the *jeraeil* had been carelessly revealed to women, Mungan was so angry that he filled the entire space between the sky and the land with fire: 'Men went mad with fear, and speared one another, fathers killed their children, husbands their wives, and brethren each other. Then the sea rushed over the land and nearly all mankind were drowned.'

Some of those who survived became the ancestors of the Gunai; others became animals, birds and reptiles, which in turn were to become the familiars of the tribe, appearing to them in dreams or in bodily form to keep them safe. The crow, particularly, was a friend, who would follow them through the bush calling out advice and warnings. The Aurora Australis was an echo of the great fire. It signified that Mungan was growing angry again, and on nights when it appeared the elders – to whom prophecies were revealed in dreams – would order an exchange of wives to appease him.

The social system of the Gunai was as complex as the mythology, and equally unique. In almost all other instances, women were bound to fidelity, but men were not. Upon marriage the man must never again speak to his mother-in-law or use her name, referring to her only as 'that woman'; yet he must give the bulk of his booty from hunting to his wife's family. On his death his widow went to his brother – provided she gave her consent.

Howitt was captivated. As his relationship with the Gunai grew, he encouraged them to maintain their traditions, re-enacting their ceremonies and reviving the *jeraeil* for a last time. He recorded their song-charms, incantations and lullabies, as best as he was able. There was 'a wild and pathetic music' to their melodies, he wrote. 'With custom they grow upon one until at length one feels in some measure the effect which they produce upon an aboriginal audience in so powerful a manner ... As it is, white men know little of the black-fellow's songs, which to most people are unmeaning barbarous chants, and to the missionaries who have some knowledge of them they savour of heathendom, and must therefore be altogether pushed into oblivion and be forgotten. Thus before long all these songs, old and new, will be lost.'

> Wa! – Wa! – Wa!
> *Stop! – Stop! – Stop!*
> Lelándū – mri – ngū
> *Sleep, – eyes of – thine*

*

The Reverend Hagenauer's intention had been to destroy the traditional culture, but what his mission perhaps achieved more thoroughly was the obliteration of the Gunai people. They began to die, both young and old, with startling frequency. And with them, just as Howitt predicted, died all that they had known.

Peter Gardner has observed that 'the most frequent Christian ceremony, apart from Sunday observances, was the funeral': the mission's thirty-year registers reveal an average life expectancy of only twenty-five years, and a desperate infant mortality rate of 31 per cent. They died of strange, inexact conditions: 'exhaustion', 'abscess', 'teething', 'fits', 'decline'. Hagenauer showed little concern about the growing toll. Every death that followed conversion was to be celebrated, 'although all the victories which are here gained will bring us nearer to the end of the mission. The number of natives is small and every triumphant death which we have to record reduces the total.'

This apparent callousness reflected Hagenauer's belief, widely held at the time, that the Aboriginal Australians were a doomed race, destined for extinction. Theories of 'scientific racism' were entering the mainstream: in 1850 Robert Knox, a professor of anatomy at Edinburgh University, had published *Races of Men*, later described as 'one of the most articulate and lucid statements of racism ever to appear', in which he argued that the world's future would be decided by a 'war of extermination' in which 'the destruction of one race by another' was inevitable. Charles Darwin's seminal *On the Origin of Species* appeared in 1859, and was a favoured topic of discussion in the parlours of the day. His theory of 'natural selection' – the triumph of the strong over the weak – seemed applicable to the case of the unfortunate indigenous Australians; Darwin himself tackled the question of humanity in his 1871 book *The Descent of Man*, in which he assigned Aboriginals to the lowest rung on the ladder of humanity:

> the civilised races of man will almost certainly
> exterminate, and replace, the savage races
> throughout the world. At the same time the
> anthropomorphous apes ... will no doubt be
> exterminated. The break between man and his
> nearest allies will then be wider, for it will
> intervene between man in a more civilised state, as
> we may hope, even than the Caucasian, and some

ape as low as a baboon, instead of as now between the negro or Australian and the gorilla.

The future of the Aboriginal people seemed clear: there was none. The missionaries' purpose was thus also clarified: to make the death of a race as comfortable and as Christian as possible. In this, Hagenauer was highly successful. Even as the numbers at Ramahyuck dwindled, its school gained rave reviews from inspectors, and in 1877 it was declared the most successful of all the Victorian missions.

Hagenauer would play a key role in the institution of the 1886 Half-Caste Act, state legislation under which Aboriginal people of mixed descent were expelled from stations and reserves, in the hope that these lighter-skinned individuals would be quickly absorbed into white society as the reserves declined and eventually closed down – thus neatly solving the Aboriginal problem. The Act may have been based on a certain cold-blooded logic, but real human tragedy accompanied these expulsions: families were disrupted, married couples split apart, children forcibly removed from their parents and sent to orphanages or residential schools for 're-education' – the first of the so-called 'stolen generations', a nationwide practice of child-removal in the late nineteenth and early twentieth centuries that would see tens of thousands of Aboriginal children separated, either under duress or through decep-tion, from their parents and placed in orphanages or 'fostered out' to white families. The practice continued in some areas up to the 1970s.

Earlier I had visited the Knob Reserve, a picturesque area of open, sun-dappled forest a short drive to the north of the Ramahyuck site, rising to a bluff that looked out over the long and languorous curves of the Avon River. Traditionally it was a meeting point between clans on important tribal occasions – corroborees, *jeraeils* and other ceremonies – but after the advent of the mission station it became the site of more melancholy gatherings, as bereft residents walked ten miles from the mission under cover of darkness to meet their exiled family members.

If it seems a cruel and unusual solution, the fact is that the approach taken by Hagenauer and his peers bears an eerie resemblance to policies that would be enacted not only in the rest of Australia over subsequent decades, but throughout the colonial world.

At around the same period, across the Pacific Ocean, the Canadian government was embarking on an aggressive programme of assimilation that also included a system of demarcated reserves and residential schooling. At one point, a third of all First Nation (indigenous) children were separated, sometimes by force, from their families, to be educated in institutions where they were indoctrinated in the English language, Christianity and the 'civilised' lifestyle, and where native languages, dress and cultural practices were banned.

In 2008, the then Prime Minister Stephen Harper made a national apology to surviving pupils and family members, conceding in his speech that the objectives of this system had been 'to remove and isolate children from the influence of their homes, families, traditions and cultures, and to assimilate them into the dominant culture. These objectives were based on the assumption aboriginal cultures and spiritual beliefs were inferior and unequal. Indeed, some sought, as it was infamously said, "to kill the Indian in the child".'

To the south, an analogous programme of 'American-isation' was under way: more boarding schools, more plots of land where stubborn adults might be confined until they either died or changed their ways. In his State of the Union Address on 4 December 1871, President Ulysses S. Grant noted that 'many tribes of Indians have been induced to settle upon reservations, to cultivate the soil, to perform productive labor of various kinds, and to partially accept civilisation. They are being cared for in such a way, it is hoped, as to induce those still pursuing their old habits of life to embrace the only opportunity which is left them to avoid extermination.'

All across the globe, the pattern repeated as, again and again, one culture swallowed another as a python swallows an egg whole.

Perhaps there is a name for this systematic snuffing out of Aboriginal society: genocide.

Deployment of this word in terms of Australian history is divisive, and it is beyond the scope of this book to make an academic or legal study of whether it is appropriate. But it is worth touching upon the issue here, in the interests of considering the enormity of the events of the Gippsland frontier.

There are two definitions of the word that might come into play in the case of Aboriginal history. The 'standard' usage concerns the physical destruction of an ethnic group by violence or force, and there are two instances in which this is invoked in an Australian context.

The first is in terms of frontier massacres, when settlers driven by a homicidal frenzy set out to exterminate the indigenous population in their area. The most clear-cut example – often given as a 'classical example' of genocide – is the grim case of the Tasmanian 'Black War', a vicious struggle shortly before the discovery of Gippsland which saw the Aboriginal Palawa people almost entirely eradicated within a decade. At one point, a human chain 2,200 men strong, dubbed 'the Black Line', was organised to sweep the entire island – an area larger than Ireland – in an attempt to corral the remaining Palawa on a small, out-of-the-way peninsula. The notoriously violent Queensland frontier too, which the events of Gippsland closely echo, is often considered a possible case of genocide.

The second instance is the case of the 'stolen generations': an inquiry into the policy initiated by the Attorney General, which reported in 1997, concluded that it had indeed been an act of genocide, 'aimed at wiping out indigenous families, communities, and cultures' – or as one chief protector had put it, 'breeding out the colour'.

Still, many continue to reject these applications of the term. In the case of the massacres, some contest the basic facts, accusing those who have recorded such incidents of hyperbole; others, such as Richard Broome, hesitate to accept the term due to the lack of an official policy ordering the elimination of the Aboriginal population. As for the stolen generations, some fear that employing the word 'genocide' in such an instance somehow detracts from the seriousness of the charge – for example, the historian Inga Clendinnen: 'When I see the word "genocide", I still see Gypsies and Jews being herded into trains, into pits, into

ravines ... I believe that to take the murder out of genocide is to render it vacuous.'

On these points, the United Nations Convention on the
Prevention and Punishment of the Crime of Genocide is
clear: the state as perpetrator is not a prerequisite, and
execution is but one of five possible means of committing
genocide. As the historian Dirk Moses has noted, 'genocide is not a synonym for the Holocaust'. It is instead
defined as:

> any of the following acts committed with intent to
> destroy, in whole or in part, a national, ethnical,
> racial or religious group, as such:
>
> (a) Killing members of the group;
> (b) Causing serious bodily or mental harm to
>   members of the group;
> (c) Deliberately inflicting on the group conditions
>   of life calculated to bring about its physical
>   destruction in whole or in part;
> (d) Imposing measures intended to prevent births
>   within the group;
> (e) Forcibly transferring children of the group to
>   another group.

By these definitions, it seems reasonable to regard Angus
McMillan's Gippsland – where the Crown Commissioner
spent his weekends 'hunting blacks' and Aboriginal men,
women and children were shot indiscriminately 'wherever
they can be met with' – and the settlement of Australia
more broadly, as being flecked with what Moses calls
'genocidal moments'.

An alternative usage, more applicable to the Ramahyuck mission station and the assimilation processes from the 1860s onwards, is one best understood as 'cultural geno-cide' – that is, the systematic destruction of the language, practices and customs that make a group distinct. The burning of cultural artefacts and the banning of tribal languages and ceremonies would seem to put Ramahyuck squarely in this camp. But this too is a highly contested area. Many commentators in Australia have taken umbrage at the concept that the actions of white missionaries and administrators, often undertaken in good faith, in the honest belief that their work would save Aboriginal communities – or, at the very least, their children – should be equated with genocide.

Because it would be amiss not to touch upon the fact that Victoria's half-caste laws, and others like them, were created out of – well, not exactly *love*, but often at least partly out of concern and a sense of responsibility. It is also worth acknowledging that even within the Aboriginal community itself there are mixed feelings towards the missions and missionaries. Some have expressed the senti-ment that the missions saved their people from ruin, whether from death, disease or the dysfunction that was beginning to take hold of their families and communities.

Complex emotions had already begun to arise amongst the Gunai in 1846, at the height of the white woman hunt, as is revealed by the letters of Sergeant William Walsh, of the state-funded expedition. Having 'accompanied' a group of Gunai men and women to the native police station in Narre Warren, he was surprised to find that they wished to remain there: 'I have asked the Blacks several times if they would like to go back to the Lake where their tribe is – but they say no – that they would get nothing to Eat, and have to go naked,' he wrote. 'The last time I asked them they began to cry.'

For my part, I am ambivalent about the academic back-and-forthing over the use of the term 'genocide'. The debate surrounding its precise applications does not particularly interest me, given that all those accused are long dead, and will never face justice. Suffice it to say that whether or not the exact definitions are matched, their basic requirements have been fulfilled; certainly the 'spirit' of genocide shines through descriptions of 1840s Gippsland and its wildest work.

Whatever the technical term, and whatever the motivation, one of the saddest aspects is that this was a tried and tested method. McMillan's rival 'Count' Paweł Strzelecki noted:

> The decrease and final annihilation of the great majority of indigenous races which has followed, and always does follow, the approach of the whites, – is a fact of such historical notoriety, that the melancholy instance of the Australian natives affords but a further corroboration of the fearfully destructive influence which the one race exercises upon the other.

For centuries the world had been regarded as an enormous game of Risk, as whole continents were conquered and lost by players who sat far away, directing counters on a map. One hears much about those great empires that conquered, but almost nothing of the growing toll of cultures that died away as collateral in the course of their rise: the remnants of people's past, the marginalia of humanity.

Groups like the Beothuk of Newfoundland, the original 'red Indians' who painted their bodies with ochre in the summer, who – like the Gunai – had no interest in befriending the Europeans when they arrived in the sixteenth century; instead, they moved inland, away from the colonists and their own main source of food. Starving, ravaged by disease, and trapped in a cycle of violence with the tribes upon whose land they had encroached, they died one by one. The last known full-blooded Beothuk, Shanawdithit, died of tuberculosis in 1829.

Or the Jangil people of the Andaman Islands, who tried to avoid all contact with mainland Indians and the British colonists, but who still disappeared sometime between 1907 and 1920, probably as the result of an introduced disease to which they had no immunity. There is no remaining record of their language or customs.

The Sharpheads of Alberta, Canada, nomadic until the late nineteenth century, when they were confined to a Christian mission. Their numbers fell dramatically, thanks to measles and influenza, until the last remaining few were redistributed among neighbouring reserves, and the land retaken by the Canadian government.

The Khodynts of northern Siberia, exterminated by smallpox in 1693. The Sadlermiut of Hudson Bay, wiped out by disease contracted from a British trading vessel in 1903. The Hachaath of Vancouver Island, who vanished off the face of the earth at some point in between.

And all those Australian Aboriginal nations that bloomed and withered barely recorded, wholly misunderstood, sometimes never even seen by the European outsiders. They were unknown then. Now they are unknowable.

'I have protested against the evident wrong of allowing whole tribes to perish out of existence without the slightest record being kept of their physical and moral characteristics,' the Melbourne journalist David Blair wrote in 1868. 'It is disgraceful that we should allow the original possessors of our magnificent territory to perish before our very eyes, without preserving any record of them, beyond, perhaps, a row of grinning skulls in the national museum.'

The only part of the Ramahyuck mission that remains is the cemetery. It is a small, square patch of dry grass, grown long in comparison to the cropped fields alongside, outlined by a neat picket fence. A sign: 'We ask that you do not leave the path, as you may be walking over many unmarked graves.' Pictures from the Hagenauer era show it as a forest of wooden crosses and posts, marking the sites of the bodies, but over the years they have all crumbled away, leaving only a single standing headstone: that of Nathaniel Pepper, Hagenauer's first and most loyal convert.

Sacred to the memory
of NATHANIEL PEPPER
who fell asleep in Jesus
7th of March 1877
aged 36 years

Pepper was a Wotjoballuk man, a convert from Hagenauer's first mission on the Wimmera River who followed the minister to his new project, where he married a local woman of the missionary's choice. But though his faith was strong, he was a sickly man. He grew frail and succumbed to consumption, like so many others at Ramahyuck. Hagenauer apparently felt only triumph at his young protégé's death: 'I was standing before his happy death-bed, and saw him, safe in the arms of Jesus, passing away from us to join the host of the redeemed in glory.'

What with all these 'victories' of the sickroom and the cemetery, and the removal of the 'quite whites', by 1908 there were few enough residents left to merit the closure of the mission at Ramahyuck. Hagenauer died the next year. This single headstone, therefore, might be seen as the culmination of his life's work. As the Gippsland author Donald MacDonald had observed a few years previously: 'When we came here, the aborigines covered these wide plains in thousands. Where are they today? We have civilized them – they are dead.'

The few remaining residents were bundled off to another mission at Lake Tyers, founded by John Bulmer, an Anglican missionary who on his arrival at the Victorian goldfields had been so shocked by the drunken and degraded state of the Aborigines that he made their improvement his life's work.

The mission station at Lake Tyers was centred on a pretty white clapboard church, and overlooked a glorious stretch of white sand and turquoise water. Its residents came from a mix of tribal backgrounds, including the Tatungooloong Gunai plus a few stragglers from the Omeo, Bidwelli and Monaro groups, but largely consisted of the Krowathunkooloong clan, who had only begun to emerge from the wildest parts of the bush and gorges to the east of Gippsland during the 1850s. This tangle of tribal loyalties caused terrible problems over the following decades; Bulmer wrote of 'almost daily' physical clashes that kept the mission in a 'continual state of excitement'.

Native Camp, Lake Tyers

Lake Tyers residents, 1890s. Traditional bark canoes can be seen in the background.

Although Bulmer was more sympathetic to, even admiring of, Aboriginal culture than Hagenauer, he and his pick-and-mix residents nevertheless witnessed the continued dying away of the old ways in favour of a bastardised 'Christian' lifestyle. The abandonment of Gunai culture, far from prompting acclaim from the adjacent white community, instead provoked a strange, ambivalent reaction amounting to a further loss of respect – even disgust – for the now detribalised, decultured and demoralised inhabitants. Even Bulmer himself was not immune: 'I must say there is nothing more repulsive than a half-civilised aboriginal,' he wrote. 'One cannot help looking back to the time when wild in the woods the noble savage ran, for after all, with all his civilization he was a very much superior individual in times gone by than he is today.'

He particularly grieved the loss of the last of the *birrarks*, the 'poets, prophets and spiritual mentors of the people': 'alas all these men have passed away, there was something interesting about them. They have left behind a nondescript lot who are neither fish, flesh nor good red herring. Education has been introduced but where there has been no change of heart it has made the aboriginal not in the least interesting. He may be athletic, so were their fathers even more so.'

In private he began to question the value of his work, as it became increasingly obvious that the 'improvement' to his charges had in many ways had deleterious effects at least equal to, and perhaps outweighing, the positive.

It is a realisation that has been faced by many engaged in charity and missionary work, particularly in a colonial context. For beyond the immediate trauma of assimilationist policies – after the loss of property or family members has been grieved for – there is a slower, more ponderous cruelty that continues to work in its shadow for years, and even generations, to come. After the old ways have been lost and the ceremonies fallen out of use, what it means to be 'native' becomes diluted; those who have been assimilated and their descendants often find themselves afflicted by a profound angst as they struggle for identity in a cultural limbo where they are no longer a discrete minority, nor yet truly of the majority.

Many of these 're-educated' masses develop complex feelings of alienation and contempt for their own culture

– what might be described as a 'cultural cringe' – which may endure for the rest of their lives. Such negative feelings (seen amongst Australian Aboriginal groups, and countless others worldwide) often manifest themselves in high levels of alcoholism, addiction, abuse and all kinds of societal self-harm, and a continuing rejection of one's own heritage even once more liberal policies are introduced.

Certainly in Australia, the government would soon discover that the blunt instrument of assimilation – applied with such force so soon after the horrors of conflict – had deeply unbalanced the Aboriginal societies it attempted to help. Over the following decades, the true damage that had been wrought would become clear. Deep social problems arrived, and never departed; indeed, the question of the long-term effects of dispossession has never been more pressing than it is today.

Aboriginal life expectancy is still a decade lower than the Australian average, and the unemployment rate three times higher. Aboriginal Australians are fifteen times more likely than the rest of the population to be imprisoned, thirty times more likely to suffer from childhood malnutrition, eight times more likely to die of alcohol-related causes, ten times more likely to be taken into care as a child, and more than twice as likely to commit suicide. Aboriginal men aged between thirty-five and forty-four have a mortality rate more than four times higher than their non-Aboriginal counterparts; for Aboriginal women between twenty-five and thirty-nine, it is five times higher.

Although life is complicated, and although there are many factors in play, it still seems inescapably the case that these statistics – and the comparable plight of innumerable indigenous peoples worldwide – are the present-day outcomes of Angus McMillan, the Reverend Friedrich Hagenauer and their peers' actions, the effects of which continue to ripple out across the ages.

Even as the earnest John Bulmer agonised over the value of his life's work, other anxieties arose. Like many 'do-gooders' before and after him, the disconnect between his vision and his residents' aspirations began to prompt in him the suspicion that he was being taken advantage of.

He dwelt frequently on such worries in his correspondence. 'They try to rely solely on the Government,' he complained. 'To them she is a good cow and they will milk her. Yet they fancy themselves independent and are impatient of control.' They were lazy too, he observed. When assigned menial tasks 'they go to work as if they were going to their deaths so they can make themselves as useless as possible'. Many made a mockery of what was, for a missionary, his *raison d'être*: his beliefs. 'I once reminded [an Aboriginal man] that he must die, perhaps sooner than he expected,' he recalled. 'Oh, said he, then I will look to Christ quick.'

Because many efforts to 'help' were rebuffed by the recipients, or repurposed to unexpected ends, resentment grew among even the more sympathetic elements of the white community, and with it a growing sense that the blacks *deserved* their poor lot in life became an ever more persistent undertone in the local discourse. As Commissioner Tyers complained to Governor La Trobe:

Notwithstanding the opportunities they have had by their increased intercourse with the settlers, I cannot say they have made any progress in civilization. They still conform to their savage habits and mode of life. Too idle to cultivate the soil and to lay up provision for tomorrow they hold to their wandering propensities when employed by the White population and are satisfied with the scanty food which their indolent life allows them to obtain from Gum Trees, or from the Rivers and Lakes.

If all this sounds somehow familiar, it is because it is the same language with which all societies denigrate their underclasses. It is the way the British characterise those who rely on the charity of food banks or the safety net of social welfare; the way right-wing America vilifies the youth of failing black neighbourhoods. It is the way many Australians still portray Aboriginal people today: as lazy, feckless scroungers who live off the largesse of the state. (In 2014, a sixty-thousand-year-old Aboriginal cave painting in Western Australia was defaced when vandals carved the phrase 'Go and work for a living' into the rock.)

The irony is that, at home in Britain, the very same stereotypes were being trotted out and directed at the dregs of society there: the Scottish Highlanders. Consider this remarkable missive, published in 1845 in the *Glasgow Herald* on the subject of the starving crofters, but which might equally have been applied by men of Gaelic heritage to the Aboriginal Australian in the very same year:

The apathy which through poverty stricken generations had become part of their character rendered these [charitable] efforts unavailing. They

preferred their habitual mode of life – their few
days of desultory labour intermingled with weeks of
lounging gossip – their half-clad, half-fed condition
– to regular well repaid toil.

Or this most scathing of leaders in the *Fifeshire Journal*, in
1847:

> It is not more notorious that the sons of Ethiopia
> are black, than it is to all who know them, that
> Highlandmen will not work if they can get their
> meat by any other means ... The destitution of the
> Highlanders is the natural and legitimate fruit of
> their national vices. There is abundant proof that
> laziness is the darling sin which the Highlandman
> cherishes amidst all his imagined piety.

Yet while the Lowland commentariat waxed lyrical upon
the insufficiencies of the Gaelic race, Angus McMillan and
his companions – the brave pioneers, the Highland Brigade
– were reprising precisely the behaviour that had so devastated the lives and livelihoods of their own countrymen,
but this time casting themselves in the principal role. They
turfed the Aborigines out of their homelands to make way
for sheep; enacted new, ever more brutal clearances upon
the new land even as they grieved for the tragedies of the
old one. And as the Gunai faced hopelessness head on, so
the Gaels turned critical eyes upon them, and saw that
they deserved it.

If nothing else, those rampaging Scotsmen are proof that
all peoples are capable of atrocity. That there are no 'strong
races' or 'weak races', only strong positions and weak ones.

'Morally and intellectually the Highlanders are an inferior race,' the *Scotsman* thundered in 1846. It was their 'mild nature', their 'meek and patient spirit' that destined them to domination by the tougher southerners, observed others. But elsewhere, with one lucky break, oh how the tables had turned.

Blessed are the meek, for they shall inherit the earth. But who is to say that, when they do, they shall not rule just as cruelly?

Bung Yarnda – or as it's now known, Lake Tyers. We stood on the sand, watching pelicans wheel overhead before silently alighting in squads upon the gentle waves.

We were early. I had heard that it was hard to find – mislabelled on maps, six miles off the nearest main road – so I'd overcompensated, and now we had half an hour to kill, basking in the bright sunlight like snakes, before the boys and I picked our way up from the water's edge, along a low row of white clapboard chalets and past the wooden spire of the church. Sweet-scented air swilled up off the water and through the wide avenue, painting my lips with faint traces of salt.

After all these years, the old mission station is now a township of around 150 Aboriginal residents, who own the land and buildings by way of a trust and run it as an agricultural cooperative. It was peaceful, quaint, a waterside community with a set of government buildings at its heart bearing fresh coats of paint. Not, I thought, an unpleasant place to live.

Yet the serene surroundings belied a turbulent history. After the escalation of assimilation policies in the early twentieth century, Aboriginal reserves were increasingly closed, with working-age residents ejected into adjacent communities to fend for themselves, and remits reduced to cover only the old and infirm. By 1924, Lake Tyers was the only staffed reserve left in Victoria.

Facilities were allowed to degrade. A 1957 inquiry found that its 150 remaining residents lived crammed into around thirty 'huts', with no running water, bathrooms or means of refuse disposal. Medical attention was insufficient, the nearest doctor being located fifty-five miles away and only visiting the reserve once a month. Residents were not allowed to own cars, and all visitors had to be approved by the manager. It was, in short, 'squalid, isolated and without hope'.

Closure was floated, but the proposal met stiff resistance. Despite the terrible living conditions, for many residents it was the only home they had ever had. It had become the final refuge for many of Victoria's Aboriginal people. A campaign to save the mission was born a few years later, calling for the management to be handed over to its indigenous residents.

The campaign came in the midst of a flurry of pro-indigenous sentiment, which had taken shape after a shocking 1957 documentary, *Manslaughter*, revealed to a horrified white audience for the first time the true scale of the deprivation suffered by indigenous people. Set among an Aboriginal community in the Warburton Ranges of Western Australia, it showed breastfeeding mothers so malnourished that their milk dried up and their babies died; blind women searching on their hands and knees for grass seeds to eat; children with scurvy bleeding from their mouths. 'Read this and see if you're still proud to be an Australian,' commanded the Melbourne *Mercury* above a report of the film's contents. 'If you're not, do something about it.'

Many did. A popular Aboriginal rights movement took hold in the 1960s, echoing similar sentiments that were being voiced internationally: the civil rights movement in the US, where Martin Luther King had a dream in 1963, and the introduction of the Race Relations Act in the UK in 1965, which outlawed discrimination for the first time. State by state, Aboriginal residents won the right to vote, the final one being Queensland in 1965, and in 1967 a national referendum over the removal of two discriminatory references to Aboriginal people in the Australian constitution was held, and passed with more than 90 per cent of the vote. For the first time, Aboriginal residents were included in the Australian census.

In Gippsland, the Lake Tyers campaign formed a key element in the burgeoning Aboriginal rights movement. When, in July 1971, the governor of Victoria finally handed over the deeds to the reserve to ninety-one shareholders, consisting of current and past Lake Tyers residents, it was the first time in Australian history that unconditional freehold title had been awarded to Aborigines. 'I express my sincere wish that history will record that today was a turning point in Aboriginal affairs,' the governor told a jubilant audience of seven hundred.

It appeared to make for a happy ending to a horrid story. But unfortunately there has been no happily ever after.

In 2005 the Victorian government took control of the trust, and sacked the entire management board. An administrator from the consultancy Deloitte was appointed and given wide-ranging powers and financial control of the trust. The shareholders were up in arms: 'Our elders fought for the land so that Aboriginal people at Lake Tyers could live without government control of our lives,' resident Leanne Edwards said six years later, during a blockade of the reserve's entrance. 'We now are in 2011 and [we continue to be] dictated to by a government whose policies on us have once again failed.'

I read about this with a sinking heart. 'Taking charge' of an Aboriginal group's welfare had ominous overtones of the earliest protectors and do-gooders – Angus McMillan among them, in his latter years – whose misguided 'help' had caused so much harm.

I had made an appointment to visit the trust, to see for myself, and the boys had decided to accompany me. Steve too doubted the government's motives – more white-man meddling, he suspected. I was pleased to have the company. I'd been advised not to go there alone, although now that I walked through the bright little seaside village such warnings seemed outlandish, perhaps even racist.

An hour in the office of the executive officer Leonie Cameron was enough to shatter my optimism. 'When the administration began in 2005, the trust had lost its way,' she told us. 'Things had gotten truly desperate. Drug and alcohol abuse, domestic violence and child abuse were all rampant. There were no working toilets, or sinks that drained. Children weren't going to school. Health workers said they were too scared to come here any more.' Later I would meet a former employee of the trust who confirmed Leonie's account. Doctors and nurses were threatened, he said. Rocks were thrown at social workers' cars. The 'creepiest, crawliest' paedophiles were allowed to stay on, unchallenged.

Leonie sighed. 'One of the problems was that, as it was private land, owned by shareholders, well – governments don't really step in to privately owned businesses, unless they're invited to.' The state felt unable to do anything, until a group of female elders – 'four old aunties' – appeared in Melbourne seeking help. They said they were scared to live at Lake Tyers.

The complaint amounted to an invitation to the government to intervene, Leonie said. A ten-year 'community renewal partnership' was announced, essentially a takeover accompanied by an influx of state investment. Hence the fresh paint, the newly dug sewers, the flashy public buildings. Despite the protests, 'the best thing that could have happened was to go under administration', she said. And though the ten years were almost up, the community showed no signs of being able to take back the reins. No one wanted to lead and take difficult decisions, because of the threat of violence and the repercussions on their family.

For these reasons, Leonie said, the way forward was unclear. 'Though the place has changed a lot, it's largely in terms of infrastructure. People don't change their ways so readily. Here they've been in survival mode for so long, they've learned to survive by force.'

We stood to soberly shake hands, then wandered aimlessly back through the township, whose tranquillity now seemed sterile and unreal. Steve was quiet. His indignation had leached away over the course of an hour, leaving him deep in thought. The church where Bulmer preached God's word had been left open, and we browsed the aisle. It had a clean, Spartan air. Stained glass filled the back wall; faint chalk graffiti in the font. High to my left, in a heavy wooden frame, a prayer of healing:

In Search of Elders

We live in faith that all people
will rise from the depths of despair and
hopelessness.

*

The information boards at the Gippsland and East Gippsland Aboriginal Co-Operative in Bairnsdale were an education. There were adverts for pre-employment courses, breakfast clubs and playgroups; factsheets explaining the functions of the dedicated Koorie Justice Unit and Aboriginal Medical Service; details of phone lines for Aboriginal gambling addicts and victims of domestic abuse. A poster offered help to those of the stolen generations still searching for their families ('Free call 1800 OUR MOB'). A brochure promoted Dreamtime Coffins (bark-effect or spot-painted) for 'culturally appropriate send offs'. Above it a bumper sticker pasted to the frame read 'Family violence is not part of our culture'. Stacks of leaflets offered medical advice written in simplified English: 'Hep C is a disease that will make the liver sick.'

'Hello?'

I looked up. Peter Ryan, the chief executive, stepped out to greet me with a firm handshake. He was white, tall, with closely cropped grey hair and dressed casually in a blue cotton shirt. He had an honest manner, friendly but forthright. 'So, what do you want to know?'

'I'm writing about Angus McMillan and the "Black War",' I said. 'So I suppose I'm interested in the longer-term consequences of all that, the state of the Gunai people today.'

'Ah,' he said, airily, motioning me to follow him through the carpark towards the museum. 'They're in a

273

pretty rough shape. They won't mind me saying that.' As if to demonstrate his point, a battered car was parked haphazardly nearby, its windows down as far as they would go. An Aboriginal man sprawled in the front seat, almost horizontal, snoring loudly.

I felt slightly crestfallen. From what I'd heard, the isolated Lake Tyers 'mob' and the rest of the Aboriginal community in Gippsland lived quite separate existences. I had hoped to find a brighter picture among the more 'integrated' population of the cities. We took our seats in a meeting room in which a dozen photo-portraits of prominent elders glared balefully down at us. An office chair in the corner wore a possum-skin cloak, which my fingers yearned to stroke.

Peter spoke of a fractured community, one not short of people keen to improve the situation, but hampered by intergenerational rivalries, poor health and a lack of education. 'It's a hard job, this. It has so many heartbreaking aspects.' He interviewed everyone who came to work there, he said, to check that they were tough enough to handle it. Many who want to work in Aboriginal affairs do so because they think it will be rewarding. They think they will be thanked for their efforts. But it's not always so straightforward. Prejudice goes both ways; many of those they work with are suspicious of their methods and motivation.

A few weeks earlier, Peter had made a controversial decision to sack a prominent member of staff after a nasty scene outside working hours. I'd heard about it on the grapevine: drunk, disorderly, police in attendance, allegations of domestic violence. 'Some people said, "You know, it's different here. It's a cultural issue." But we can't ...'

He sighed. 'It put me in a difficult position. I'll always be the white chief executive who sacked a black officer.'

Locally, there is still a deep divide between the white and black communities. Bairnsdale has an Aboriginal population of around 4 per cent of the total, slightly higher than the national average. Generally they are young, with a median age of only nineteen compared to forty-three in the non-indigenous population, and poor, with a weekly income just two-thirds the white average. Relations with the police are shaky: in 2011, booze-fuelled violence prompted officers to order a blanket ban on selling alcohol to Aboriginal residents, raising the spectre of the notorious race-based 'interventions' of the Northern Territory. GEGAC filed a complaint to the Australian Human Rights Commission; police chiefs later blamed the controversy on a 'miscommunication'.

In many ways, the rift in Bairnsdale reflects the situation nationally. Racism is endemic in Australia; indeed, it is written into the country's DNA. Not only was the nation formed as a settler colony – white pitched against black in a desperate battle of attrition – but immigration legislation written at the time of Federation in 1901 was explicitly aimed at maintaining an overwhelming proportion of whites to ethnic minorities (the 'White Australia' policy, which made immigration from Asia or the Pacific Islands extremely difficult). Such policies were dismantled during the 1960s and 70s, but the underlying attitudes are still remarkably widespread; not only anti-immigrant, but anti-Aboriginal too.

In 2013 the *Sydney Morning Herald* posed the question 'Are you a casual racist?' to its readers. Of more than 11,000 respondents, 64 per cent admitted that the answer was yes. Of those, the majority answered bluntly: 'Yes, but I'm not going to change.'

To those on the receiving end, this amounts to an extraordinarily high incidence of race-related incidents. A 2012 survey of Aboriginal people in Victoria found that 97 per cent of respondents had been targets of verbal or physical abuse, or discrimination, over the previous year. Eighty-four per cent said they had been verbally abused, 67 per cent had been spat at or had objects thrown at them, 66 per cent told that they 'did not belong' in their home towns. Seventy per cent had suffered eight or more such attacks over that period.

But it's one thing to know that there's a problem. Another thing entirely to know how to solve it.

10

Reconciliation

Driving down from the Monaro south towards the coast we had travelled for a while through the ancient temperate rainforest of Errinundra, where stands of sassafras and black olive berry crowded together, overlooked by shining gums whose great, buttressed girths jutted from the canopy like the calves of giants. We stopped to walk amongst them, dwarfed in both scale and age, diminished by all that they had been alive to witness.

It was here that Steve showed me the smoking ceremony. It is an ancient custom, in which the perfumed smoke from native plants is used to cleanse an area, to ward off bad spirits. Traditionally the ceremonies mark major events, such as a significant death. In recent years they have been used to mark new public ventures. The Boon Wurrung and Woi Wurrung people were asked to perform such a ceremony at the site of the Melbourne Museum before it was built, so as to heal a troubled land. This was described as 'a historic step in recognising the desecration of spiritual, practical and cultural bonds with the land that occurred during invasion'.

Steve cut a section of bark about the size of an A4 sheet of paper from a gum tree, using his axe blade in a smooth movement to peel away the dry outer layers, leaving a perfect rectangle of pale new flesh on the trunk. I reached up to touch it, felt it soft and naked and slightly damp beneath my hand. This sheet became a tray, into which he shaved curls of wood in a small pile for tinder, then piled a few tiny sticks from the forest floor on top. It caught light easily enough, sending a thin line of smoke up through the branches above our heads. Immediately he smothered the flame, dropping a handful of the samphire-like leaves of the cherry ballart, a type of sandalwood, on it. They began to smoulder and steam, turning the elegant cigarillo whorl into a medicinal cloud. I shut my eyes. Breathed in. Solemnly he brought the bark sheet up to my chest, allowing the smoke to drift across my face on the lethargic breeze.

I imagined myself cleansed, loosing my layers of insincerity to let the smoke in underneath, exposing the least attractive parts of me to the air so they might be disinfected. I recalled a Gunai song that Alfred Howitt had recorded, a charm for driving away pain and bad magic. It was brought to the elder Tulaba by his late father in a dream, a 'curious tune' sung with extraordinary energy, the final syllable exploding from his mouth like the shot of a cannon:

Minyan – būlūn – ma naranke
Show – belly – moon to

'Show your belly to the moon.' This had struck a chord with me; perhaps it was a command that had been meant literally, but I heard it as a directive that one must display one's softest, most vulnerable parts, like a cat rolling over to show its tummy, ecstatic and terrified all at once, in order to be healed.

Steve demonstrates the smoking ceremony in the shade of a shining gum.

I felt a flush of envy, too – of those whose dreams were full of messages from the land beyond the clouds, from their dead elders. Healing charms, great truths. All my dreams seemed to consist of was adrenaline and recycled scraps from the wastepaper basket in my mind. All these gory re-enactments, the switching of perspectives. They were haunting me now, recurring, sometimes overlapping, sometimes overlaid upon other, more mundane reveries. These were no semaphores from the afterlife, I knew. Only the byproduct of my growing, waking preoccupation.

Still, I thought, now I knew how it felt to kill a man, or be killed by one. Maybe that was message enough.

'That should do it,' said Steve finally. 'Have to be careful. There might be a fire ban on. We can't let it actually catch light.'

Reluctantly we headed back towards the low country. But on the way we were struck by an idea: a ceremony of cleansing at the site of the worst massacre. To clear the air, clear the earth. A gesture of forgiveness, of reconciliation, that would mark the past with a full stop, ready for a new sentence to begin. We would organise it, invite all the elders, have speeches, make a day of it.

I called Libby to organise a return trip to the Warrigal Creek homestead, and we drove down with our proposal at the ready. I assumed that she would be excited, but to my surprise she seemed reluctant. Similar ventures had been floated before, she said. But not everyone in the community was ready to forgive. We needed to wait until everyone was united, or we would risk offending afresh.

When I introduced her to Steve, she said to him, 'Did you know your Pop has been out here?' She meant his grandfather, Uncle Albert.

'Oh? No.'

'Well, we've been batting ideas back and forth a long time. I really don't want to derail anything by rushing in. Things have to be done when the elders decide they are ready, I think.'

We were all disappointed, but we understood what she was saying. I felt young and rash, as if we were three cubs being gently batted away. You couldn't just smoke the pain away, I supposed. These things take time. The ceremony would one day be a symbol of the healing that has taken place, rather than itself the source of healing.

'Hey,' said Steve suddenly, rising from the table and wandering through to the next room to stare up at a framed print on the wall. 'I designed that!' It was the logo he'd drawn for the Gunaikurnai land rights movement spearheaded by his grandfather.

Libby followed him through, and took an ornate carved boomerang out of a cupboard. 'Recognise this?'

He smiled at it, then at her. 'Pop's work?' He turned it over, found the signature on the back. She smiled in return.

They hit it off. Libby was a charming hostess, interested in what we all had to say, deferring to Steve's knowledge of local Aboriginal politics. And both Steve and Cam were just as seduced by the beauty of the homestead as I had been. They cooed over the pressed tin ceiling, the hand-painted tiles, the rippling glass in the original Victorian windowpanes.

After tea, the boys and I walked out to the massacre site, and I watched Steve and Cam do the same mental restaging I had done, eyes flitting between strategic points, gauging the steepness of the banks.

'They're at the bottom of the waterhole. I can feel it.' Steve was certain. He stood on the bank, peering through the thick undergrowth into the pool beyond. Three pelicans paddled in leisurely circles, scooping their beaks through the water almost as an afterthought, Austen-era women trailing their hands from rowing boats.

'Saying that,' he continued, 'it doesn't feel so terrible, you know. I wasn't sure that I'd be able to come. Many people wouldn't. But it doesn't feel like there's anything malevolent still lurking here.'

Libby was waiting for us when we got back to the house, ready to take us out in the ute to some other spots named in Peter Gardner's book. First Gammon Creek, the site of one of the possible follow-up massacres, in the bend of another river marking the edge of an enormous field. We clambered out to stand on the bank in the fading light, the skyscape stretching before us painted in incredible colours, dip-dyed along its length the same blazing orange of the sun as, above, raspberry faded to lilac, streaked through with ripples of indigo cloud.

An agricultural track took us back to the coast behind the dunes to Freshwater Creek, another alleged site, and past Red Hill, a sandy hummock where the massacred bodies were said to have been carted down in their dray-loads, burned, then crudely buried. Somewhere around here, a local schoolteacher and his friend stumbled over a cache of human remains in 1912. 'With our hands we scraped away the sand,' he wrote, 'and an inch or two below the surface discovered a quantity of human bones and skulls of men, women and children, even to very young children, all intermixed.'

But the bleakness I'd felt last time I'd come to this stretch of beach had washed away with the tide. In the gloaming, everything was beautiful. The waves sighed as they caressed the sand, keeping time, taking the pulse of the land.

We stood for a while in the cool salt air, not speaking much, then drove slowly back along the track to the house. Grey kangaroos, dozens of them, sprang out of the scrub away from the car and leapt ahead of us in the headlights. They were unsettlingly human: similar size, similar in expression. We found ourselves among them, travelling at the same speed, as if we were one of a crowd, all of us on our way to the same place.

I wanted to meet Uncle Albert Mullett for myself. I'd heard so much about him. He was a man with many strings to his bow: activist, cultural authority, government adviser, master craftsman, respected Gunai elder. Everyone I had spoken to so far had, at some point in our conversation, asked if I'd met him. 'You must,' they told me. 'He has such a wealth of knowledge.'

Still, Steve was reluctant to take me to see him. Uncle Albert was an old man now. He'd been unwell, I was given to understand. A heart attack several years previously had had a serious impact on his health, and these days he rarely left the house. Aunty Rachel, his wife and Steve's grandmother, had been acting the bouncer since he had taken ill, turning away the many who, like me, wanted an audience with the man himself.

But just as I'd given up hope, Steve relented and we stopped off at the pretty bungalow in Buchan where his grandparents were living out their retirement, clutching a box of cream cakes as an offering.

Aunty Rachel answered the door with a guarded expression. She was a slim, tan-skinned woman of around eighty, with long silver hair swept into a ponytail. 'I didn't know you were coming,' she chided Steve. He looked uncomfortable, and muttered something that sounded like an apology. She nodded at Cam, eyed me, then relented. 'All right,' she said, reluctantly accepting the box. 'But not long.'

Albert was born in 1933, as government attempts to force Aboriginal people to assimilate were intensifying, and lived much of his early life on the fringes of white society. His mother lived a transient lifestyle, moving between relationships, so he grew up under the care of his aunt and grandparents. The family were ejected from the Lake Tyers mission station when Albert was an infant, so they lived for a period on an island on the lake, making clandestine visits to friends who remained there, before moving on to temporary sites on riverbanks, near rubbish dumps, and at Jackson's Track, an unofficial camp that had sprung up by the sawmill at Drouin.

Albert left home at thirteen for a succession of seasonal jobs, later marrying his childhood sweetheart Rachel, a girl of Gunai-Ngarico descent, and settling in Bairnsdale, where they brought up their eight children. He became a well-known and very effective firebrand and activist, fighting for the recognition of Aboriginal rights and the preservation of Gunai culture. Among other things, he helped establish the 'keeping place' museum and archive I'd visited in Bairnsdale, and campaigned for fifteen years to have his people's right to the ownership of their traditional lands recognised. In 2013 he was inducted to the Indigenous Honour Roll of Victoria.

We found him propped up at the kitchen table watching television. I was taken aback by how much he'd aged since the last picture I'd seen of him, dated only a year or two previously. But his eyes were bright, and he was neatly dressed. A single bed had been pushed into the corner of the room, and adorned with cushions like a sofa.

At first I wasn't sure that he had noticed I was there. I smiled, as his eyes flickered away from the game show on the television to greet Steve and Cam and then returned to the screen. The volume was very loud. After a minute,

Aunty Rachel stepped forward and switched the set off. In the silence, Steve introduced me, and explained what we'd been doing. We'd been on a road trip, he said, of historical sites. I was a relative of Angus McMillan, visiting Australia to find out about his legacy.

Interest flickered in Uncle Albert's eyes, and he turned to look at me properly. 'McMillan?' he said. I nodded. He said something indistinct.

Aunty Rachel spoke from behind him. 'He said: "He was a butcher."'

'Oh!' I said, a bit taken aback. Then I turned back to him. 'Yes. He was, yes.'

He nodded once in approval. He might have been a frail man, but the anger was still raw. The inequalities devised by Angus McMillan's generation had still been very much in evidence during Uncle Albert's lifetime. Until the 1960s, he said, Aboriginal people had counted only as 'animals, vegetables or minerals' in Australian society. Haltingly, he recalled episodes from his earlier years when he and his family suffered from discrimination.

When he was a baby, two of his six brothers had been forcibly taken by the authorities and placed into care. He never saw them again. At school, white children had taunted them, told them they smelled – but, he added, raising his fists and weakly paddling the air, 'I gave them an education, all right.'

His speech was faltering, occasionally inaudible, and Rachel would interject to make his meaning clear. I craned to hear him, nodding to show that I had understood. Later, I watched an interview with him from some years previously, when he had been able to speak more clearly. In shops, he said, Aboriginal people wouldn't be served until last. In cinemas, attendants would force them to sit at the front. 'They ran us down like shit. Treated us like we weren't even human beings.'

He and Aunty Rachel had lived hand to mouth for many years, working every waking hour: in the sawmills, in the hayfields, bean-picking, at truckstops, in restaurants, at a hostel for Koorie children. And in the few scraps of free time they had, they campaigned for the rights of their people. When Gunai native title was recognised, Uncle Albert had fulfilled a lifetime's ambition.

I felt childlike and humbled, for the second time in only a few days. To me, and to Steve too, in many ways, reconciliation was simply a concept for discussion. But to Uncle Albert it had been his life's work. I wanted to beg for his forgiveness, on behalf of my relative, but what did he care for my second-hand guilt? All his life he had looked for solutions and action, not handwringing.

I knew that for me, struggling with a sense of shame that was not truly mine, action was only a small part of what I was searching for. But what use was that to anyone? Libby and I, I thought, and all those other uneasy descendants, were looking for an exoneration that will never come.

A few months after we met, Uncle Albert Mullett passed away, aged eighty-one. More than two thousand mourners gathered to pay their respects at his funeral, accompanied by a farewell smoking ceremony and the sound of the bullroarer, at the Knob Reserve near Stratford. I feel privileged to have met him.

*

So what can be done? If the past cannot be undone, and the wrongs never truly forgiven, what can be made right?

In recent decades there has been a rush of initiatives aimed at preserving and promoting Aboriginal culture, and raising awareness of the events of the past. Funding for Koorie art and oral-history projects has come in a flood, while the Australian government and academics have made ever greater efforts to ensure that Aboriginal viewpoints and experiences are represented. Strict laws have been enacted to protect and conserve archaeological sites, rather than simply allowing construction companies to build over them, by which so many have already been destroyed.

In 2008, Prime Minister Kevin Rudd made a national apology to Aboriginal Australians for the stolen generations. In his speech, Rudd repeated the phrase 'I am sorry' three times – on behalf of himself, the government and the parliament. The Melbourne *Age* reported that after he did so, 'there was, quite audibly, the exhalation of breath. That same release – the hope of an expulsion, really, of a national burden – could be felt across the country.'

Aboriginal ownership of the land has become far more explicitly accepted and proclaimed. Signs in public spaces now specify the land's traditional owners: in Gippsland, they pay tribute to the Gunaikurnai. Such tributes can also be found in the prologue to the text of many state and other official documents, while at public meetings or events a local elder often gives a short speech or performs a ceremony to open proceedings.

I stumbled upon this convention at an event at a local theatre near Drouin. At the start, without explanation, an Aboriginal woman took to the stage to give thanks to her ancestors and beseech them to welcome this roomful of white, middle-class retirees to the auditorium. I was bemused; even more so when Jeannie waved the woman over to a seat by us, only to be politely rebuffed. 'Sorry – can't!' she responded in a stage whisper. 'Got two more of these to give tonight!' To my eye it appeared tokenistic, but Aboriginal people I later spoke to disagreed. Finally, they said, their existence, their historic claim to the ownership of the lands was being acknowledged. Whatever form that took, it was an important step.

The Aboriginal claim to the land was acknowledged in a more concrete way through the advent of native-title legislation, an avenue of law that has sprung up since the landmark Mabo ruling in 1992, which struck down the colonial doctrine of *terra nullius*, thus undermining the entire basis of the Crown's claim to the Australian continent. Since then, Aboriginal groups that have been able to demonstrate an unbroken connection to their homelands since colonisation can lodge a claim with the federal court to have their status as traditional landowners recognised.

Uncle Albert Mullett spearheaded the native-title claim in Gippsland on behalf of the united 'Gunaikurnai' people, with the assistance of, among others, a younger Gunai man called Barry Kenny. They succeeded in 2010, becoming recognised as the traditional owners of almost 8,500 square miles of Gippsland, nearly a fifth of all the state of Victoria's Crown land. They were also awarded a $12 million settlement and joint control of ten national parks and reserves in the area, including the Knob Reserve and the temperate rainforest of Terra Bulga.

The land secured in this settlement is now managed via a statutory body called the Gippsland Land and Waters Aboriginal Corporation (GLaWAC), headed up by Barry

Kenny and based in Bairnsdale. I finally found its offices, in an unprepossessing glass-fronted building on MacLeod Street, an industrial thoroughfare full of paint and hardware stores. A crowd of Aboriginal men in matching shirts hung around the back of the building, loading tools into shiny four-wheel drives – the cultural rangers now employed to work alongside their government counterparts in the parks. Inside it was clean and corporate, maps of the area successfully claimed blown up huge on the walls. Stacks of newsletters were full of instructions for how those of Gunaikurnai origin could make the most of their new rights, by applying for free fishing permits and so on.

Barry sat down with me in a boardroom to talk me through the corporation's function. He saw GLaWAC not only as symbolic recognition of his people's history, but as a major opportunity to bring employment and income to a community that badly needs both. As native-title holder, the corporation has the power to oversee the exploitation of natural resources in the area; negotiations with mining companies, such as an iron-extraction group, have resulted in 'significant' income for a foundation that is used to pay for scholarships, educational equipment and funeral costs for community members.

It is relatively rare for such a body to be run by a member of the group it represents, Barry said. 'It's a difficult job. Everyone has a different opinion on every decision we have to make, and that can be hard when you know everyone socially.' This development in his career had taken him somewhat by surprise – as a young man he had, like many Gunai men, found employment as a labourer, picking beans and later working in sawmills.

Uncle Albert had recruited him to the cause and acted as a mentor during the native-title process, and now he found himself unexpectedly at its head.

Around 650 of the three-thousand-strong Gunai population had opted to join the organisation so far. To do so they had to fill in a form that detailed their family tree back three generations, specified the clan they belonged to, and which of the 'apical ancestors' they descended from – a list of twenty-five individuals or couples who appear in every *bona fide* Gunai family's lineage. Anyone who can't trace their ancestry back to one of these individuals is not recognised as Gunai and may not join, even if their family has lived in the region for generations, as might be the case with families imported to the Gippsland missions from elsewhere in Australia.

'Who is your apical ancestor?'

'Well my father was Krowathunkooloong, and we descend from ...' He ran his finger down a tick-list. I read it over his shoulder, a collage of traditional and Christian monikers: Tommy Bumberrah. Bungil Narran. Old Darby Tar-loomba. Mary Tur-un-gook. King Tom Kee-lum-bedin. James Scott. William McDougall. Jimmy. '... This man, George Thomas. He was one of two survivors of a massacre in the Lake Tyers area. He and another boy hid under a log. After they were found they were brought up on the Lake Tyers mission.'

I swallowed. Putting names to the victims of the massacres was a new development, and an uncomfortable one. It was in a different register from what I'd felt reading my history books, where the dead were rarely definitively identified and their numbers were debated, lending their accounts an airy, hypothetical aspect. In this way it had been possible for me to amass a vast amount of information, facts, figures, details, while still keeping a sort of intellectual distance from a lot of it. The questions I'd found myself considering! Like: How many deaths does it take to count as a massacre? (Six or more, apparently.) Or: Would it be better or worse to die in your sleep? (Better, probably.) But now I felt like a pathologist who, on rolling over a body, recognises its features as those of a friend.

I asked Barry whether, given his family story, he had any hesitation in dealing with the government and the wider white population, or in working at the coalface of the reconciliation process.

He pulled a conflicted face. 'Well,' he said, thinking aloud. 'A lot of our mob wouldn't do this job. They don't like white people, call 'em *gubbahs*. Just say, "They took our land," or "They killed our people," and keep themselves very separate. But I don't think that attitude helps. We got a bit of distance now. It wasn't you, and it wasn't me. Plus, you know, a lot of people don't know what really happened, with the massacres and the missions and everything. So we run cultural awareness courses for companies and government departments where we lay it all out.' A few years previously, he said, he had been helping to run one of these courses when one attendee, a girl from a prominent local farming family, had stood up partway through and simply walked out. Barry had followed her, irritated, only to find her in tears outside the front of the building.

'I'm so embarrassed. My family did that,' she told him, sobbing. 'It's too awful.'

He told her she didn't know that, not for sure, but she shook her head. 'Yes,' she said. 'I do.'

Seeing the tears streaming from her eyes, her trembling lips, her blotchy face, Barry had felt only compassion. 'Well,' he told her, 'you can't take it back.'

'It's quite something to meet a descendant.' Ricky Mullett, a cultural officer from GLaWAC, had come to meet me on his lunchbreak.

I shook the proffered hand, laughed to cover up my sudden rush of awkwardness. 'Great-great-great niece, actually. Not a direct descendant.'

There was a short pause while he seemed to be deciding whether or not to laugh. Then he led me across to a café, where he bought me lunch in a courtyard under trailing vines.

'I should really be buying you lunch,' I said, 'for taking time to meet me.'

His gaze crossed mine like a sword. 'You're a guest in my country. We, the Gunai people, are your hosts.'

'Thank you,' I said. 'But it's a strange situation.'

He inclined his head. 'Yes. Well. I don't really like to talk about any of this any more. I've had enough of it. But you did keep calling, and ... I believe in what you're doing. I think it's important.'

'Thank you,' I said again.

'This trip must have been confronting for you.'

Confronting: an adjective, not a verb. A word Australians use when discussing anything that deals with unsettling – often race-related – issues head-on. Modern art, human-rights reports, documentaries investigating Aboriginal health, that sort of thing. Issues that are easier to brush under the rug. It has a directness to it that I like.

'Confronting ... Yes, it's been that, I suppose.'

Too flippant. He looked at me a little oddly. 'You know what happened? That your ancestor and his men slaughtered my people? I say "slaughtered" on purpose, because that's what they did.'

I nodded mutely.

'You know the stories? You know that the official death toll is only a fraction of the true total? It was inhuman, what they did to my people. Killed them. Massacred them. Tortured them. Raped them. Murdered them. Your relative ... he decimated my people. And he got away with it.'

His eyes were shining. I felt him watching me for a response, but I didn't have one. I just nodded to show that I understood, agreed, didn't intend to argue the point. Sunlight streamed cleanly between the vine leaves, dappling his face and the table. A waitress stopped by to deliver him his milkshake, bringing a touch of the banal to the intense negotiations we seemed to be thrashing out.

'Now,' he continued, relenting, 'I don't hold any personal grudge against you or your family.'

'Why not?'

'Why?'

I blew out my cheeks. 'Don't we owe you something?'

'Owe what? Who's "we"?'

'I don't know, and I don't know. Me? The Australian descendants? More land? Private land? Land that's still in the hands of the old squatting families? Rule their original claims invalid?'

He shook his head, shutting his eyes as he did so. I already knew why. Native-title legislation was divisive enough when only Crown land was handed over, and in limited form. The process was still misunderstood by many landowners, who hung back from reporting archaeological finds for fear that their land might be taken away as a result. Striking down property deeds would cause outrage that could undo all the good work done in recent years to repair relations.

'Then what more can be done? How can it be fixed?'

There didn't seem to be an answer.

I kept on. 'How about efforts to reconcile within the community? I heard that there are groups that ...'

'"Reconciliation,"' he scoffed. 'It's just a political watchword. "Reconciliation" is a myth. The only reconciliation I believe in happens one on one. That's what we're doing now.' He gestured to the table, hands opening gracefully, conductor to orchestra.

'Which is?'

'Speaking to each other on a level. One on one. And this – me and you, sitting together at a table – this is very symbolic. Isn't it?'

I said I guessed it was. I didn't feel like a representative of my culture, meeting a representative of his in a great gesture of regret and forgiveness. I didn't feel qualified for that. I just felt like one of two people eating lunch together in a deli in Bairnsdale, on our second round of drinks. But maybe that was the point.

We sat talking in the courtyard for three hours. We discussed what I'd learned, the experiences he'd had, the problems that seemed so intractable, the past that seemed so irreversible. We got on. When Ricky asked me to name all the places I'd visited during my research, he seemed almost disappointed that he couldn't now show them to me himself. But there were a few lesser-known spots, he said, that I should visit.

On the way out, we stopped to pay the bill. Ricky knew the waitress well, and paused to introduce me. 'This is Cal Flyn,' he announced. 'Her great-great-great uncle, her *apical ancestor*, was Angus McMillan.'

'Ah yeah?' She smiled at me encouragingly.

'Her relative was responsible for the deaths of hundreds of my people, the Gunaikurnai people. She's come here all the way across the world, at great cost and personal discomfort. And emotional discomfort.'

The waitress nodded, smile fixed in place, not sure what the correct response was.

'Tomorrow we're going to go on a tour of massacre sites together.'

There was a pause. I wanted to make a joke to take the pressure off, but I managed to contain myself. Flippant, I rebuked myself. Don't be flippant.

'Well,' she said finally. 'You enjoy that. Bye now, Ricky. Bye, Carole.'

That night I thought about inherited guilt, about debts that transcend generations and cannot be repaid.

They have a word for it in Germany: *Erbschuld*. It is a particularly salient concept there, where the postwar generations have been forced to confront uncomfortable truths about their parents' or grandparents' role within the Nazi regime. The discomfort manifests itself in different ways; in the more extreme cases, such as of the offspring of former SS guards, there are children who have cut themselves off completely from their parents to make a 'fresh start' – for his 1987 book *Born Guilty: Children of Nazi Families*, Peter Sichrovsky interviewed a couple who had refused to invite their own parents to their wedding. Others choose to reimagine the past in more palatable form. As Dirk Moses has written, 'The imperative to insulate the family unit from the Nazi contamination is so strong [that] grandchildren imagine their grandparents as resisters or anti-Nazis despite evidence to the contrary.'

It is a theme dealt with in Bernhard Schlink's novel *The Reader*, which centres upon a young man who discovers that his former lover, an enigmatic older woman, is guilty of appalling war crimes. As well as an examination of an obsessive, cross-generational romance, the book serves as a parable for the postwar generation who, despite their youthful innocence, found themselves tarnished by association with their parents' generation. As Michael, the protagonist, reflects: 'The pain I went through because of my love for Hanna was, in a way, the fate of my generation, a German fate.'

Erbschuld is an abstract concept, but it is not a novel one, not for anyone who has had even the most cursory of Sunday school educations. It is also the term for the Christian concept of 'original sin', of the eating of the forbidden fruit by Adam and Eve, and the corruption of all subsequent generations.

Wherefore, as by one man sin entered into the
world, and death by sin; and so death passed upon
all men, for that all have sinned (Romans XV:12)

The Pentecostal Church's version is more elaborate, holding that sin is passed through blood down the generations. This belief is based on passages in scripture that refer to 'punishing the children for the sin of the parents to the third and fourth generation'. The principle is used to account for the apparent transmission of problems like alcoholism, depression or cancer between members of a family. To break these 'generational curses', believers are encouraged to create lists of all the sins of their ancestors for up to four generations, so they can confess to them on their relatives' behalf, and thus break free.

The state of North Korea takes a similarly literal approach to the idea of familial guilt, arresting the relatives of criminals and punishing them together or in the offender's place. One former prisoner, interviewed in 2011 after she had fled the country, told Reuters she had been detained at the age of thirteen, after her grandfather escaped to South Korea, and spent the next three decades in a notorious labour camp, where hangings and firing squads were commonplace.

These examples are extreme ones, of course, and few people subscribe to them. But the truth is that the notion of inherited guilt has no small amount of traction. What are national apologies, for instance, but admissions of a collective – if not inherited, precisely – guilt that continues generations later to stew? If this concept did not make a certain intuitive sense, their value would be very slight. Yet in 2008, as Kevin Rudd stood in the House of Representatives to make his apology to the Aboriginal people, many reported experiencing a profound sense of relief, of a 'weight' dropping away, or the dawning of a new sense of closure. My own trip to Australia, grounded in similar reasoning, seemed to appeal to my interviewees' senses of circularity.

The Gunai believe that the offences of an individual can bring a curse upon his relations, Ricky told me. Breaking the laws of the community – he gave the example of disobeying one's elders – is thought to bring bad fortune upon the family, over many years and in unpredictable ways.

'So,' I hazarded, 'although you say that you don't hate me, or the descendants of Angus McMillan, you do to some extent believe that we have been punished? That the entire family has been or will be forced to pay for his sins?'

He pursed his lips, nodded. 'Don't you think so? Has your family been afflicted with bad luck?'

I thought about it. 'Not really. Not my close family, anyway. Touch wood.'

'You're superstitious.'

I laughed. 'No, not really. Are you?'

'Yes.' He didn't elaborate.

'I've always thought that if you don't believe in it, it can't affect you. Sort of like the opposite of the placebo effect.'

I could tell he didn't agree with me, but he didn't argue the point. I was telling the truth, though: I'm not superstitious. I studied statistics for three years as part of my degree, and had drilled into me the folly of attaching significance to coincidence, of assuming causality where there is only correlation. Plus, I've been very fortunate in life, despite my lack of credence.

Angus McMillan's immediate family was not so lucky, I would later discover. His wife and children would be visited by tragedy again and again, decades after he had passed away.

After his death, Christina had a terrible time raising the children on no income – the pension promised to her by the government was never paid – and eventually became afflicted by a 'painful melancholia' that unhinged her mind. She was fixated by the idea of throwing herself into the river, twice attempting it, but finding, as she expressed it, that 'a hand seemed to draw her back'. Finally she disappeared, and her body was found face-down in the water.

The elder son, Ewen, grew up to become a capable bushman, but in 1926 he was 'burnt beyond recognition' while clearing a gorge of brambles. He survived despite 'being burned internally' and his limbs 'burnt to the bone', but died five years later, leaving only his younger brother Angus, who according to his obituary 'did not inherit the resource or enterprise of his father'. He 'lacked initiative', it continued, and had been 'mutually dominated by his brother'. After Ewen's death he turned to gold-prospecting, which he 'pursued without success for the remainder of his life', dying in 1936 after a long illness.

I didn't know any of that then. Still, I would have said, that doesn't prove anything.

Box's Creek is a small, sheltered inlet that cuts into the hillside behind a limestone bluff on the edge of Lake King. It is deep, picturesque, shielded from even the wildest of the winds that roar in off Bass Strait, and so it has become a firm favourite among the yachties who frequent the upmarket seaside village of Metung.

The owners of the cabins, whose roofs nudge up through the tea trees, live there for only a few weeks per year. When in residence they sit out on their verandahs of an evening to watch their neighbours pottering on the private jetty below, or turn instead to look out along the sweep of Bancroft Bay. It's a beautiful spot. Although it is debatable, perhaps, whether it would be quite so popular as a holiday destination had it retained its original name, Butcher's Creek.

'Can you see it?'

I aligned my gaze with Ricky's outstretched finger. 'Yes, I think so.'

'McMillan's men chased them all the way from Bushy Park, trapped them up on that bluff, and shot them down into the water. Crowds of them.'

Before European settlement, Gunai legend held that the creek was haunted by malevolent spirits, dead men who refused to stay dead. I suppose in Angus McMillan's time they must have believed it haunted too by the dozens of men shot down and killed there. Perhaps they were the same spirits, wandering, anchorless, through time.

'Are you all right with this?' Ricky studied my face, looking for shock or squeamishness. But I was only grim now, my teeth gritted, exhausted by the scale of it all. The endlessness of the horror that kept emerging from under every stone. I felt as if I'd been awake for a hundred years, my brain slowly turning over each thought one by one.

I recalled the words written by Henry Meyrick:

I remember the time when my blood would have
run cold at the mention of these things but now I
am become so familiarized with scenes of horror,
from having murder made a topic of everyday
conversation. I have heard tales told and some
things I have seen that would form as dark a page
as ever you read in the book of history.

Perhaps five hundred yards further along, just off the
main road, was Legend Rock, an enormous rust-coloured
meteorite that pokes from the shallows by the boardwalk.
Gunai mythology holds that it was one of three fishermen
who had eaten all their catch without sharing it with
their dogs; for their greed, the womenfolk had turned
them to stone. Two other rocks that completed the trio
had sat nearby, but construction workers destroyed both
in the 1960s to make way for the road we were driving
on.

Directly between the two sites, two perfect case studies
in the destruction of Aboriginal culture, was a luxury
holiday resort. Its name: McMillan's of Metung. Of course
it was. 'Relatives of yours!' Ricky crowed as we roared
past, en route to our next stop on the massacre mystery
tour.

'Tennis Court – Heated Pool – Private Marina – Spa',
read a sign out the front.

One more stop. The top of a red limestone cliff. Eagle
Point, it was called. The Mitchell River slid by sluggishly
below, at the bottom of a sheer drop, fat and lazy and
gathering the energy to empty itself into Lake King. We
stood close to the edge, peering through a wire fence
strung up to prevent suicides. The clifftop offered an

unparalleled vista of the Gippsland low country, stretching out before us, golden and rippling in the breeze, illuminated with the gold leaf of the evening sun.

'Beautiful!' I gasped.

'Beautiful country ... yes. But stained.'

I'd never even heard of this massacre, but the story had been passed down in Ricky's family. It was the worst one yet. Here, the fleeing Gunai were herded together like cattle and forced from the clifftop, he said. Men, women and children. Think of the hysteria, the crush, the desperation, as feet scrabbled for purchase and hands grasped for handholds. Men stood on the opposite bank of the river below, shooting any survivors. The bodies all washed out to sea.

'And I haven't told you everything. About how else they were killed. I don't think I want to tell you.'

(I left it, allowing him to decide what he wanted and didn't want to talk about. But he told me later, anyway, over dinner. We were eating pie and mash, I was dangling his ten-month-old grandson over my knee. 'They cut the men's genitals off to see how far they'd run,' he told me calmly, watching my face. 'Stabbed women through their vaginas to see how much they'd bleed. Buried babies up to their necks and kicked their heads off.' '*Dad*,' complained his son Pat. 'We are *eating*.')

'It was your people who did this. But of course, the same happened to them. It was in their make-up, in their past as a people. The same that's in *your* make-up, in your *mother's* make-up.'

I scowled, thinking, 'Don't bring my mother into this.' Although, I realised, I had done that myself already, in pursuing my great theory of intergenerational guilt. But

Ricky must have seen my rebellious expression, because he backtracked, trying to defuse the tension.

'Not that I have bad feeling towards you. Or your mother. We won't *forget*, but we don't bear a grudge.' A pause, before he wondered out loud, 'But what is *your* motivation for all this? What question are you hoping to answer?'

My thoughts had crystallised now. 'I suppose what I really want to do is to understand how a person can do these things. *Evil* things. Because Angus McMillan was not evil. I've read his diaries. He seems like a normal guy. A bit like me in many ways –'

Ricky raised his eyebrows disbelievingly.

'It's true! He talks about this girl he fancies, he misses home. He makes resolutions about how to be a better man, he takes pity on convicts. He's frustrated because his boss doesn't trust his judgement. He's just a normal guy. Even ... a *good guy*. Relatable.'

'So, if you think he's like you – and part of him is *in* you, in your blood – you want to understand what it would take to turn you into a mass murderer?'

There was a long pause. 'Yes,' I admitted.

He shook his head at my folly. 'You won't understand. You'll never understand.'

But I didn't believe him.

I was running out of money. I'd been staying with people I'd met during my travels, or wild camping when possible, to cut costs. Towards the end of my trip I found myself setting up home in a rather dated static caravan just off the freeway near Bairnsdale. It was the best I could stretch to.

But I was beginning to find my boxy, cramped cabin quite reassuring: the murmurs of the other residents sitting out on their little porches; the small, high, net-curtained window that looked out on the featureless side of the caravan next door; the false timber 'panelling' on the walls, the false slate 'tiling' of the floor; the high, square bed, with its counterpane printed to look like a patchwork quilt. The flimsiness of the lock on my screen doors, less so.

I am rarely concerned by loneliness, usually finding more than enough amusement in books and navel gazing, but travelling alone can generate other, more pressing anxieties. At night in my box I drew the net curtains tight across the glass doors and policed my modesty like a Victorian spinster pulling her skirts around her legs.

Once I sat up all night doing an assignment for a magazine back home, battling the time difference as I conducted interviews and responded to queries, in the hope that I could beg them to pay up quickly and keep me from the bottom of my overdraft for another week or two. Blinking tired eyes and boiling my little kettle yet again, I concocted batches of soupy espresso from free sachets of freeze-dried coffee as I tried to focus on the task in hand. Outside the cicadas were as sleepless as me, endlessly tuning up ahead of some glorious insect symphony.

Halfway through, with restless legs, I stood and strode out across the crispy grass to the enormous, institutional toilet block. It had bare brick walls and echoed like a gym hall. I chose a cubicle and locked the door before realising that the lights, set off by a motion sensor, had already been lit when I'd come in.

'Hello?'

No answer. I froze, listening for the other person hiding in the row of stalls, my senses sent haywire by caffeine and lack of sleep. There's someone here to hurt me, I thought, madly.

I pissed quietly, against the side of the bowl to lessen the noise, my ears pricked for the sounds of breathing in the next cubicle. Nothing.

That fear is something that has been drilled into me. There's a certain unwelcome attention that shadows young women travelling alone for any length of time. I had become practised at deflecting conversations with strangers after nightfall with bland smiles and judicious use of my mobile phone. At walking odd looping routes down straight roads while watching for followers. At clocking and logging any curious or unusual glances from unknown men in hotel lobbies. These are all within the normal skillset of the urban woman. Standard practice. They would not, of course, throw off any determined pursuer, but that's not really the point. They're just to make yourself feel you're doing something useful.

Usually I can divorce myself from the unformed, unhinged fears that lurk behind the news reports and the unspoken presumptions of self-defence classes; but sometimes, when my logical brain is too busy or too tired to keep it at bay, the fear takes hold. Every man's eye seems to follow me, like portraits in a gallery – the ubiquitous gaze. Every rustle in the night is a stranger listening at the door. These are childish fears of monsters under the bed, fleshed out by true crime stories and statistics. A state-sanctioned paranoia, the sort of madness that can be taught.

Stumbling out of the fluorescent-lit toilet block, I paused, considering my caravan, wrestling with my doubts.

'There's no one,' I told myself sternly. But I hesitated by the small swimming pool. The water shone still and milky in the moonlight. I was so tired.

I vaulted silently over the locked gate and pulled off my clothes, slipped silently into the water. It was cold, calming. Up to my neck, I felt invisible as I trod water and breathed as quietly as possible. If anyone came out of the caravan, I reasoned, I would see them, and duck my head under. Or scream. It would be hard to get at me here.

My hands beat softly at my sides like fins, sending cool water spinning up, silky against my skin. I was acting like an insane person. I knew that. I pushed the churning fear back down my throat, forced myself to lie back and let the water inch up my cheeks and run its fingers through my hair. I began to feel safe again. I hate dealing with myself when I'm like this – irrational, full of fear, seeing silhouettes in every shadow. In reality I have never truly been at risk. I have always simply been able to trust that my fears are unfounded, *force* myself to believe that the worst is not going to happen. And it doesn't. My streets have always turned out to be safe ones, shadows only shadows, suspicious strangers only shy.

I waited for the fear to abate, there in the water in the dark, until I began to shiver. Then I pulled myself out and padded, dripping, across to the caravan's sliding doors. They were ajar, just as I'd left them. There was nobody inside.

11

Iguana Creek

There was one last aspect of Angus McMillan's life I had left to investigate: his final years.

Although he would be resurrected as a great local hero in the twentieth century, at the time of his death he had fallen on hard times.

In November 1860 he resigned his seat in the Legislative Assembly, citing 'failing health'. He addressed his constituents in a graciously worded letter in the *Gippsland Guardian*: 'Thanking you, Gentlemen, from my heart,' it began, 'for the honour you have done me in electing me as your representative ... I can assure you that nothing would have induced me to tender my resignation but the present cause, as I find myself from physical debility, quite unable to give a due attention to your interests.' This debility, though distressing, was left unlabelled.

Despite a convincing electoral triumph, his tenure had lasted only fourteen months, during which he attended only a third of divisions and failed to make a maiden speech in the house. He had also been moved to apologise after a public spat with the road board in the letters pages of the local papers, during which his record had come in for no small amount of criticism. He had not, it must be said, taken to public office with aplomb.

Still, his resignation produced little triumph from the *Gippsland Guardian*. Far from gloating, it ran an editorial with an almost apologetic, elegiac tone. 'Whatever feelings may have actuated our remarks from time to time on Mr. McMillan's public career must now lie buried in the regret which we, in conjunction with all who know the private worth of that gentleman, must feel at the reason assigned by him for thus placing in the hands of the electors the duty of again returning another representative.'

Quietly, he stepped aside. Financial ruin followed soon afterwards. Bushfire was blamed, but a series of poor financial investments were also a contributing factor. Suddenly the Laird of Gippsland found the ground crumbling beneath his feet. In 1862 he was declared insolvent and forced to sell almost his entire estate, including his beloved Bushy Park.

It was a terrible time. He was hit particularly hard by the loss of the Bushy Park homestead, which he had built quite literally with his bare hands, summoned it from the earth. Pride hurt, he retreated to a cottage at his remote Tabberabbera sheep station on the steep-sided hills near Dargo, the only remaining vestige of his once extensive property empire.

He was not the first or the last explorer to find it difficult to adapt to normal life, or to die in poverty. Good bushmen did not necessarily make good businessmen, and the Australian climate was unpredictable and unforgiving. As fast as riches arrived, they might depart, and in the New World, the wild world, far from family, there were

no safety nets. Many saw the country they pioneered turn
its back on them.

The Dargo Valley, near McMillan's Tabberabbera station, in 1865.

George Edward Mackay, he who complained of the
'œdematous swelling' brought on by the physical
demands of overlanding, later wrote candidly of his
regret that he had failed to attain the great riches the
region had seemed to promise when he had settled there:
'These, Sir, are the salient points of my experience as a
squatter: I have lost my capital. I have lost my health. I
have lost fifteen years of the best period of my life. I
have undergone many hardships, exposed myself to many
dangers, and am now a poorer man than I was when I
became a squatter.'

'The early squatters, their sufferings, and their services
to the colony, are alike forgotten,' agreed the pastoralist
and politician William Thomas Mollison in the same year,
1853. 'Men seem to regard them, as the new heir regards
the furniture and portraits of the distant relative to whom

he has succeeded, as something to be at once quietly consigned to the lumber room or the auction marts.'

Financial ruin had precipitated Angus McMillan's departure from Scotland; now it blighted his new life. This time he was the laird, undercut by other, more savvy businessmen. Meanwhile, whispers about his health and the exact nature of the 'debility' that had cut his parliamentary career so short began to circulate. The true nature of his health problems is not fully known, but reading contemporary accounts, one gets the sense of more being left unsaid than said.

There are several possibilities. McMillan was known to suffer from rheumatism, which became increasingly problematic towards the end of his life – but would that alone account for his giving up his political career so abruptly? It might, however, have been an excuse – a way of backing away from politics with his pride intact, after finding himself at sea among the legislative class.

For although Australia was in many ways a far more meritocratic country than the one he had fled, McMillan never truly broke through into the upper social circles outside of the relatively closed society of Gippsland. Decades later, a distant relation of Lachlan Macalister revealed that his family always believed that McMillan 'was at his best as a farm manager', and that his many achievements could be attributed to his employer's superior strategy and finances.

It is possible that such tensions may have underlain McMillan's lack of success in parliament, which was still dominated by the upper (or at least, upper-middle) classes. He 'did not enjoy' his time in politics, his contemporaries noted, was reportedly 'gravely offended by the criticism and manoeuvring that was a natural part of parliamentary politics', and largely confined his activities to backroom lobbying and the furthering of private projects, such as masterminding, as a member of the Royal Society of Victoria's exploration committee, the ill-fated attempt by Burke and Wills to cross the continent in 1860. The self-confessed 'man of few words' was more at home on horseback than in an office or a debating chamber, it seemed.

There have also been some rumours of alcoholism, which are not easy to dismiss. A Highland man famed for his 'hospitality', who remunerated his men with whisky rations; a proud, capable outdoorsman who, risen to the top in his district, found himself disregarded by the political elite and pilloried in the local press by his constituents. Might a man in his position turn to the bottle to prop up his self-confidence? Yes, it is possible. With this in mind, a few asides in his friends' correspondence gave me pause.

Shortly after McMillan's death, the author John Shillinglaw would write to Commissioner Tyers, mentioning somewhat euphemistically 'the well-known weakness of ... our late dear friend, McMillan'. He did not elaborate, but to my mind the implication looms large.

During this downturn in his fortunes, it must have been very hard for McMillan not to dwell upon the successes of his former rival Strzelecki, the man with whom his career had once run parallel. After his journey through Gippsland and subsequent celebrity in Melbourne, the Pole continued to Tasmania, where he undertook scientific explorations, before emigrating to London, where he became a naturalised British citizen and was awarded fellowships of the Royal Geographical and Royal Societies. More acclaim was to follow: an honorary doctorate from Oxford University, elevation to the Order of the Bath for his charitable work during the Irish Famine, finally the title of Knight Commander. He would die in 1873, a few days after being informed by his friend, the prime minister William Gladstone, that Queen Victoria had expressed interest in meeting 'the famous count'.

Though he had succeeded in unseating his rival from the title of 'discoverer of Gippsland', McMillan may well have reconsidered the value of this victory in his later years, as with every new garland Strzelecki received, he saw his own fortunes recede. A silver tongue and gold-plated pretensions seemed, in the end, to have brought the so-called 'count' far more success than McMillan's steadfastness and loyalty ever had.

Still, life went on. In 1864, two years after the sale of Bushy Park, McMillan found his vocation once more when he was offered the role of leader of the Alpine Expedition, cutting tracks and mapping an area of high country to the north of Stratford that remained almost entirely unexplored and uncharted.

A series of gold discoveries – most recently at Good Luck Creek, by a party led by the anthropologist-to-be Alfred Howitt – had prompted a rush of incomers to the region, an ill-mannered rabble largely comprising inexperienced bushmen in search of fortune. Many had come to grief in the mountainous area lyrically described by Howitt as 'all frosted silver with black gorges and chasms running among their rugged spurs'. As a result, the government saw fit to commission McMillan to cut a route linking three main sites, totalling 280 miles of track. It may seem a menial sort of job for a former politician, but for McMillan it was both a much-needed source of income and an opportunity to return to prominence in the region.

In fact, it was a godsend. McMillan was back on top, and regaining some of his old swagger. Ahead of his departure he took a room at Scott's Hotel, the Melbourne lodgings of choice of the wealthy country set, where a correspondent for the *Mountaineer* spotted 'the redoubtable explorer' full of 'high hope and confidence in the future of what might very appropriately be called "McMillan's Land" instead of Gippsland'.

Savouring his return to favour, McMillan revived his journal, in which he distilled his relief into words. Others too seemed to share his delight. *Everyone glad to see that these unknown forest lands of Gippsland were at last to be penetrated into and thankful that I was to be the party that was to receive that honour, being the first European that first broke ground in the far famed land. I would not like another to carry the Laurels.* He directed his gratitude to the government that had given him another chance. *I hope they will find me do my duty.*

The party set out from the Dargo Inn, not far from McMillan's Tabberabbera run, in March 1864. Conditions were horrendous. Scrub so dense they were forced to dismount and proceed on foot, slashing at the undergrowth with long knives and axes. Heavy rain, for days at a time, sometimes so hard they were forced to abandon work to shelter under canvas and wait out the storm. Thunder, lightning, hail. McMillan's deputy, a man called Jones, branched off alone to clear a side path, and returned *like a drowned rat*, every item of clothing sodden, and streaked with blood; *even his forehead is bleeding with bites of*

313

leeches, *which are always numerous at this altitude in thick damp
underwood.*

Despite all this, morale was high. McMillan had seen
worse; he was in his element. His men trusted his judgement. Pride and purpose were returning. He was older
now, yes, but also more sure, more authoritative. He was
back in control, leading by example, rising well before
dawn at 4.30 a.m., getting the fire blazing and sounding a
wake-up call at 5.30. By seven, the men would be at
work. *Arrived back at camp at ½ past six, had supper and then
our pipes cheered us with a few tunes, all hands in splendid
spirits.* He found, to his delight, that the men continued to
work in his absence; in return he gave them Sundays and
Good Friday as rest days.

1864 engraving describing McMillan's party at work cutting tracks
between the Alpine goldfields.

Happiness flooded back into him. It was in the bush,
without domestic comforts, that he felt most at home.
This was his kind of work; these were his kind of men.

He understood them, knew how to manage and motivate them. It was doing he was good at, not debating. *It is a great pleasure to one that they are so anxious to get on with the work and I make it my duty to keep them on the most friendly terms, as a party of explorers should be like one family, look on their leader as a father and the leader should behave to them as he would his children.*

Of course, his real children were many miles away. Now aged six and three, they were ensconced with Mrs McMillan in the remote cottage at Tabberabbera, and growing up in his absence. He had never spent much time at home. But he thought of them sometimes. The only hill on the Dargo road he christened Mount Ewen, after his eldest. *I hope he will deserve the honour one day. I hope, poor fellow, he will not have so many ups and downs in this cruel world as his papa has had.*

When McMillan left Barra he had cut himself loose from his roots, and in doing so had given himself the freedom to redefine himself as a man – a successful man. Now, after life had taken his measure and found him lacking, when he found himself fallen from grace, poor as on the day he began, disappointed by the way things had turned out, he cut himself loose once again.

Out in the bush, off the edge of the map, living on his wits, he rediscovered himself. He remembered his own strength and worth. He turned his face to the infinite sky, to his capricious God, and offered his thanks for all that he had endured.

6 May, 1864
Mr Bennison's stock men came to our camp this evening.
Mr. B's station is 8 miles lower down the river, near

what he called 'McMillan's coming' — where I camped 16 years ago. Those were happy days, but thanks to the Giver of all good and perfect gifts I am now contented with my lot, for he gives me strength according to my burden.

Despite everything I now knew about Angus McMillan as a man, I found myself happy for him. This tactical retreat, to a space where he might re-evaluate his life, was an impulse that I could understand. In a sense, my trip had fulfilled the same function for me.

The longer I spent away from home, the more I found myself a solitary figure. I drove long distances, camped in empty clearings, sat alone in bars. It was easier than lining up a constant stream of companions, and it allowed me to make my own timetable, going where I chose, sleeping when I wanted, eating at odd intervals and working for long stretches. More than that, I was finding that my thoughts came clearer, tauter, when I had time to digest what I had learned each day in the long hours of the lowering light, under canvas. Alone.

I was ever more out of sync with my old life back at home. This was not only due to the time difference — although the time difference was considerable, my friends and family asleep when I was awake, and vice versa — but emotionally too. I found it increasingly hard to explain to those I loved what I was hearing, seeing, reading, feeling, thinking. For months now I had been half-living in the nineteenth century, seeing the world through that prism, and it had unlinked me from my peers, broken the spell of the fears and stresses I had been labouring under. I had cut myself loose from normal life, and in doing so had found myself solid at the centre of it again, just as I had been all along, but had forgotten.

One night on the road at dusk, somewhere on the endless road between Melbourne and Sydney, I found euphoria. The roads were empty and I drove without clear direction, looking for either a place to camp or a motel to stop at for the night. An electrical storm was brewing in the cauldron of the sky, the air thick and crackling with anticipation, an unsettled wind pacing first one way and then the other. It had sent my GPS haywire; it kept telling me to turn off the road I was on, then abandoning me to my fate as soon as I did – 'Establishing satellite connection' – so I had given myself up for lost, just followed my instincts. Leaving it to the horse, as the pioneers would have called it, I cork-screwed up an entry road and down again at the next exit, waiting for an answer to present itself.

I found myself in a long, wide valley, a fieldscape of waving green grasses. The sky bruised a deep, painful violet. Lightning flickered around me in all directions, long forking tails of it, the thunder drowned out by the noise of the car's engine. Along the verges of the road, silvery gums stood in lines, pressed against the barrier like spectators at a race. They reached to the sky, trunks split-ting then splitting again – into limbs, into branches, into twigs, until they formed thousands of pale twisting tendrils: ground lightning, a mirror image of the pyrotechnics above. To the side of the road, a fireman and a concerned man in overalls stood close together inspecting a patch of scorched, steaming earth.

All of this going on, and me watching from the other side of the window. I am here, I thought, but I will be gone again soon.

It filled me with a deep peace. I was both lost and found.

But while we loners are locking ourselves out of the world, turning inwards, the world does not stop spinning on its axis. While McMillan was out on the uncharted ranges, cutting tracks, Christina and their two sons were back home, getting on with things, making do with what little he had left them. They were getting used to life without him.

There was something destructive in this tendency to withdrawal, I was beginning to realise. Something selfish. It was the easy way out: just snip the ties and run off somewhere new, where nobody knows you. Like McMillan I had gone haring off, with little thought for what would happen in my absence, or when I got back. Behind me I had left a job, a relationship, a *life* trailing in my wake, and for the first time it occurred to me that it might no longer be waiting for me when I went home.

I had cut myself loose. Again. The realisation came over me in a flood of self-censure. Wasn't this part of a pattern? I had been constructing a rootless existence for myself. Wasn't that the reason I had found Angus McMillan's story so enchanting at the start of it all, as I stared at the map of Gippsland in the archive in Skye? Well, I'd made it. From Skye to the South Pacific, just as I'd imagined. To all those storybook placenames: I'd seen Snake Island from the mangrove-tangled shore near Port Welshpool; looked up the blue-grey peak of Mount Useful; bathed my feet in the warm, shallow waters of Sealer's Cove, lain back in the sand. I'd hiked there alone, weaving between the peaks of Wilsons Promontory, asked a stranger to take my picture when I got there.

But McMillan's generation had done so with reluctance. They had been tipped from their homeland by force or by finance, and once they had emigrated, home was a six-month sail and a lifetime away. But I was not rootless, not really. I had a family, a place to retreat to. Somewhere I could call and hear a voice tell me I could come home whenever I wanted. After years of trying to prove that I could do it all without them, I found that the thought of returning home to my parents, my brothers, the place I knew best of all, brought with it a stillness, a calmness, that I had never before traced back to its source. I was anchored to the place I was born by an invisible rope that had kept me steady, tugging hard at my heart when I stretched too far away. It was time to go home.

A wave of love broke over me. And something more melancholy, too. I understood, really understood, for the first time the significance of the Highlanders' dispossession. An appreciation of the pain of all those people who feel that same tug of longing and love for people and place, but have no way of returning; the ache of those whose families have been scattered, never to be reunited. How fiercely they must have felt the loss of their past selves: those once-worn paths now grown over; those once-blazing hearths now filled instead by grasses made heavy with seeds and droplets of rain.

I thought again of that lost town of Yallourn. I felt differently, now, about what it could teach us. Just as its residents reconstructed their virtual town so they might walk endlessly along old streets, and the modern-day Gunai reconstructed a lost language and laid claim to old hunting grounds, the Highland settlers of Gippsland kept their motherland alive by attaching old names to new places; by employing their fellow countrymen; by forming Caledonian Societies; by banding together in their Highland Brigades in times of strife. Because it is impossible to be truly rootless. Even if your roots lead to somewhere that no longer exists, even if they have been cut cleanly away, you still feel them as phantom pains. For everyone belongs to the land they were born in, the culture they were born into. It has helped form every aspect of who they are.

The new land, despite its many advantages, its opportunities, did not have the same emotional significance to the settlers. They were not invested in it in the same way, had no understanding or appreciation of the culture and the landscape they had stumbled upon. And so it was easy for them to destroy it without thought, like big boys jumping on sandcastles at the beach.

This story, the story of Angus McMillan and the Scotsmen and the Gunai and the guns, is, as much as anything, a study of nationalism. Of in-groups and out-groups, and of sticking with one's own people. The simple truth of it all is that when it came down to it, they chose to protect their own.

To McMillan, riding from the foothills of the Australian Alps, the broad, fertile flats of the Gippsland plains were a *Caledonia Australis: a country capable of supporting all my starving countrymen.*

Years later, in 1935, a group of Paweł Strzelecki's descendants led by New Yorker Boleslaw Strzelecki cabled Britain's King George V an extraordinary request. They were preparing a claim against the Australian government, they said. Would he lend his support? Not only did they want $560,000 as a refund of the cost of Strzelecki's Gippsland expedition, and the return of some £17 million of the count's money which had been left in British and Australian banks, but for Gippsland to be turned over to the family as a sanctuary for Polish refugees who were leaving their country, which found itself sharing its borders with two aggressive, expansionist regimes: the Soviet Union and Nazi Germany. The normal route out – the immigrant's American Dream – had been shuttered by the Great Depression. Their compatriots might arrive 'at a rate of 25,000 a year', they suggested.

A *Polonie Australis*, perhaps.

The Strzelecki family claim, fanciful though it was, caused an uproar in the region. Local author Hal Porter, himself of British immigrant stock, recalled the episode with outrage forty years later:

> No mention of what was to happen to the
> inhabitants of all the towns and one-horse villages
> of Strzelecki Province; to the city of Sale; to the
> Bairnsdale Salvation Army which, in 1935, was
> celebrating its jubilee ... or how a Polish take-over
> would be regarded by a town with streets dubbed
> Buchanan, Moroney, Ballantyne, and Brown ...

Of course, one might ask the same of a province once inhabited by three thousand Gunai: the Tatungooloong of the lake country, the Bratowooloong of Corner Inlet and surrounds, the Brabawooloong who so haunted Bushy Park, the Krowathunkooloong of the Snowy River, the Brayakooloong of the high country. How was the British takeover regarded in a country where the Mitchell River was once the Wy-yung, the Avon the Dooyeedang, and the La Trobe the Tanjil?

But so it goes. We see only through our own eyes.

The '4x4 Adventure Map' I'd found in a petrol station was without contours, and vague in parts, but it was going to have to do. It was the only sufficiently detailed map I could find of the area, and it did at least label McMillan's walking track specifically. It had been picked out by a line of tiny diamonds, albeit interrupted by large gaps where the path could not be found. 'Track contains poorly defined and overgrown sections (Not recommended),' the map warned.

It was too hot to hike the whole length of it, and too risky, with the fire-danger rating inching up every day. But I wanted to get out onto his trail, following in his footsteps, to get an idea of his state of mind.

Cam had come along for the ride. It was getting dark by the time we turned off an unsealed road onto an even more rutted track – 'McMillan's Road', the GPS announced happily – that led us deep into the Grant Historic Area, home of the goldrush townships of Grant and Talbotville. Or, more accurately, the former goldrush townships of Grant and Talbotville. At the end of the nineteenth century both were hives of activity and excitement, as new houses sprang up every day. Today, however, it is as though they never existed.

'Jesus,' I said, as the headlamps of my hire car strobed the vacant ground; a clean-edged clearing in the woods about the size and shape of a village. 'What the hell is this?'

Cam snorted. 'I told you it would be underwhelming.'

I considered, slowing down to peer through the long grass. A faint depression ran off at right angles to the track, unnaturally straight: the outline of a street that no longer exists. My mind flitted to Sorley MacLean's 'Hallaig'. All those girls walking 'in silent bands', ghostly footsteps muffled by the moss grown over old roads. Right then, in our twilit clearing, in the crossover time between light and dark, past and present, I could feel our two realities brushing up against each other. Insects fluttered through the headlights' beams; I imagined the soft tread of feet, the press of cold hands against the window. 'I don't know if "underwhelming" is right,' I said. 'There's something sort of horrifying about it.'

'An actual ghost town.'

'Exactly. I'd say I wouldn't want to come here at night, except – well, here we are.'

'Camp?'

I sighed and pulled over. It was too late to look for anywhere else. We pitched up in a side clearing by the remains of a previous visitor's firepit, and I left Cam preparing a fire to wander back into the heart of old Grant, flicking a saucer-sized circle of torchlight ahead of me. Everything had vanished but the gravestones, which were real and solid, penned in by wooden rails as if they might make a break for it otherwise. Along what had once been Main Street, someone had recently, painstakingly, staked in plaques marking the former sites of shops, the post office, the old inn. Historical society stuff: more monuments to the mundane. 'We were here. We were here. We were here.'

The goldrush township of Grant in its heyday, 1865.

Now, after all that I had learned, I couldn't help but brood on the flipside: that secret history that has gone unrecorded, and too often forgotten. But what you don't know can't haunt you. I slept well that night, amid the shopkeepers and the tailors and the men panning for gold.

Morning found us in Talbotville; another blank space at the foot of the hill, another railed-off cemetery. The phantoms had evaporated off like water in the harsh sunlight, their place taken by a rowdy off-roading party, all of them men, who had parked their SUVs in a circle. Every so often another of their members careered by, mud and dirty water scraped by the windscreen wipers to create two shell-shaped look-holes. Each man clutched a can of beer in an insulated holder. All of them were clearly drunk. It was 11 a.m.

We prepared to walk. McMillan's track branched off
from the 4x4 track somewhere around there, and I wanted
to explore it on foot. Cam unfolded the map on the
bonnet of the car and stooped to study it, but I was
distracted. I felt eyes on me. When I looked up, I saw that
two men had detached themselves from the party and
were making their way, unsteadily, towards us.

'You lost?' The shorter, and drunker, of the pair
swigged from his can as he peered over my shoulder. He
wiped his mouth and offered me a swig.

We told them we were looking for McMillan's track.
Yeah, said the other guy. He'd heard of it. But it was
'pretty crook'. Not much chance of getting the car along
it. He eyed my shiny white rental vehicle. 'You done
much off-roading before?'

'We're not going to drive. It's a walking track.'

'Bushwalking!' They both laughed openly. 'In this heat?
You're going to die out there.'

We fended off their concerns and headed off along a
track, looking for the turn-off, dodging the occasional
SUVs that came roaring past like tanks on their way to
battle, finally locating a tree marked with a small metal
triangle denoting where the trail diverged.

The adventure map had not been lying when it warned
of 'poorly defined and overgrown sections'. Fallen
branches splayed across the path. Brambles totally
choked the way. We struggled on into the thicket,
bashing our way through with heavy sticks, not speaking
except to exchange expletives and occasional groans of
pain. The plan had been to follow the track for a few
miles past the former Pioneer Racecourse, but after
about an hour of fruitless hacking, stuck with thorns and

bleeding from every bare patch of skin, we were ready to admit defeat.

'This is hopeless. How far do you reckon we've gone?'

Cam turned to size up the hillside. 'Less than a kilometre? We need a machete or an axe or a chainsaw. I don't envy them, those track-cutters.'

We turned and began to muddle our way back, but the path seemed to have sealed up just as tightly as before we had passed through. 'It's sad, isn't it?' I said, ducking under a fallen trunk. 'After all that effort, to allow it to grow over.'

Cam disagreed. He thought the trail should be allowed to disappear. 'It's not as if it's well-used, is it? And it's perverse to keep it as a monument to McMillan.'

'Do you think so?'

He paused from batting back a bramble that seemed determined to garrotte him, and looked back at me with a funny expression. 'Yes. Why, don't you?'

He had a point. It *was* perverse to have all these memorials to a man who had caused so much pain and damage. But it seemed wrong too to demolish them, or let them fade back into the bush as if they had never existed. Wasn't that just another sort of denial of the past?

A black cockatoo alighted on a branch far above my head. Its call came, harsh and rasping, the creaking of a door closing.

A few days previously, I had been driving through the hills in the hour before sunset when I came across another section of the track. I had come skidding along a dusty, unsealed road from Dargo High Plains down through a stand of straggling trees; they were torn limb from limb, branches arched off in strange poses like arms thrown up for protection. Just as the road straightened out, I passed a tree with a metal triangle nailed into its trunk. I slammed on the brakes, and twisted over the passenger seat to read the label: 'McMillan's Tk'.

Hello. I reversed back through my own dustcloud, pulled into a flat space just off the road beside a tumble-down corrugated-iron hut, tiger-striped with dark rust, and clambered out to wander in the evening sunlight, just in the flip-flops and shorts I'd been driving in. The path was clear enough up here on the plains, a bare track through sparse, burned-out bush, gnarled bare shrubs set far apart. There was little evidence that anyone had been up there recently. 'McMillans Walking Track', read another sign. 'Victoria River Via Mayford 25km 2 Days. Remote Walking – Please Use Intentions Book'.

I ignored the request, and set off along the track without a clear purpose in mind, feeling exposed and very alone in this sunbleached, windblasted clearing. The last woman on earth. The air was still, and silent. There were no sounds except for the muffled crunch of my footsteps on the dry earth. No birdsong. No wildlife that I could see –

I froze mid-step, a fraction of a second before I stepped on a fat-knuckled spider about the size of my hand. He sat brazenly in the middle of the path, as if expecting me. My breath caught in my throat and I swallowed a scream, carefully pedalling my foot backwards before taking two or three steps back in quick succession, like a spooked horse. The spider didn't move.

I watched it, heart pounding. What was it? Something venomous? I didn't recognise it, had no hope of identifying it, but it didn't look friendly, that was for sure. We stood at an impasse. A voice in the back of my head cackled and catcalled. 'Get on with it! Coward!'

Should I jump over it? I took one step closer, then immediately backed away again when the spider twitched a leg. Should I prod it with a stick? The thought made my stomach turn over. A lazy breeze played through the dry grass, across my bare ankles, my bare legs, the skin on the back of my neck. I glanced around in the dry undergrowth. Every stick and tree root looked like a snake, every clump of weeds a harbourer of some nasty predator.

Fight or flight? I swivelled my head to look back the way I'd come. I couldn't have gone further than half a mile. Flight was easier. I set off towards the car at a sprint, senses on full alert, leaping every suspicious rock and root, clawing my toes to keep the flimsy flip-flops on my feet.

Idiot. By the time I got back to the car I was giggling like a maniac. I gathered my wits, waited for my breath to slow, and wandered over to the metal locker that held the intentions book, hungry for human contact. It was a crumpled A4 notebook with a broken spine, the pages coming away in my hands. There were two and a half pages' worth of entries in the entire book. The first was dated 2010, and a handful of others were scattered throughout the following years. 'Pedersen's and Fyfe's had soup here 2/6/11'; '16-12-12 Manning and Graver … Five horses with us, all good, heading to Mayford 2night.' According to the book, no one had passed this way on foot for months.

I looked at the sign again. 'Please Use Intentions Book'. It implied, but didn't say: 'So we know where to look for your body.'

Iguana Creek

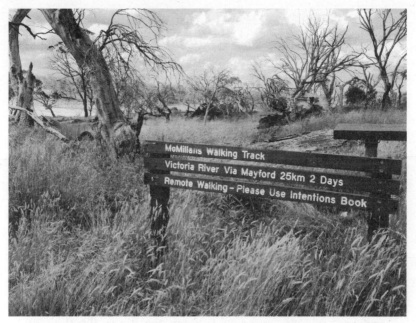

Signpost where McMillan's track intersects with the road,
Dargo High Plains.

I thought about Angus McMillan, up here in his element.
Bashing through the bush looking for new routes. Making
up the maps. No tracks, no roads, no nothing. An hour or
so in the bush and I was running for safety. Come on,
come on, come on. Boots on.

I packed my rucksack quickly and set off again into the
dusk, following the track through thousands of bleached
trees, until I emerged at a flat spot with a view across the
opposite hillside. A bushfire had rushed through years
before; what must once have been a glorious lookout now
offered an unbroken vista of the most incredible scene of
devastation. For miles around, hills dropped and rose
again, stubbled and wrecked and unrecovered after more
than a decade. Dead trees carpeted the landscape as far as

329

the eye could see, arms lifted in salvation, naked to the waist and streaked with scorch marks. They were silver and utterly bare, thin and leggy, javelins dropped into the hillside at speed.

On my own, I saw no point in lighting a fire. I just set up my tent, zipped myself in and climbed into my sleeping bag. I tried to read, but the battery in my head torch faded to nothing, so I switched it off and lay still in the dark, trying to shut out the noises of the night, the rustling in the grass beside my head. At some point, I slept.

I woke suddenly in the night, shivering. I was high up, I realised: the air was cold. I hadn't thought to bring a jumper with me. Desperate for the toilet, I reluctantly slid out of the bag and clambered from my tent to find the moon high and full in the sky. It flooded everything with a thin, clear light. Instantly, all fear was washed from me, replaced by wonder. Trees torn asunder were now curving, silver sculptures. The grass a carpet of white velvet. The stars piercing bright: the sky shot through with gossamer.

If ever there was to be a time of visitation, it was now. I felt drained of warmth, of colour, of worry. I waited patiently, my head upturned, letting the breath leave me in a long, low sigh. Who was I waiting for? Dark tribesmen, trailing pewter blood? Orphaned children, one-eyed, crying? Angus McMillan and his men, bearing arms? Bearing bodies? Offering explanations?

I didn't know, but I waited anyway, my mind still as the night, its surface unruffled by thoughts. I was heavy, pregnant with expectation, ready for answers.

I waited in the moonlight until the shivers came in violent pulses and my teeth clashed together. No one had come. Nothing. No answers. Perhaps there were none. I turned and let myself into the dark recess of the tent and my thin summer sleeping bag. My feet and hands were cold to the touch.

Not long after McMillan found his peace, things began to fall apart. His men struck gold near what would become the township of Grant, and though they honoured him by naming the reef 'Pioneer', for his new horse, most of the party deserted to stake their claims and chase their fortunes. McMillan hired a new team for the last leg and pushed on, but a delay in the delivery of government funds left him hard-pressed to pay their wages.

1864 engraving showing McMillan's party discovering a quartz gold reef.

As they inched towards the finish, McMillan grew taciturn. Funds were still short, the government were hanging back from paying him; they were nitpicking, he felt, over his scrappy bookkeeping. But the job was completed, was it not? With nothing else to be done, he sent the men home with his own money in their pockets; to raise it, he had been forced to sell his stake in the reef.

They were grateful for his efforts, at least. *All hands well and expressing themselves sorry to be so near the end of the journey. One of the men expresses that the expedition was more like a picnic for they never fared better. I always made it a rule to camp on a nice spot.*

But it was time to return to society, and he found himself a lonely figure. *I am now in the camp with only 1 man.* After four days, he sent the man home.

He could not follow, *being attacked with rheumatism.* The next day he was still *unable to move.* And the next. It was more than a week later, on Friday, 3 June 1864, before he could drag himself from the hut in which he had taken refuge to head slowly, painfully, back towards civilisation. On the way, yet another calamity would befall him. The packhorse he was leading slipped and fell from a rocky precipice, dragging the already aching McMillan down with it. The fall broke three of his ribs, and tore his right knee open, leaving him so badly injured that he found it difficult to walk. He struggled on for the remaining miles, tight eyes fixed upon the ground in front of his feet. He was in too much pain to record the details. *Arrived in camp on Sunday 5th June. Suffered fearfully on the road.*

He had accomplished his task, that was one thing at least. His friend John Shillinglaw wrote to Commissioner Tyers of his success: 'Mac has never looked better than he does now, and but for his bad knee, which is sometimes very bad, he would be able to enjoy the laurels he has lately won more heartily. The fact is that he is quite a hero just now, for there is every chance of a great rush during the spring and summer to the country he has newly opened.'

So it proved. Over the coming months, thousands rushed down McMillan's track to at least thirty-five more gold-quartz reefs that were discovered along its length, heralding an economic boom across all Victoria. McMillan was welcomed back into Gippsland society with open arms. But the cost had been very great.

Not only financially – although the government continued to drag their feet, leaving him out of pocket – but physically as well, and his failing health hung heavy upon the bushman who had always prided himself upon his strength and fortitude. McMillan was, as the *Gippsland Guardian* wrote later, 'broken in constitution and in spirit'. Still he did not return home, instead checking in to the Club Hotel in Sale, and later, perhaps when his money began to run out, to a down-at-heel inn on the road to Dargo, at a place called Iguana Creek.

It was there that he died on 18 May 1865, aged fifty-four. Neither his wife nor his children were present.

He never had made it back to Barra, despite his fervent hope all those many years ago, as he sat in his pitching bunk on board the *Minerva*, legs braced against the partition, casting his thoughts like a fishing line, first back, and then forward into the far-off future:

Farewell to the land where my first love is
A long farewell dear Barra to thee.
I think on thee while I write this
On the deep and stormy sea.

God grant that I may see your land and shore
In after years in other time
Again from thee to go no more
To other dear and distant time

But should He please my humble bones to lay
In foreign land, beneath a foreign sun
Why then, I have no more to say.
God's will be always done.

God's will be done. 'Endocarditis', the death certificate said. As a diagnosis, it made sense: a common complication of rheumatic fever. Still, a certain mystery surrounds Angus McMillan's death. Some have suggested suicide. Others that he drank himself to death. The coroner, his great friend Dr Arbuckle, declined to conduct a post mortem, and so a sliver of doubt survives.

I read all of this with sinking spirits. To die in a strange bed, in a dingy roadhouse, is a sad and anticlimactic exit for anyone. The Gippsland poet Laurie Duggan described McMillan's Iguana Creek: 'a few houses and a T-intersection;/proof only that the famous/die in ordinary places'.

Today, a memorial stands in the spot. I saw it as I came down the road from the high country, and made a sudden swerve onto the grassy flat alongside. A huge slab of orange sandstone poked toothily from the ground, lichen spread across the top like snowfall. Behind it the eponymous creek was a dry rocky bed, strangled by tall grass as high as my shoulders. A metal plaque bore a portrait of McMillan in relief, wearing a Highland cap and looking every bit the laird. I ran my fingers over his face: that same strong nose, that same strong brow. Above it was a chronological list of his explorations: the rivers he discovered, crossed and named. And beside his picture a legend:

DIED HERE
May 18, 1865

The plaque had been shot. There were three perfect round bulletholes in the metal: the first through his name, the second through the dedication. The third went through his face. Oh, Angus.

I thought of that young man sailing out from the Hebrides, drawing up in serpentine longhand his list of resolutions for a life to be lived the New World.

I resolve hereafter to do whatever I think to be my
     duty and most for the good and advantage of
     mankind.
I resolve to do this whatever difficulties I meet with.
I resolve to live with all my might while I do.
I resolve never to do anything which I should be
     afraid to do if it were the last hour of my life.
I resolve never to do anything out of revenge.
I resolve I shall live as I shall wish I had done when
     I come to die.

There was a dead tree on the hill, a whole, perfect skeleton. Its trunk split into thick muscled arms; at their tips, jointed twigs were crooked like bony fingers. Clumps of dried-out mistletoe hung from its branches as baubles.

Numbly, I got back into the car and drove on.

There was a danger in my quest, I realised now. By tying myself to McMillan, by submerging myself in his life and thoughts, I had begun to feel for him, care for him. Empathise with him, even. I had begun to allow my compassion for the man to colour my judgement of his actions.

A French proverb: *Tout comprendre, c'est tout pardonner.* To understand is to forgive.

But it is not my place to forgive. It is not my place, either, to become an apologist for a murderer, a defender of the indefensible. Whatever I recognise in McMillan, however engaging I find him as a man, it cannot be escaped that he must be defined by his worst actions. He was a murderer. A *mass* murderer. A proponent of genocide.

It is true that my improved knowledge of his situation, and the pressures it entailed, had engendered in me a better appreciation of how such wicked work might take place. I had begun to understand that many individuals might be capable of the same, under the right conditions. Myself, even. For can I truly say that in his position – far out on the frontier, where law and order is a distant construct, where white is good and black is evil – I would not behave in the same way? No. I can't say anything like that. Not for sure.

Yet that does not absolve him of guilt.

We must hold him, and others like him, accountable for their actions. It is important to look back with clear hindsight and see what havoc they wreaked, and know that it was wrong. That they should have acted differently, reacted more wisely to their fears, followed their ambition with more caution. But before we sermonise too loudly upon the moral weaknesses of our predecessors, we must remember too what things looked like to them, so we might understand why they behaved as they did, and in doing so, ask how such things might be prevented from happening again.

It we chalk this up as nothing but the actions of evil men, it will all have been for naught. We will not have confronted the moral ambivalence that lies at the heart of every person. Of this, McMillan is a better example than most: the conflicts between his actions and his ideals are obvious. He shot to kill; he handed out blankets. He lived in sin; he observed the Sabbath. He hunted those who speared his stock remorselessly; his generosity to his fellow men was renowned. He rallied to the rescue of the defiled white woman; he kept the mother of his bastard child as housekeeper for three years rather than marry her.

Contrast the barrowloads of bones he carted from Warrigal Creek, under cover of darkness, to be burned and disposed of in pits and under sandbanks, with the tidy grave he had dug for Clifton, his favourite horse, near the homestead at Bushy Park. The actions of both a cold-blooded killer and a soft-hearted fool. He was both.

That juxtaposition particularly called to mind a memory from another day, a long way from Gippsland. I was fishing with three others, bobbing in a small boat off the west coast of Scotland. After an hour of listless waiting we drifted through a shoal of mackerel, and suddenly we could not reel them in fast enough. Six hooks on every line; I had my feet braced against the side of the boat, cranking the reel, my rod bending with the weight of them. It was miraculous: the apostles fishing from the other side of the boat. Soon our catch had overflowed the buckets and we were wading through silver fish, which gasped and flipped between our feet.

I was laughing now, from shock, or joy, or something else entirely, holding my rod aloft with one hand, grasping ineffectually at their muscled bodies with the other, fingers slipping as they struggled and catching on the barbed hooks. Rob, the estate manager, teased me for my timidity, and leaned in to help. He grasped them roughly and pulled so the hooks ripped through their flesh, laughing when I winced. We were like merpeople, waterproofs caked in a thick layer of iridescent scales. Blood everywhere, from their torn mouths, our torn hands.

Finally it was still again. We had drifted out the other side. We slumped back, talking in undertones, regaining our composure. Rob watched his spaniel fondly as he crunched the head of a half-dead mackerel, which still lashed limply in its jaws. Its fur was foul with blood and fish guts. 'Good dog,' said Rob, addressing the top of his head. He thumped his tail half-heartedly, concentrating on the fish.

'I almost killed him once,' Rob recalled, wincing at the memory of it. 'When he was a puppy. Ran him over with a quad bike.' Thinking the dog was dying, he panicked, scooped him up in his arms and leapt into a powerboat, racing ten miles to Mallaig and the nearest vet with blood thudding in his ears. 'He was all right in the end.'

Rob put out a hand and rubbed the dog's haunches with a look of soft, familial pride. A fish flipped over at his feet. He lifted his boot and stamped it dead.

Isn't it strange, I thought then, how we see only certain kinds of pain? We tune in and out of them, choosing which to receive as if they were radio stations.

It was late summer now. The moisture had been sucked from the ground, the leaves were crisp and brittle on the trees, shifting in the wind with the sound of the ocean. Across the creek, a grass fire had swept through the fields not long before. The ground was scorched to a threadbare black-brown, what leaves remained on the shrubs were desiccated and curled. I had crossed into a world where it was forever autumn. The air was dry, woody: the smell of the sauna.

I headed south into thick, bitter air. Near Yallourn the fire had got into the coal seams, had been burning for a week. It was dark; evening had fallen though it was not yet noon. Dark particles swirled in the air, settled in the well behind the windscreen wipers like dirty snow. Cars appeared from the gloom, hazard lights blinking. Thick smoke rose up in a black wall ahead, and I drove into it.

Epilogue

GIPPS LAND.
(FROM OUR OWN CORRESPONDENT)
Port Albert, 6th March, 1856.
— Angus McMillan, Esq. —

The entertainment given to Angus McMillan, Esq., came off on Monday evening last, and brought together about fifty gentlemen. The dinner, which was entrusted to the care of Mr. Gellion, reflects the highest credit on that gentleman; and, in truth, it must be very gratifying to hear the praises of everyone lavished upon the excellence and good taste that characterised this — one of the most sumptuous entertainments ever given in Gipps Land.

After the cloth was withdrawn, the Chairman proposed the toast: 'Mr. McMillan, and discovery of Gipps Land.' The Chairman said:

Gentlemen — we are assembled here to-night to do honour to the man whose enterprise laid open to us the district we inhabit, — an enterprise, the difficulties of which can be but imperfectly appreciated by us who enjoy the fruits of it; but that we do appreciate the advantages thus afforded us, as well as the excellent qualities of the man to whom we are indebted for them, is shown by our presence here to-night. To those very obstacles which opposed a mighty barrier to the inroads of civilisation, and stayed the advancing progress of the white man, until McMillan, undeterred by difficulties and dangers, led the way, we are indebted for some of the principal advantages we enjoy as dwellers in Gipps Land.

The gigantic granite ramparts which seclude us from the rest of Australia shelter us also from the scorching winds of the desert, and give rise to numerous rivers, which, flowing in every direction through the land, fertilise the soil and give the superiority we claim for it as an agricultural and grazing district.

From our situation between those mountains and the sea, we enjoy a climate which I consider approaches more nearly to perfection than that of any spot on earth. Unchilled by severe frosts – sheltered from hot winds – knowing no dread of drought – the heat of the day followed invariably by cool refreshing nights; a climate to which not only no disease is to be ascribed, but which is calculated to retain the body in perfect health where no other disturbing cause is in action; a climate not only enabling a settler to endure the severe toil that ever must accompany the conversion of the forest into the farm, but fulfilling in the plenty of harvest the hopes with which he laboured in seedtime.

Epilogue

We have lately made a great stride in advance, and I confidently believe that the time is not far distant when the few gaps made in the forest by the present settlers will extend over the whole of the lower district, when in place of the sombre gum forest and tea-tree scrub, the makeshift hut, and the half-cleared paddock, the eye of the traveller will rest for miles on waving corn-fields, interspersed with the substantial dwellings and well stocked homesteads of a prosperous and happy race of families, whose industry will relieve us from our present state of dependence upon foreign countries for our food. When the vast mineral treasures of our granite ranges shall be worked by thousands instead of hundreds of sturdy miners, guided by science and aided by machinery, the valuable products of their industry and enterprise, brought to the coast by railway or canal, for the construction of which this country seems expressly formed.

When above all other resources we shall be found to possess in abundance, as I believe we do, that gift of provident nature, 'more precious than silver, more valuable than gold' – the food of the mighty steam-engine, coal.

Then, with an unequalled climate, a fertile soil, numerous and valuable mineral productions, safe and convenient harbours, it needs no prophetic vision to foresee that this district, the fortunate discovery of our honoured guest, shall hold a most important rank amongst Australian settlements. (Cheers.)

But I trust should we live to see Gipps Land rise from our present obscure to our future proud position, we may never see her people lose those characteristics which mark them now; the hospitality that welcomes everywhere the stranger and the traveller; the honesty that makes a locked door at night a rarity in the district; the energy that led the way, and has continued to distinguish the squatter and the farmer in their struggles ever since; the unity and friendly feeling that will never let a Gipps Lander stand by and see a neighbour beat for want of a helping hand either here, at home, or as I have often experienced myself, on the distant gold-fields.

Let us continue to cherish those feelings and we may then rejoice in the present and trust confidently in the future of the 'Land we live in', whilst our children's children shall learn to honour, as we do, the name of McMillan its discoverer. (Loud and continued cheers.)

Author's Note

I open this book with a dramatized account of the events of the Warrigal Creek massacre, the most significant violent clash between white settlers and indigenous people in the history of Gippsland – and one of the worst recorded in Australian history.

A great deal of secrecy surrounds the events of that day – as I have explained elsewhere, the participants were well aware that their actions were punishable by hanging – and so the sources are often coy or second-hand, and the true timeline is still a matter of some debate.

There is, for example, disagreement between sources over the exact location of the attack; others disagree on the nature of the injuries to Ronald Macalister (the *Port Philip Patriot* says the body and face were 'so totally disfigured that his countenance could not be recognized among his most intimate friends'; the source of early allegations of a massacre, William Hoddinott, described the Gunai 'driving spears into the body'; yet others state that he was beaten to death with sticks or waddies). There is also conflict among the sources as to who discovered the body: McMillan; an employee of his, John Morrison; or the Aboriginal station hand known as Boy Friday.

Author's Note

The scenario described in the prologue is necessarily a reconstruction of what seems, to my eyes, after carefully examining the available evidence, the most likely course of events that day. It must be underlined that I do not claim to have produced a 'definitive' account – although largely my scenario echoes that mooted by the historian Peter Gardner (who appears in person in Chapter 6) and outlined by Dirk Moses in his book *Genocide and Settler Society*.

I am aware that some voices in Australian historical circles are apt to focus on the uncertainty surrounding the attack at Warrigal Creek (and other cases both locally and nationwide), using it as evidence that these events did not take place. I find this denialism disingenuous and with the potential to cause great social harm.

In his book *The Gippsland Massacres*, Gardner compares and contrasts a wide range of sources – diaries, private correspondence, letters from the office of the Aboriginal Protector, interviews with the descendants of local settlers and so on – which, although not always in strict accordance with one another, in their volume, content and tone together paint a convincing picture of a brutal 'day of reckoning', and, more broadly, a region in the midst of a violent, unofficial conflict befitting the title 'black war'. (This term is commonly used to refer to the persecution of the Palawa in Tasmania between 1824 and 1831, but is also fastened to a series of earlier clashes in the Hawkesbury and Parramatta area, beginning in 1795; what they have in common is that they are outbreaks of racially motivated violence of such intensity as to resemble open warfare.) I encourage those who doubt the version of events recounted in my prologue to read that book and to make up their own minds.

Author's Note

I owe a great deal to Gardner's tireless research, and turned frequently to *The Gippsland Massacres, Through Foreign Eyes* and *Our Founding Murdering Father*. These works are not widely available but can be procured from Gardner directly through Ngarak Press or found in public libraries across Gippsland.

Other books that became essential texts include Don Watson's *Caledonia Australis*, Robert Hughes' extraordinary *The Fatal Shore*, and a fascinating compendium of first-hand accounts of frontier life written during McMillan's time at the request of Lieutenant-Governor Charles La Trobe, *Letters from Victorian Pioneers*. I also highly recommend Laurie Duggan's epic poem *The Ash Range*, in which he collages dozens of contemporary sources to create a haunting account of the founding of modern-day Gippsland.

McMillan's own journals, from which I have quoted liberally throughout the book, can be found in the archives of the State Library of Victoria in Melbourne. Several versions of the 'exploration journal' exist and it appears that McMillan reworked and revised his account of his early exploratory travels throughout his life. Each reiteration provides information not found elsewhere, and so I have not confined my quotations to one version, instead using whichever is most relevant and insightful in each case.

In terms of my own investigations, I conducted three separate trips to Gippsland of between four and six weeks in length between 2013 and 2015. The bulk of the 'action' in the book took place between November 2013 and February 2014, though the meetings with Ricky Mullet and Barry Kenny of GLaWAC took some time to set up and did not take place until I returned a year later in

February 2015 in the latter stages of writing this book. For the sake of narrative coherence, I have not referred to the intervening period. Similarly, a small number of other episodes did not occur in the order in which they are presented.

Dialogue is reproduced to the best of my ability, either from the use of my contemporaneous notes (in the case of more 'formal' interviews, such as my visit to Lake Tyers) or from detailed records of my activities and conversations entered in a daily journal during my travels.

I am extremely grateful to all of the people – historians, community leaders, writers and friends – who donated their time and knowledge. Any errors are mine and mine alone.

Spelling

McMillan

In modern accounts Angus is usually referred to as McMillan, and I have adopted this spelling to avoid confusion. In newspaper articles of the time he was often referred to as Angus M'Millan (or even Augustus M'Millan), which I consider a Victorian quirk and use only in direct quotations where necessary. However, in Chapter 1, I use Macmillan while discussing my mother's relatives. This is the spelling used by our branch of the family, which I'm told was settled upon by her grandfather. Prior to this, both Mc— and Mac— were used interchangeably, as in many Highland families in the nineteenth century.

Author's Note

Gunai

In recent decades there has been a linguistic split among the remaining Gunai people, some of whom refer to themselves as Kurnai, a derivation of the phonetic rendering of the tribe's name devised by the Victorian anthropologist Alfred Howitt (Kŭrnai). In the run-up to the native-title agreements in Gippsland, this disparity became a source of friction, and after a lengthy hearing the local community compromised on Gunaikurnai as a collective label (see Chapter 7). Nevertheless, I felt on reflection that this composite name would not reflect the original usage. Therefore, following discussion with indigenous language expert Dr Doris Paton and in accordance with independent expert testimony submitted during the native title hearings, I have opted for Gunai, which more closely follows the name's original pronunciation in McMillan's time.

Koorie

Aboriginal people from different regions of Australia refer to themselves as a group by several different names. Koorie is used in Victoria, while in New South Wales this is more often spelled Koori. Other words are in use in different regions, such as Murri in Queensland, Nyungar in the Perth area, and so on. Each word can be roughly translated to mean 'people'.

General comment on Aboriginal names

In the case of Aboriginal names (both for individuals like Bungelene and Jackie Warren, and cultural groups such as Eora and Palawa), there are often several variants in texts dating from the period. I have tried to use what is, arguably, the most prevalent in each case, but with some caution.

Although apparently interchangeable to outsiders, in some cases these inconsistencies have become symbolic of deeper divisions between branches of cultural groups. Usually the issue arose only after Anglicised distortions were produced by Europeans attempting to record Aboriginal language and customs.

The settlers saw through European eyes and heard with European ears. As, of course, do I. I hope I have not caused offence by my choice of spellings: if I have, it was entirely unintended.

Sources

1. Blood Relatives

p. 16 almost a third: 2006 census: 288,180 respondents out of 903,090

p. 26 'A Scottish pioneer': 'Aborigines Vow to Wipe Pioneer Scot off the Map', *Scotsman*, 22 June 2005: http://www.scotsman.com/news/scotland/ top-stories/aborigines-vow-to-wipe-pioneer-scot- off-the-map-1-1391101

p. 29 'O Flower of Scotland': 'Flower of Scotland' – unofficial national anthem of Scotland, by Roy Williamson of The Corries

p. 30 'every Scotch man': Quoted Linda Colley, *Britons: Forging the Nation 1707–1837* (1992), p. 120

p. 30 'skilful obstructions': Hugh Thomas, *The Slave Trade: The History of the Atlantic Slave Trade 1440–1870* (1997), p. 550

2. But for the Sea

p. 47 the novelist Catherine Sinclair: Don Watson, *Caledonia Australis: Scottish Highlanders on the Frontier of Australia* (2009), p. 54

p. 47 A fifth brother: 'A Dauntless Man: Angus McMillan', Traralgon and District Historical Society (1972)

p. 49 Until then, lairds: John Lorne Campbell, *A Very Civil People: Hebridean Folk, History and Tradition* (2014), p. 202

p. 50 £2 million and numerous estates: 'Legacies of British Slave Ownership', University College London: http://www.ucl.ac.uk/lbs/person/view/1301318774

p. 51 'a scene of horror': Eric Richards, *The Highland Clearances* (2008), p. 209

p. 51 'in a state of absolute starvation': From a collection of pamphlets assembled by James Maidment (Vol. 1, p. 86) and held in Inverness Library: http://www. ambaile.org.uk/en/item/item_narrative.jsp?item_ id=22818

p. 57 *Sporthail* (noun): Also features in 'Sound Poem' by Rody Gorman, a collection of Gaelic descriptions of sound

3. The Fever Ship

p. 66 'No parent, sister, brother': 'Written for Mr. George Lang, the author's brother, on his embarking for New South Wales. – London, April 25th, 1821'. Full text: http://www.inspirationalstories.com/poems/ verses-i-john-dunmore-lang-poems/

p. 73 'overcrowded state': J.V. Thompson Esq., Deputy Inspector General of Hospitals, writing from on board the *Minerva*, 24 January 1838

p. 73 a third of the population: David Neal, *The Rule of Law in a Penal Colony: Law and Politics in Early New South Wales* (1991), p. 200

p. 74 New arrivals often: In 1790 the colony's chaplain, Rev. Richard Johnson, wrote of the selfishness that the depth of their penury engendered: 'Instead of alleviating the distresses of each other, the weakest were sure to go to the wall. In the night time, which at this time is very cold, where [the convicts] had nothing but grass to lay on and a blanket amongst the four of them, he that was the strongest of the four would take the whole blanket to himself and leave the rest quite naked.' Quoted Robert Hughes, *The Fatal Shore* (1987), p. 147

Sources

p. 75 'The colony that would': Ibid., p. 74

p. 75 'Famine ... was approaching': Watkin Tench, *A Complete Account of the Settlement at Port Jackson*, Chapter VI: http://www.gutenberg.org/files/3534/ 3534-h/3534-h.htm

4. The Cattle Station

p. 79 more than A$100 billion: Australian Bureau of Statistics, Yearbook 2012: http://www.abs.gov.au/ ausstats/abs@.nsf/Lookup/by%20Subject/1301.0~ 2012~Main%20Features~Mining%20Industry~150

p. 83 'swans are black': *Caledonia Australis*, op. cit., p. 85

p. 84 'in the habit of': John Goodwin, quoted *The Fatal Shore*, op. cit., p. 311

p. 85 'I was put in': McMillan's account reprinted in the *Gippsland Times*, 3 January 1924, p. 2

p. 85 'accursed colony': Quoted Rev. J. Cox, *Notes of Gippsland History*, Vol. 1, *Exploration*, p. 44

p. 89 seventeen to one: P.J. Marshall (ed.), *The Cambridge Illustrated History of the British Empire* (1996), p. 258

p. 94 'The country looked very pleasant': From Bill Gammage, *The Biggest Estate on Earth: How Aborigines Made Australia* (2011; Kindle edition), p. 417

p. 94 'It may perhaps be doubted': Quoted ibid.

p. 94 'To clear the forest's': 'The Telegraph: A Consolatory Epistle', quoted *The Fatal Shore*, p. 179

p. 96 'Bathurst –': *South Australian Gazette and Colonial Register*, 11 May 1839

p. 103 'add fuel to the politics': Keith Windschuttle: 'Black and White Perspectives on the Apology', from *The Fabrication of Aboriginal History*, Vol. 3, *The Stolen Generations* (2009): http://www.stolengenerations. info/index.php?option=com_content&view= article&id=70&Itemid=22

Sources

5. First In, Best Dressed

p. 107 a nineteenth-century map: http://handle.slv.vic.gov. au/10381/116740

p. 109 'great care [had to] be exercised': Charles Browning Hall, recalling his time travelling from the Monaro to Port Phillip in 1840, quoted T.F. Bride (ed.), *Letters from Victorian Pioneers* (1898), p. 210

p. 110 'Mr [George] Blaxland': Quoted Laurie Duggan, *The Ash Range* (1987), p. 37

p. 111 *I looked to the S.W.*: From the *Gippsland Times* account (republished 1866 – first published 'nearly four years ago')

p. 115 'as wild as hares': Thomas Alexander Brown, *Robbery Under Arms* (1882). Full text: http://www.gutenberg. net.au/ebooks/e00008.txt

p. 118 'calls in various directions': Henry Reynolds, *The Other Side of the Frontier: Aboriginal Resistance to the European Invasion of Australia* (2006), pp. 14–15

p. 121 It put him in mind: http://www.trove.nla.gov.au/ ndp/del/article/65362111

p. 122 'I may mention': Letter recalling settlement of that region, dated 30 August 1853 and quoted *Letters from Victorian Pioneers*, op. cit., p. 187

p. 125 'the worst Governor': *Sydney Morning Herald*, 1846, quoted *The Australian Dictionary of Biography*: http:// www.adb.anu.edu.au/biography/gipps-sir-george-2098

p. 128 painted the panoramic view: http://www.beta. worldcat.org/archivegrid/collection/data/ 220087393

p. 128 'If hospitality be a virtue': Richard Mackay, writing in 1916, *Recollections of Early Gippsland Goldfields*, quoted P.D. Gardner, *Our Founding Murdering Father: Angus McMillan and the Kurnai Tribe of Gippsland, 1839–1865* (1990), p. 57

p. 128 'Chairman and Gentlemen': Melbourne *Argus*, Tuesday, 11 March 1856, p. 4

p. 131 recited poetry: The example given was 'The Pioneers', from Frank Hudson, *The Song of the Manly Men and Other Verses* (1908)

p. 131 'Let Onward, Onward, be the cry': Unknown author, 'To the Discoverer of Gippsland', quoted Rev. George Cox, *Notes on Gippsland History*, Vol. 1, p. 75

6. Black War

p. 142 'convenient situations': 'Secret Instructions for Lieutenant James Cook Appointed to Command His Majesty's Bark the Endeavour', 30 July 1768, National Library of Australia

p. 144 'every such treaty': Proclamation of Governor Bourke, 10 October 1835

p. 145 'suffering severely': *Letters from Victorian Pioneers*, op. cit., p. 133

p. 147 The region was 'infested': Ibid., p. 199

p. 147 'pandemonium upon earth': Rev. W. Bean's correspondence (1848–9), republished in the *Gippsland Standard and Alberton Shire Representative*, Wednesday, 4 March 1914, edited by Rev. J. Cox

p. 147 'We have learned': Quoted P.D. Gardner, *Through Foreign Eyes: European Perceptions of the Kurnai Tribe of Gippsland* (1994), p. 24

p. 148 'most beautiful': *Letters from Victorian Pioneers*, op. cit., p. 238

p. 149 'in the night, his father': L. Fison and A. Howitt, *Kamilaroi and Kurnai* (1880), p. 247

p. 149 'They are beautifully preserved': James Warman during the 'white woman' expedition, quoted Julie E. Carr, *The Captive White Woman of Gipps Land: In Pursuit of the Legend* (2001), p. 127

p. 154 'There was a desperate fight': P.J.C. Wallace writing in the *Gippsland Times*, 6 December 1923

p. 155 'It was scarcely to be': Quoted *Letters from Victorian Pioneers*, op. cit., pp. 177–8

Sources

p. 157 'Walked out ... to scrub': Diary entry, 1844, quoted
Through Foreign Eyes, op. cit., p. 15

p. 159 'A.M. – rain[,] P.M. – fine': 27 January 1845, quoted
ibid., p. 31

p. 159 'These things are kept': Letter dated 30 April 1846,
quoted A. Dirk Moses (ed.), *Genocide and Settler
Society: Frontier Violence and Stolen Aboriginal Children in
Australian History* (2004), p. 202

p. 160 'most awful statement of doings': Quoted *Through
Foreign Eyes*, op. cit., p. 51

p. 161 'GIPPSLAND: NUMBER OF ABORIGINES': *Letters
from Victorian Pioneers*, op. cit., p. 79

p. 162 'melancholy anthropological footnote': Quoted Dr
Mark McKenna, 'Different Perspectives on Black
Armband History', Parliament of Australia (1997):
http://www.aph.gov.au/About_Parliament/
Parliamentary_Departments/Parliamentary_Library/
pubs/rp/RP9798/98RP05

p. 162 'The charge of "political correctness"': Peter Gardner,
'Frontier Violence, Political Correctness and
Memorials: Brief Comments on Henry Reynolds and
Bill Bryson', http://petergardner.info/wp-content/
uploads/2012/11/Frontier-Violence-Political-
Correctness-and-Memorials.pdf (2004)

p. 163 'so much garbage': From Gardner's collected notes:
http://www.petergardner.info/wp-content/uploads/
2012/11/Notes-on-Massacres-rev.ed_.pdf (2000–15)

p. 165 'Warrigal Creek: range 60–150': Ibid.

p. 166 'a fanatic': *Our Founding Murdering Father*, op. cit.,
p. 55

p. 171 'shot plenty of blacks': 'Bushman', quoted ibid., p. 38

7. The White Woman

p. 174 'The clue to the foregoing mystery': *Port Phillip
Patriot*, 18 July 1841

p. 183 'Yallourn people bought': Peter Read, *Returning to
Nothing: The Meaning of Lost Places* (1996), p. 99

Sources

p. 187 'Will *no one* come forward': *Port Phillip Herald*, 12 May 1846, quoted *The Captive White Woman of Gipps Land*, op. cit., p. 66

p. 188 'compelled to yield': Quoted Kate Darian Smith, 'Capturing the white woman of Gippsland: a frontier myth', Captured Lives: Australian Captivity Narratives: http://www.kcl.ac.uk/artshums/ahri/centres/menzies/research/Publications/Workingpapers/WP85-87Darian-Smithetal.pdf, p. 30

p. 189 'Unhappiest of the fairer kind': 'Homo' in the Melbourne *Argus*, quoted *Caledonia Australis*, op. cit., p. 203

p. 190 40 per cent nationally: Milton James Lewis, *The People's Health: Public Health in Australia, 1788–1950* (2003), p. 26

p. 192 'wandering about the bush': 'An Englishman', writing in the *Sydney Herald*, 10 September 1846, quoted *The Captive White Woman of Gipps Land*, op. cit., p. 95

p. 192 'a slave of savage lust': *Port Phillip Herald*, 1 October 1846, quoted *Our Founding Murdering Father*, op. cit., p. 47

p. 192 'total absence of women': Quoted *The Captive White Woman of Gipps Land*, op. cit., p. 26

p. 192 'well bro' up': John Pettit, quoted *Caledonia Australis*, op. cit., p. 204

p. 193 'like smoke': Ibid., p. 203

p. 195 'denounced in forcible terms': *The Captive White Woman of Gipps Land*, op. cit., p. 87

p. 196 'If Mr. La Trobe': 'Humanitas', writing in the *Port Phillip Herald*, 10 March 1846

p. 198 piles of black bodies: From sworn affidavits by de Villiers and Warman, 1847: http://www.prov.vic.gov.au/online-exhibitions/nativepolice/documents/00019_u094_47-1348_034.html

p. 198 'wanton barbarity': From a letter published in the *Port Phillip Patriot*, 22 January 1847. Emphasis in the original

p. 198 'have acted with a great want': Letter from clerk William Elyard Jr on behalf of the Colonial Secretary, 5 March 1847 ('I am directed by the governor to inform you …')

p. 199 'tall, with a considerable stoop': De Villiers party dispatches, quoted *The Captive White Woman of Gipps Land*, op. cit., pp. 120–2

p. 199 'shouted with delight': H.B. Morris, quoted ibid., p. 119

p. 200 'As a proof': *Port Phillip Herald*, 18 February 1847

p. 200 'FORCE MUST BE USED': *Port Phillip Patriot*, 22 February 1847

p. 201 'upbraided him': Donald Mcleod, quoted *The Captive White Woman of Gipps Land*, op. cit., p. 168

p. 202 'Of grief': Report on the death of Bungelene's son Thomas, *Ballarat Star*, 14 January 1865, p. 2

p. 204 'The young Kŭrnai man': Alfred Howitt, *The Native Tribes of South East Asia* (1996), p. 273

8. Slaughterhouse Gully

p. 211 '"Some settlers gladly hailed"': L. Edgar, 1865, quoted P.D. Gardner, *Gippsland Massacres: The Destruction of the Kurnai Tribes 1800–1860* (1993), p. 98

p. 212 'The blacks who were living': Buchan resident Mr J. Armstrong, recorded 1977 by P.D. Gardner, ibid., p. 80

p. 214 '"No bones have been found"': E. Whittaker, 1977, quoted ibid., pp. 80–1

p. 214 '"The avenging party"': A. Macrae, 1966, quoted ibid., p. 39

p. 217 'Here the offending tribe': C.H. Grove, quoted ibid., p. 82

p. 221 'unsurveyed country': Details from Map of Australia Felix, 1847, compiled and engraved by Thomas Ham

p. 221 'eyes like live coals': *Arrow*, Friday, 19 December 1924, p. 16

Sources

p. 222 'Their whole art of war': Quoted *The Other Side of the Frontier*, op. cit., p. 100

p. 226 'precipitous and broken country': Tyers writing in 1844, included in *Letters from Victorian Pioneers*, op. cit., p. 194

p. 237 'Nothing meets the eye': James Atkinson, *An Account of the State of Agriculture and Grazing in New South Wales* (1826), pp. 6–7

p. 238 'No sooner was all fear': *Letters from Victorian Pioneers*, op. cit., p. 153

9. In Search of Elders

p. 240 'four or five': *The Native Tribes of South East Asia*, op. cit., p. 78

p. 244 'I see by the Gazette': *Sydney Gazette*, 22 May 1841. Letter signed F.J. Sloman, quoted *The Captive White Woman of Gipps Land*, op. cit., p. 32

p. 246 'his station at Bushy Park': *Gippsland Guardian*, 16 September 1859, p. 3

p. 246 'I tell them': *Our Founding Murdering Father*, op. cit., p. 55

p. 248 'reading, writing, singing': *Through Foreign Eyes*, op. cit., p. 62

p. 250 'Wa! Wa! Wa!': Gunai lullaby, from A. Howitt, *Notes on Songs and Songmakers of Some Australian Tribes* (1887)

p. 250 'the most frequent': *Through Foreign Eyes*, op. cit.

p. 250 31 per cent: Ibid., pp. 65–6

p. 251 'one of the most articulate': Michael Banton, quoted http://www.core.ac.uk/download/pdf/9654087.pdf

p. 251 'the civilised races of man': Charles Darwin, *The Descent of Man* (1871), Vol. I, Chapter VI: 'On the Affinities and Genealogy of Man', pp. 200–1

p. 255 'When I see the word': Quoted *Genocide and Settler Society*, op. cit., p. 19

p. 256 'genocide is not a synonym': Ibid., p. 23

p. 256 'genocidal moments': Ibid., pp. 35–6

Sources

p. 257 'I have asked the Blacks': Letter to the Crown Commissioner of Gippsland, dated 24 July 1846: http://www.prov.vic.gov.au/online-exhibitions/ nativepolice/documents/00019_u092_47-907_027. html

p. 260 'I have protested': Melbourne *Argus*, Saturday, 5 December 1868, p. 6

p. 261 'When we came here': Donald MacDonald, *Gum Boughs and Wattle Bloom* (1887), quoted R. Evans, K. Saunders and K. Cronin, *Exclusion, Exploitation and Extermination: Race Relations in Colonial Queensland* (2002), p. 65

p. 263 'I must say': Quoted *Through Foreign Eyes*, op. cit., pp. 75–6

p. 265 'Notwithstanding the opportunities': 15 January 1853: http://www.parliament.vic.gov.au/papers/govpub/ VPARL1853-54NoC33.pdf

p. 266 'The apathy which': *Glasgow Herald*, 9 June 1845, quoted 'Contempt, Sympathy and Romance: Lowland perceptions of the Highlands and the clearances during the Famine Years, 1845–1855': http://www.theses. gla.ac.uk/842/1/1996fenyophd.pdf, p. 70

p. 267 'It is not more notorious': *Fifeshire Journal*, 23 September 1847, quoted ibid., pp. 111–12

p. 268 'Morally and intellectually': James Bruce in 1846, quoted http://www.theses.gla.ac.uk/842/1/ 1996fenyophd.pdf

p. 268 'mild nature': A. MacKenzie (ed.), *History of the Highland Clearances* (2015), p. 21

p. 269 'squalid, isolated': Save Lake Tyers Committee campaign leaflet (1965), quoted in 'A 1960s Campaign to Save an Aboriginal Reserve: Lake Tyers in Victoria, Australia', by Azita Shamsolahi, University of Bristol

p. 269 'Read this and see': Melbourne *Mercury*, 28 March 1957, p. 4

p. 275 Of more than 11,000 respondents: Poll published online in 2013; these figures correct as of November

Sources

2014: http://www.smh.com.au/national/are-you-a-casual-racist-20130530-2ndyy.html#poll

p. 276 A 2012 survey: A VicHealth, Lowitja Institute, University of Melbourne and beyondblue survey, published at Congress Lowitja 2012, Melbourne: http://www.vichealth.vic.gov.au/Media-Centre/ Media-Releases-by-Topic/Discrimination/Vast-majority-of-Aboriginal-Victorians-are-targets-of-racism-shows-new-survey.aspx

10. Reconciliation

p. 282 'With our hands': Mr Thomas, head teacher of Woodside School, to the *Gippsland Standard*, 9 October 1912, quoted *Gippsland Massacres*, op. cit., p. 58

p. 283 Albert was born in 1933: Doris Paton, 'A Journey with Woolum Bellum Koorie Open Door Education School. Its Life Cycle in Meeting the Educational Needs of Aboriginal Children', PhD thesis, RMIT university, pp. 15–16: https://www.researchbank. rmit.edu.au/view/rmit:6769/Paton.pdf

p. 286 'They ran us down like shit': Interview with Bobby Nicholls of Yarnin Pictures: https://www.vimeo. com/101897953

p. 288 Uncle Albert Mullett spearheaded: Mullett on behalf of the Gunai/Kurnai People vs. State of Victoria (2010)

p. 296 'The imperative to insulate': A. Dirk Moses, *German Intellectuals and the Nazi Past* (2007), p. 28

p. 299 'painful melancholia': *Maffra Spectator*, 31 January 1884, p. 3

p. 299 'burnt beyond recognition': *Gippsland Times*, 16 December 1926, p. 1

p. 299 'did not inherit': *Gippsland Times*, 20 January 1936, p. 1

Sources

11. Iguana Creek

p. 308 'Whatever feelings may have': *Gippsland Guardian*,
2 November 1860

p. 309 'These, Sir, are the salient points': *Letters from Victorian
Pioneers*, op. cit., p. 188

p. 309 'The early squatters': Ibid., p. 185

p. 310 'was at his best': Letter from Norman Macalister,
dated 1982, held in Maffra Library

p. 310 'did not enjoy': *Our Founding Murdering Father*, op.
cit., p. 77

p. 313 'the redoubtable explorer': The *Mountaineer*, 24 May
1865, quoted *Caledonia Australis*, op. cit., p. 242

p. 321 'No mention of what was to happen': Hal Porter,
Bairnsdale (1977), p .61

p. 334 *'a few houses'*: The *Ash Range*, op. cit., p. 115

p. 335 'I resolve hereafter': *'Minerva* journal', Monday, 13
November 1837

Epilogue

p. 341 'The entertainment given': Melbourne *Argus*, Tuesday,
11 March 1856 (cut for length and clarity)

Illustration Credits

Acknowledgements

I would like to express my sincere gratitude to a number of people who very generously assisted, advised and hosted me during the production of this book.

I am deeply indebted to Jeannie and Ian Haughton, Cameron Cope, Steaphan Paton, Ricky Mullett and Elizabeth Balderstone, who – as well as devoting hours to explaining Australian culture and discussing the modern-day legacy of settlement – fed me and put me up in their homes (and tents!). The historians Peter Gardner and Don Watson were both generous with their time and expertise, and our conversations directed my research in interesting directions. The same goes for Rachel Mullett, Doris Paton, Barry Kenny, Russell Mullett, Leonie Cameron, Peter Ryan, Kath and Mike Coggan, Ella and Jenny Jamieson, Ros Winspear at RANZCOG and the Maffra Historical Society: thank you.

Back in the UK, my agent Sophie Lambert of Conville & Walsh has been an endless source of ideas, encouragement and advice, and I owe her a great deal. Likewise, so many thanks to my brilliant editor Arabella Pike and others at William Collins: Stephen Guise, Robert Lacey, Joseph Zigmond, Katherine Patrick, as well as Catherine Milne of

Acknowledgements

HarperCollins Australia. Dr Naomi Parry, who saw the text in its later stages, also made many helpful observations.

I received financial awards from Creative Scotland and Arts Trust Scotland, without which I would not have been able to make the initial trip to Australia that enabled me to write a book proposal in the first place. The importance of support from such bodies in the development of a young writer cannot be overstated.

Thanks should go too to Alex Christofi and Charles Cumming, both of whom shared their experience and contacts at a crucial stage; Samira Shackle and Louise Gray, who provided insightful feedback and share daily with me the highs and lows of freelance life; my uncle Myles Macmillan and his wife Boo; Anna Blundy and Hope Mortimer, at whose beautiful home in Tuscany I wrote a good chunk of the first draft. Alex Kendall: apologies for taking your name in vain.

Most of all: to my parents, Fiona and Derek Flyn, and brothers, Rory and Martyn. Thank you for everything. And to Richard West, who makes me very happy.